MAKING ENDS MEET

Volume 86, Sage Library of Social Research

Sage Library of Social Research

1 Caplovitz **The Merchants of Harlem**
2 Rosenau **International Studies & the Social Sciences**
3 Ashford **Ideology & Participation**
4 McGowan/Shapiro **The Comparative Study of Foreign Policy**
5 Male **The Struggle for Power**
6 Tanter **Modelling & Managing International Conflicts**
7 Catanese **Planners & Local Politics**
8 Prescott **Economic Aspects of Public Housing**
9 Parkinson **Latin America, the Cold War, & the World Powers, 1945-1973**
10 Smith **Ad Hoc Governments**
11 Gallimore et al **Culture, Behavior & Education**
12 Hallman **Neighborhood Government in a Metropolitan Setting**
13 Gelles **The Violent Home**
14 Weaver **Conflict & Control in Health Care Administration**
15 Schweigler **National Consciousness in Divided Germany**
16 Carey **Sociology & Public Affairs**
17 Lehman **Coordinating Health Care**
18 Bell/Price **The First Term**
19 Alderfer/Brown **Learning from Changing**
20 Wells/Marwell **Self-Esteem**
21 Robins **Political Institutionalization & the Integration of Elites**
22 Schonfeld **Obedience & Revolt**
23 McCready/Greeley **The Ultimate Values of the American Population**
24 Nye **Role Structure & Analysis of the Family**
25 Wehr/Washburn **Peace & World Order Systems**
26 Stewart **Children in Distress**
27 Dedring **Recent Advances in Peace & Conflict Research**

28 Czudnowski **Comparing Political Behavior**
29 Douglas **Investigative Social Research**
30 Stohl **War & Domestic Political Violence**
31 Williamson **Sons or Daughters**
32 Levi **Law & Politics in the International Society**
33 Altheide **Creating Reality**
34 Lerner **The Politics of Decision-Making**
35 Converse **The Dynamics of Party Support**
36 Newman/Price **Jails & Drug Treatment**
37 Abercrombie **The Military Chaplain**
38 Gottdiener **Planned Sprawl**
39 Lineberry **Equality & Urban Policy**
40 Morgan **Deterrence**
41 Lefebvre **The Structure of Awareness**
42 Fontana **The Last Frontier**
43 Kemper **Migration & Adaptation**
44 Caplovitz/Sherrow **The Religious Drop-Outs**
45 Nagel/Neef **The Legal Process: Modeling the System**
46 Bucher/Stelling **Becoming Professional**
47 Hiniker **Revolutionary Ideology & Chinese Reality**
48 Herman **Jewish Identity**
49 Marsh **Protest & Political Consciousness**
50 LaRossa **Conflict & Power in Marriage**
51 Abrahamsson **Bureaucracy or Participation**
52 Parkinson **The Philosophy of International Relations**
53 Lerup **Building the Unfinished**
54 Smith **Churchill's German Army**
55 Corden **Planned Cities**
56 Hallman **Small & Large Together**
57 Inciardi et al **Historical Approaches to Crime**
58 Levitan/Alderman **Warriors at Work**
59 Zurcher **The Mutable Self**

60 Teune/Mlinar **The Developmental Logic of Social Systems**
61 Garson **Group Theories of Politics**
62 Medcalf **Law & Identity**
63 Danziger **Making Budgets**
64 Damrell **Search for Identity**
65 Stotland et al **Empathy, Fantasy & Helping**
66 Aronson **Money & Power**
67 Wice **Criminal Lawyers**
68 Hoole **Evaluation Research & Development Activities**
69 Singelmann **From Agriculture to Services**
70 Seward **The American Family**
71 McCleary **Dangerous Men**
72 Nagel/Neef **Policy Analysis: In Social Science Research**
73 Rejai/Phillips **Leaders of Revolution**
74 Inbar **Routine Decision-Making**
75 Galaskiewicz **Exchange Networks & Community Politics**
76 Alkin/Daillak/White **Using Evaluations**
77 Sensat **Habermas & Marxism**
78 Matthews **The Social World of Old Women**
79 Swanson/Cohen/Swanson **Small Towns & Small Towners**
80 Latour/Woolgar **Laboratory Life**
81 Krieger **Hip Capitalism**
82 Megargee/Bohn **Classifying Criminal Offenders**
83 Cook **Who Should Be Helped?**
84 Gelles **Family Violence**
85 Katzner **Choice & the Quality of Life**
86 Caplovitz **Making Ends Meet**
87 Berk/Berk **Labor and Leisure at Home**
88 Darling **Families Against Society**
89 Altheide/Snow **Media Logic**
90 Roosens **Mental Patients in Town Life**
91 Savage **Founders, Heirs, & Managers**
92 Bromley/Shupe **"Moonies" in America**

Making Ends Meet

How Families Cope with Inflation and Recession

DAVID CAPLOVITZ

Volume 86
SAGE LIBRARY OF
SOCIAL RESEARCH

 SAGE PUBLICATIONS   Beverly Hills   London

For information address:

SAGE PUBLICATIONS, INC.
275 South Beverly Drive
Beverly Hills, California 90212

SAGE PUBLICATIONS LTD
28 Banner Street
London EC1Y 8QE, England

Printed in the United States of America

Library of Congress Cataloging in Publication Data

Caplovitz, David.
    Making ends meet.

    (Sage library of social research ; v. 86)
    Includes index.
    1. Cost and standard of living--United States.
2. Inflation (Finance) and unemployment--United States
Psychological aspects. I. Title.
HD6983.C33   339.4'1'0973   79-14438
ISBN 0-8039-1292-7
ISBN 0-8039-1293-5 pbk.

FIRST PRINTING

CONTENTS

Chapter   *Page*

Acknowledgments   8

1. Introduction   9

PART I. THE IMPACT OF INFLATION AND RECESSION

2. The Victims of Inflation and Recession   21
3. Subjective Inflation Crunch   37
4. The Voice of the People: Inflation's
   Impact in the Various Subsamples   53

PART II. CONSEQUENCES OF INFLATION AND RECESSION

5. Coping Patterns   91
6. Impact of Inflation-Recession on the Family   119
7. Impact of Inflation-Recession on Mental Health   139

PART III. MITIGATING FACTORS: PUBLIC AND PRIVATE ASSETS

8. The Role of the Welfare State   161
9. The Role of Homeownership   173

PART IV. THE IMPACT OF INFLATION-RECESSION
ON THE MIND

10. Impact of Inflation-Recession
    on Values and Attitudes   187
11. Perceived Causes of Inflation and Recession   211
12. Summary and Conclusions   243
    Appendix   261
    Index   295
    About the Author   301

For Paulann, Abigail, and Gideon—the joys
and the strengths of my life

ACKNOWLEDGMENTS

This research was carried out under Grant Number 5-R01-MH 26335 of the Center for the Study of Metropolitan Problems of the National Institute of Mental Health. I am most grateful to Dr. Elliot Liebow, the director of the Metro Center, for his enthusiasm and encouragement for this research project. In carrying out the study, I was assisted by a number of colleagues and research assistants. In the early stages of the study, Professor William Kornblum took responsibility for supervising the field work that was done. The field work itself was carried out by a team of research assistants, Paulette Pierce, Joan Goldstein, William DeFazio, Eva Margolies, and Joan Liebman-Smith. These people were responsible for the depth interviews that so enrich this book and I am eternally grateful to them.

I am pleased to acknowledge the help of a former colleague, Robert Smith. He had learned that I was given a grant to study inflation, and he got in touch with me and told me that he had done some research in this area. He generously made his questionnaire available to me at the time I was drafting my questionnaire. I was particularly impressed with a battery of his questions dealing with what I call "subjective inflation crunch," and I borrowed these questions from him. I am most indebted to him for giving me many of the items for measuring this concept.

My greatest debt is to my colleague, Louis Genevie, who assumed responsibility for all the computer work involved in processing the data and generating the tables. Without his extraordinary skill in making the computer "talk," this research might never have been completed.

Chapter 1

INTRODUCTION

In 1973, after more than a decade of stability, the cost of living began to rise precipitously. Whereas the rate of change had been 4.1 percent in 1971 and 3.2 percent in 1972, in 1973 it rose to 6.2 percent. In 1974 the cost spiral accelerated sharply. That year saw double digit inflation for the first time in many decades, with the cost of living increasing at a rate of 10.9 percent. In terms of absolute change, the cost of living rose by 14.6 percent in 1974, meaning that it took that many more dollars to buy the same amount of goods as the previous year. In the fall of 1974, President Ford launched a campaign to combat inflation with the slogan "Whip Inflation Now" and proceeded to distribute WIN buttons at press conferences. But even as President Ford was focusing the nation's attention on inflation, unemployment began to rise. Contrary to all Keynesian economics, the country was being lashed by both high inflation and high unemployment. By the end of 1974, unemployment stood at 5.6 percent, up from 4.9 percent in 1973. In 1975 inflation abated somewhat but was still at the unusually

9

high rate of 9.1 percent and unemployment soared, reaching 8.5 percent. In 1976 the inflation rate dropped further to 6.2 percent, but unemployment was still depressingly high at 7.7 percent. As 1977 draws to a close, inflation is still running above 6 percent, and unemployment persists at around 7 percent.[1] A new term was coined by the economists to describe this situation of high unemployment and high inflation—stagflation—but it soon became clear that an old-fashioned word best described the economy of 1975 and 1976—recession. For the first time in its history, America experienced a recession at a time of sharply rising prices. The double shock of high unemployment and high inflation was a major issue in the 1976 presidential election, and Jimmy Carter emerged the winner largely because of these economic troubles.

The anecdotal accounts that have appeared in the press have suggested that the poor and the retired, living on fixed incomes, were particularly hard pressed by these strains in the economy, but the stories also suggested that the working classes and even the more well-to-do were being forced to tighten their belts. The previous calamity in the American economy, the great depression of the thirties, inspired a broad range of social research on the effects of the depression on society. The Social Science Research Council sponsored a series of some eleven volumes dealing with the impact of the depression on American institutions and various sectors of society. And the Work Progress Administration in the thirties sponsored many more studies. The disastrous state of the economy in the mid-seventies, which has not fully abated as this is written, has failed to stimulate comparable interest in research. As far as this writer knows, no social scientists have attempted systematic studies of the responses of people to these hard times. The anecdotal material that has appeared in the press has suggested that widespread changes in life styles may have taken place as people curtail their consumption in a wide variety of areas. But unlike the great depression of the thirties, the stagflation and recession

1. As this book goes to press in mid-1979, inflation is still the nation's number one problem with the rate climbing to 9 percent.

of the past few years have failed to generate any mass protests. It is conceivable that the wide range of social programs enacted since the depression, from unemployment insurance to welfare to food stamps, have been effective in lessening the pain and easing the adjustment to today's hard times. But it is also conceivable that families have adopted new patterns of adjustment, and that many families have failed to adjust and are experiencing considerable pain and strain that is undermining familial stability and mental health.

The present research is intended to fill the gap in our knowledge as to how families have been affected by and have responded to the twin calamities of inflation and recession. Which sectors of society are feeling the burdens of inflation and recession and how are they coping?

The proposal for this research was submitted to the Center for the Study of Metropolitan Problems, a division of the National Institute of Mental Health, at the height of the inflation and recession in the winter of 1975. The project was funded in the summer of 1975, and the survey of families in four cities took place in May and June of 1976. Thus, by the time the survey took place, the rate of inflation had declined considerably, and unemployment had dropped from its peak. But in the spring of 1976, inflation was still well above normal, and unemployment was so high and economic growth so slow that the term recession was still appropriate to describe the economy.

The Design of the Study

It was widely assumed that rampant inflation was particularly difficult for the poor and the retired, and the research design insured that these two groups would be adequately represented. Rather than draw a national sample, the decision was made to concentrate the research in four major urban areas, reflecting the four major areas of the country, the Northeast (New York), the South (Atlanta), the Midwest (Detroit) and the far West (San Francisco). The research was done in the Standard Metropolitan Statistical Area of these cities, a census unit that refers to a central city and its surrounding suburbs. The research plan called for 500 interviews in each SMSA, for a total of 2,000 interviews. In each city, approximately 15 percent of the respondents were to be poor people, with incomes averaging below $7,000, and 15 percent of the respondents were to be retired persons. The remaining 70 percent of the interviews were to be divided evenly among blue collar and white collar families. A major data collection firm, Audits and Surveys, was retained to do the sampling and interviewing. Audits and Surveys consulted census data to select areas in each metropolitan area in which the desired population was likely to be located. Their interviewers who went to poor communities were instructed to carry out the interview only if the household met the income criterion, with the result that the proportion of poor households in the final sample is very close to the intended number. The same rule was followed by those sent to communities with a high proportion of retired people. Only if the head of the household was retired did an interview take place. But the interviewers who were sent to predominantly working class and middle class neighborhoods were allowed to interview someone in the randomly selected household provided that it was a complete household. In short, if the sampled household contained both a wife and a husband, the interview took place. Inasmuch as white collar workers frequently live in predominantly blue collar neighborhoods, and, conversely, blue collar people sometimes live in mainly white collar communities, we were less successful in meeting our quotas of blue collar and white collar families. White collar families were oversampled, especially in Detroit, with the result that 39 percent (rather than the intended 35 percent) of the interviews were with white collar families. Working class families above our poverty line amount to 29 percent of the sample, with poor households and retired households accounting for 16 percent each. As noted, blue collar and white collar families had to be complete (both husband and wife present) to be eligible. For the sample of poor households, broken families were eligible, e.g., a mother and children, but single persons were excluded. Only among the retired were single person households eligible.

Given these sampling decisions, the sample is by no means representative of the entire adult population. Single, divorced, and separated persons were deliberately undersampled or excluded, and the poor and retired were oversampled. Moreover, the research was done only in major cities, meaning that the rural and small town populations are unrepresented. With these caveats in mind, the samples can still be treated as representative of four urban populations: blue collar families, white collar families, the poor, and the retired.

Although our goal was to interview 500 families in each city, bringing the total sample to 2,000, the number fell short of 500 in Atlanta (480) and San Francisco (495) and was slightly over 500 in Detroit (507). Only in New York were exactly 500 people interviewed, and the total for the four cities comes to 1,982 (rather than the aimed-for 2,000).

Characteristics of the Samples

In much of the subsequent analysis we shall be comparing the four subsamples—the poor, the retired, the blue collar, and the white collar groups. In this section we describe some of the salient characteristics of these groups. The sampling plan called for equal numbers of these groups in each of the four sample cities, but slight discrepancies occurred. For example, 28 percent of the poor came from New York, compared with 25 percent from Detroit (the correct number) and 24 percent from Atlanta and San Francisco.[2] The other three subsamples, blue collar, white collar, and retired, were sampled quite evenly in the four cities, with the actual percentages not varying by more than one point from 25 percent in each city.

In defining the poor for this study, we have established the cutoff point as a family income of $7,000 or less, irrespective of family size. Table 1.1 shows the 1975 family income of these

2. Poor families were those with incomes under $7,000. Where information on income was not available we relied on residence (was it a poor neighborhood?) and occupation to decide whether the family belonged with the poor. On the basis of this information, we classified 323 households as poor. The classification of families as blue collar or white collar was based on the occupation of the chief wage earner.

four subsamples. Approximately 15 percent of the respondents refused to provide information on family income, and hence the base figures in Table 1.1 add to less than the total sample.

More than half of the households classified as poor had incomes under $5,000 in 1973, and the rest earned between $5,000 and $7,000. Most of the blue collar families earned between $7,000 and $20,000, but almost one-fifth of them had earnings over $20,000. It must be kept in mind that these data refer to family income, and in many instances both spouses were employed. A substantial proportion of the white collar households were rather well-off financially. Thus, more than one-fifth had earnings over $30,000, and more than half earned over $20,000. Among the retired we find that 57 percent had earnings below the poverty line of $7,000, and most of these earned under $5,000. But a substantial minority of the retired, 21 percent, had earnings over $11,000. Even the majority of the retired who had incomes below $7,000 were for the most part better off than the poor families for the simple reason that their families were much smaller in size. In fact, 40 percent of the retired lived alone. In no other sample were single people permitted.

By definition, the white collar sample was restricted to households in which the chief wage earner had a white collar occupation, and the blue collar sample was restricted to those with blue collar occupations. But what occupations are repre-

Table 1.1: Family Income (1975) by Subsample (percentages)

| | Subsample | | | | |
Income	Poor	Blue Collar	White Collar	Retired	Total
Under $5,000	53	–	–	42	14
$5,000–$6,999	47	–	–	15	9
$7,000–$10,999	–	29	11	22	17
$11,000–$14,999	–	24	11	12	14
$15,000–$19,999	–	28	23	5	18
$20,000–$29,999	–	16	32	3	18
$30,000 and over	–	3	23	1	10
	100	100	100	100	100
N	(261)	(553)	(632)	(236)	(1,680)

sented in these broad categories, and what occupations did the poor and retired have? Table 1.2 shows the occupational distribution within each of these subsamples.

Some of the poor, those earning under $7,000, had rather prestigious occupations, as 5 percent were professionals and 3 percent managers. But the bulk of the poor had rather low status occupations as operatives, service workers, and laborers. A substantial proportion of the blue collar sample, 44 percent, were at the pinnacle of the blue collar world as craftsmen and foremen. The great majority of the white collar workers, 71 percent, were on the higher rungs of the white collar ladder (professionals and managers). The retired were fairly evenly divided between white collar and blue collar occupations, with a slight majority having had white collar jobs.

The final characteristic to be considered in this portrait of the subsamples is race. Some 74 percent of the sample is made up of white families, 21 percent are black, 4 percent Spanish-speaking, and 1 percent Oriental. Inasmuch as blacks make up almost half of Detroit and more than half of Atlanta, one might think that blacks were undersampled, but, in fact, they were not for the geographical unit was the Standard Metropolitan Area which included the suburbs as well as the central cities. Table 1.3 shows the racial composition of the four subsamples.

A substantial majority of the poor are members of minority groups, blacks (53 percent) and Spanish-speaking (14 percent).

Table 1.2: Occupation by Subsample (percentages)

| | Subsample | | | |
Occupation	*Poor*	*Blue Collar*	*White Collar*	*Retired*
Professional and technical	5	–	34	21
Managers	3	–	37	14
Clerical and sales	6	–	29	18
Craftsmen and foremen	11	44	–	17
Operatives	26	29	–	14
Service	27	17	–	9
Laborers	22	10	–	8
	100	100	100	100
N	(323)	(581)	(769)	(309)

Table 1.3: Race by Subsample (percentages)

| | Subsample | | | | |
Race	Poor	Blue Collar	White Collar	Retired	Total
White	32	71	87	92	74
Black	53	23	10	7	21
Spanish-speaking	14	5	1	1	4
Oriental	1	1	1	–	1
	100	100	99	100	100
N	(323)	(581)	(769)	(309)	

A substantial majority of the blue collar workers are white although blacks make up 23 percent of this group. The white collar group and the retired are dominated by whites. Only 10 percent of the white collar families are black, and only 7 percent of the retired are black. In the subsequent analysis, where we examine how these different subgroups have adjusted to inflation and recession, the experiences of the poor will be largely the experiences of blacks.

Organization of the Book

The organization of this book is based on a four part model or paradigm of the impact of inflation and recession. The first part stems from the question of who has been affected by inflation and recession. These economic calamities do not impact on all families to the same extent. Many families are obviously affected by rising prices as their incomes do not keep pace, and many others do experience the recession, either losing their jobs or having their jobs curtailed in some way. But many families enjoy rising incomes and do not feel the effect of inflation, and many do not lose their jobs or have their jobs affected in any way by the recession. Thus, Part I of this book, which consists of three chapters, examines the kinds of families that were affected by inflation and recession. Chapter 2 looks at the kinds of families whose incomes fell behind rising prices and the kinds of families that were hurt by the recession. Chapter 3 deals with the subjective impact of inflation, the extent to which families were suffering from inflation, whether their income fell behind or kept even. Chapter 4 turns to the qualitative data developed through depth interviews to show how people in the various subsamples, poor, blue collar, white collar, and retired, responded to inflation and the recession.

Part II of this volume deals with the second component in the underlying model, the consequences of inflation and recession and responses to these economic crises. Chapter 5 deals with responses in the form of efforts to fight back and compensate for rising prices. These efforts include such strategies as raising income, curtailing consumption, and becoming more efficient in allocating resources. Chapter 6 deals with the impact of inflation and recession on family life. To what extent do these economic pressures result in strains between the spouses and between parents and children, and to what extent have these pressures brought the spouses closer together? Chapter 7 looks at the impact of inflation and recession on mental health. To what extent do the respondents report mental stress as a result of economic pressures? And what kinds of people were likely to have their mental health suffer because of the economy?

Part III deals with another component of the underlying paradigm of inflation impact: the role of assets as mitigating factors in the inflation crunch-strain equation. Chapter 8 looks at the role of public assets, that is, various welfare programs, in easing the pain of rampant inflation and unemployment. The survey tapped access to various public assets from social security to unemployment insurance, welfare, and food stamps. Are the families who have taken advantage of these programs suffering less than their peers who have not taken advantage of them? This chapter focuses on a critical difference between the depression of the thirties and the recession of the seventies—the existence of these welfare programs and their significance for the well-being of the population. Chapter 9 examines the role of an important private asset, homeownership, in mitigating the strains of inflation and recession. Homeownership in the seventies is characteristic of a majority of American families, and because of inflation, this asset has appreciated in value. Are homeowners better able to meet the pressures of inflation and recession than nonhomeowners?

A word of explanation is perhaps in order for the title of Part IV, "The Impact of Inflation-Recession on the Mind." Mind is used here in contrast with psyche which is that part of the personality that is the home of feelings and emotions, the components of mental health, or psychological well-being. Such things as anxiety, self-esteem, anger, love, confidence, and fear belong to the psyche. The mind, in contrast, is the home of cognition and thought. The components of the mind include ideas, values, attitudes, and beliefs, and it is these elements that are dealt with in Part IV. Chapter 10 examines the economy's impact on selected values of some importance. To what extent have these economic pressures shaken people's aspirations for the good life? Have people been forced to lower their aspirations and standard of living? To what extent have these economic crises led people to lose faith in our economic system? And to what extent have the failures of the economy reverberated on the federal government, causing people to lose confidence in political leaders and their government? These questions will be examined in Chapter 10. Chapter 11 looks at the respondents' beliefs regarding the causes of inflation and recession and their proposed solutions to these problems. This chapter will be of some interest to policy-makers who must design strategies for coping with these problems, for it will show them what kinds of strategies people are prepared to accept.

Chapter 12, the concluding chapter, summarizes the main findings and addresses their implications for public policy. To summarize this table of organization, it consists of the following elements: (1) Who is hurting from inflation and recession? (2) what have people done to fight inflation and recession, and what has inflation-recession done to them? (3) what assets do people have that mitigate the impact of inflation and recession? and (4) how have inflation and recession affected the thinking of people, what they consider important and unimportant, what they believe in and have faith in, and what they think are the forces at work that are causing them these economic difficulties and what can be done about them?

PART I

THE IMPACT OF INFLATION AND RECESSION

Chapter 2

THE VICTIMS OF INFLATION AND RECESSION

When the cost of living rises sharply and unemployment increases, many families suffer. But by the same token, many other families are able to weather the storm with little or no difficulty. Their income rises to keep pace with prices, and they do not lose their jobs. The first order of business is to measure the impact of these economic pressures on the families. How many families have failed to keep up with rising prices, and in how many families did the chief wage earner feel the recession? And what kinds of families failed to keep up, and what kinds of families did keep up with the rising cost of living? And which sectors of the population were most vulnerable to unemployment? These questions concern us in this chapter.

Objective Inflation Crunch

The respondents in this survey were interviewed in May and June of 1976, almost two years after the peak of double digit inflation and some eleven months after the recession had bottomed out and the economy had started to turn upward. By every reasonable standard one might suppose that people were generally better off than they had been two years earlier. But as we shall see, the majority of the respondents in our sample did not think they were better off. In fact, a majority thought they were worse off.

A measure of the impact of inflation is provided by the following question:

Over the past couple of years, has your income kept up with the rising cost of living or has it fallen behind?

Those who said that their income kept up were then asked:

Are you better off financially now than you were a few years ago, or are you just staying even?

Those who said that their income had fallen behind were asked:

Are you a little worse off or a lot worse off now than you were a few years ago?

These questions yield a four point scale measuring the impact of inflation in the families. In all, 41 percent of the respondents said that they had managed to keep up with the cost of living, and 59 percent said they had fallen behind. The distribution of the more detailed breakdown is as follows:

Better off now	16%
Stayed even	25
A little worse off	37
A lot worse off	22
	100%
	(1,955)

All but twenty-seven of the respondents answered these questions. As the figures show, the modal category consists of those who said they are a little worse off than they were a few years ago. A little more than one-fifth said they are a lot worse off. A quarter of the respondents managed to keep up with rising prices, and some 16 percent said that their income had increased so much that they were actually better off than they were a few years ago. These results are a marked departure from the pattern that has accompanied the development of our affluent society in the decades since World War II. Throughout the fifties and sixties, a clear majority of our wage earners experienced a steady increase in their real income from one year to the next. Had these questions been asked in a survey conducted in 1970 or 1972, a great majority would have said that they were better off financially than they had been a few years earlier. That only a small minority gave this response is a clear indication of the impact of inflation on American families.

It is important to keep in mind that these samples from four major cities are by no means representative of the country as a whole. As noted, when these respondents were interviewed in 1976, inflation had eased considerably and the economy was in an upturn. Most Americans were presumably better off than two years previously, but this turn for the better is not reflected in this sample. It may well be that those living in large cities were more seriously set back by the cost of living and unemployment than those in small cities and rural areas. Also, our sample overrepresents the hardest hit groups, the poor and the retired.

A national survey conducted by the National Opinion Research Center only a few months before our survey found that for the country as a whole, most people felt that their financial situation had improved or had stabilized. The NORC question did not specifically refer to the rising cost of living as did our question. It read as follows:

During the last few years, has your financial situation been getting better, getting worse or has it stayed the same?

By not linking financial situation to cost of living, the NORC question might have invited respondents to report whether their income had increased over the past few years, even if it had not caught up with the cost of living. In any case, fully 36 percent of the NORC sample said their financial situation was getting better compared with 16 percent of our sample who said they were better off now than a few years previously. Forty-one percent of the NORC national sample said their financial situation had stayed the same, compared with 25 percent of our sample, and only 23 percent of the national sample said they were worse off financially, compared with 59 percent of our sample. As noted, part of the difference in these results can be attributed to the wording of the questions, but it is also due, in part, to our samples, specifically the overrepresentation of the poor and the retired. But as we shall soon see, even those relatively well-off in our survey—those earning over $20,000 and those with professional and managerial occupations—are much more likely to say their financial situation has deteriorated than the respondents in the NORC sample. The comparison of our data with the NORC data provides some clue to how our sample differs from a national sample, but given the differences in the wording of the questions, it may well be that the NORC study underestimates the impact of inflation.

Toward the end of the interview, the respondents in our survey were asked what their family income had been in 1975, and what it had been two years earlier, in 1973. Almost one-third of the respondents were either unable or refused to answer these questions. But by comparing the income data for 1973 and 1975 provided by the 70 percent who did answer both questions with their estimates of whether they are better or worse off than a few years earlier, we can assess the validity of respondents' estimates of their financial situation. Income increases that exceeded the rate of inflation are equated with better off; income increases which kept pace with inflation are equated with "even"; and income changes that fell behind inflation are equated with "worse" off. Table 2.1 shows how these changes in income are related to the respondents' estimates of their financial situation.

Table 2.1 shows a strong correlation between the respondents' estimates of their financial situation compared to a few years ago and actual changes in their income over that period. Those who claim they are better off now are much more likely to have experienced a substantial increase in their income than those who think they are worse off. And conversely, those who

Table 2.1: Changes in Income 1973–76 by Estimates of Financial
Situation (percentages)

Income 1975 Relative to 1973	Better Off	Stayed Even	A Little Worse	A Lot Worse
24% + higher (better)	53	30	23	14
15–23% higher (even)	23	34	31	20
10–15% higher (little worse)	17	26	31	30
0–10% higher (lot worse)	7	10	16	36
	100	100	101	100
N	(229)	(352)	(521)	(315)

say they are worse off now, were much more likely to experience only modest changes in income, increases substantially
below the rate of inflation over this three year period. But
Table 2.1 also discloses that some respondents misjudge their
financial situation. Some 24 percent of those who said they are
better off financially than a few years ago, experienced income
changes below the rate of inflation and at the other extreme,
about one-third of those who said they were a lot worse off
financially had income increases that at least kept pace with the
rate of inflation. But these judgments that seem at odds with
income changes need not be errors. Whether a family experiences itself as better or worse off financially than in the past is
related not only to income changes but also to changes in
demands on income. For example, a family that has married off
a daughter may feel it is financially better off even though its
income has not changed, and a family that has grown because of
births may need more income than before and may feel
strapped even though its income has increased substantially over
the three year period. The import of Table 2.1 is that the
respondents' estimates of their financial well-being is very much
related to changes in their income. In the subsequent analysis
we shall treat these estimates of their financial situation as the
measure of the impact of inflation on the families in the study.

The Victims of Objective Inflation Crunch

The primary concern of this analysis is to find out who the
victims of inflation were, and, conversely, who were the people

who kept up with even sharply rising prices. The first question is whether it makes a difference where one lives. Has the sharp rise in prices affected people in all parts of the country in the same way, or are those in certain regions suffering more than those in other regions? When objective inflation crunch, as measured by the respondents' assessments of their financial situation, is related to city, we find that the New York respondents were somewhat worse off than those in Detroit and San Francisco, as 64 percent of the New York sample said they were worse off financially than in previous years, compared with 56 percent in Detroit and 55 percent in San Francisco. The Atlanta respondents were almost as bad off as those in New York, as 62 percent of them said they were worse off than previously. But these differences are too small to be very significant, and the safest conclusion is that people in all the regions were affected by inflation to almost the same degree.

The sampling plan for this study insured that substantial numbers of the poor and retired would be sampled since it is widely assumed that these groups were especially hard hit by inflation. The various subsamples represent in part different social classes. To round out the picture of inflation and social class we also present in Table 2.2 three other indicators of social position, income, occupation, and race-ethnicity.

The expectation that the poor and the retired would be most hard hit by inflation is confirmed by Table 2.2. Fully 80 percent of the poor were worse off financially than they were a few years ago, as were 66 percent of the retired. In contrast, 59 percent of the blue collar and only 49 percent of the white collar respondents claimed they were worse off. At the other extreme, 26 percent of the white collar respondents felt they were better off financially than a few years previously, compared with 14 percent of the blue collar respondents and only tiny fractions of the retired and poor (6 percent and 4 percent, respectively). Underlying these differences in the various subsamples is probably income inasmuch as the white collar group tends to have much higher income than the blue collar and poor samples. The second part of Table 2.2 shows that income is a major factor affecting the impact of inflation. As income

Table 2.2: Objective Inflation Crunch by Selected Social Characteristics (percentages)

	Better Off	Stayed Even	Little Worse	Lot Worse		N
Subsample						
Poor	4	16	37	43	100	(318)
Blue collar	14	28	38	21	101	(575)
White collar	26	26	37	12	101	(758)
Retired	6	29	41	25	101	(305)
Income						
Under $7,000	3	17	39	42	101	(389)
$7,000–$12,999	8	23	40	29	100	(390)
$13,000–$19,999	15	28	43	14	100	(435)
$20,000 and over	33	29	30	8	100	(462)
Occupation						
Higher white collar	24	27	36	13	100	(670)
Lower white collar	18	26	37	19	100	(292)
Higher blue collar	13	26	38	23	100	(341)
Lower blue collar	8	23	38	31	100	(653)
Race-Ethnicity						
White	19	28	36	17	100	(1,446)
Black	8	17	42	33	100	(400)
Spanish-speaking	3	14	36	47	100	(87)

increases, the percentage who say they are worse off, especially a lot worse off, declines sharply, and the percentage who feel that their financial situation has improved increases sharply. The same patterns hold for occupation. The higher the occupational prestige, the smaller the percentage who are worse off financially and the higher the percentage who are better off. Finally, Table 2.2 shows that the minorities, the blacks and Spanish-speaking, were much harder hit by inflation than the whites. Taken together, these findings demonstrate the major importance of social class in determining the impact of inflation. Clearly, it is the lower social classes that have most difficulty keeping up with rising prices. The middle classes are likely to experience rising incomes which offset the increases in prices. Inflation turns out to be a significant force exacerbating the differences in the social classes. Them that hath not are the hardest hit.

Another measure of social stratification, education, is also related to inflation impact. The college graduates were much more likely than those of low education to say that their financial situation had actually improved and much less likely to say that they were worse off financially. In sum, inflation is a disease that infects the underprivileged much more than the privileged members of society. For all the complaining that the middle classes do about rising prices, the data show that they are not nearly as affected by inflation as are the classes below them.

The families in the sample varied considerably in size. Some 36 percent of them consisted of one or two persons, 42 percent of three or four persons, and 22 percent of five or more persons. One might suppose that large families have more difficulty keeping up with rising prices than small families in that their consumer needs are greater. Inasmuch as large families tend to have larger incomes than small families, it would be necessary to take income into account when relating family size to inflation crunch. Controlling for income allows us to consider yet another question: whether income is the critical link between the various social statuses, such as subsample, occupation, and race-ethnicity and inflation crunch. Table 2.3 presents three variable relationships: family size and inflation crunch, subsample and inflation crunch, and race-ethnicity and inflation crunch when income is held constant. The rows of Table 2.3 tell us what we already know, that income is a major determinant of inflation impact. Of more relevance for our present purposes are the columns of Table 2.3. The columns in the top third of the table confirm our expectation that large families have more difficulty keeping up with rising prices than small families. Thus, on every income level, the families with five or more members were more likely to say they were worse off than smaller families. The second part of Table 2.3, dealing with subsample, tells us that the reason the subsamples experienced inflation differently is because of the differences in their income. When income is held constant, there is little difference in how the subsamples experienced inflation. The difference between the blue collar and white collar completely disappears

Table 2.3: Percentage Worse off (Little or Lot) Financially by Selected
           Social Characteristics and Income

	Under $7,000	$7,000-$12,999	$13,000-$19,999	$20,000 and Over
Family Size				
1, 2 persons	76 (196)	62 (149)	55 (121)	29 (114)
3, 4 persons	84 (129)	69 (156)	54 (209)	29 (220)
5 or more persons	86 (64)	83 (80)	66 (101)	43 (128)
Subsample				
Poor	84 (256)	–	–	–
Blue collar	–	71 (212)	56 (232)	39 (104)
White collar	–	69 (107)	57 (175)	38 (347)
Retired	75 (142)	62 (66)	52 (79)	27 (11)
Race-Ethnicity				
White	75 (190)	65 (245)	56 (371)	37 (414)
Black	87 (149)	77 (109)	65 (49)	54 (39)
Spanish-speaking	85 (29)	86 (29)	* (5)	* (5)

*The asterisk symbolizes a case base too small for percentaging.

and the gap between these groups and the retired narrows
sharply. Inasmuch as no poor earned over $7,000 by definition,
the poor can only be compared with the retired in this income
group, and they are only slightly more likely than the retired to
say that they are worse off financially. Although not presented
in the table, occupation behaves much like subsample when
income is controlled. The differences between the occupational
groups with respect to inflation crunch tend to disappear on
each income level.

While income washes out the differences between the subsamples and occupational groups, it does not eliminate the
differences between the racial-ethnic groups, as can be seen
from Table 2.3. On every income level, the blacks and Spanish-
speaking are more likely to be worse off financially than the
whites. This would suggest that whites and the minorities really
differ on income even when family income is held roughly
constant. For example, black families might be larger than
white families, thus having smaller per capita income than
whites, and black families might be more dependent on multiple

wage earners, meaning they must work harder to match the income of white families. But the data on hand lend little support to these theories of the race-ethnicity differences in objective inflation crunch when income is controlled. For one thing, whites are as likely as blacks and more so than the Spanish-speaking to have spouses of the chief wage earners employed, and when the retired are excluded, the whites exceed the blacks in having spouses in the labor force.

On size of family, the data show that the minority families do tend to be larger than the white families, but the differences are quite small. Thus, 19 percent of the white families have five or more members compared with 24 percent of the Spanish-speaking and 29 percent of the blacks. It is most doubtful that this difference accounts for the fact that blacks and the Spanish-speaking were harder hit by inflation than whites when income is held constant.

The analysis of vulnerability to inflation crunch has identified the kinds of families who have been most affected by rising prices. As we have seen, they tend to be the poor, the retired, and those of relatively low occupation and education. But the most important factor, the one that largely explains the other correlates of inflation crunch, is income. The people who are most affected by sharply rising prices are those toward the bottom half of the income distribution. Wealthy families and particularly those who enjoy rising income are able to weather the storm of inflation. On the basis of these data we can conclude that inflation is a force contributing to the economic cleavage of American society—between the haves and the have nots.

Impact of the Recession

Sharply rising prices were not the only scourge of the economy in 1974-1975. An even more serious problem, one that is still very much with us today, is unemployment. Nineteen seventy-five saw unemployment rates climb to the highest levels since the great depression of the thirties, and while unemployment has declined since the 1975 peak, it is still well above normal, hovering at 7 percent. Unemployment has been a more serious problem in major metropolitan areas than in the country at large, and the data of our four city survey reflect this. In the late spring of 1976 when this survey was conducted, the unemployment rate in these cities was 9.6 percent (the retired are excluded from this calculation). The unemployment rate was highest, as expected, in Detroit, 12.2 percent; New York was second with a rate of 9.9 percent, followed by Atlanta, 9.5 percent, and San Francisco, 8.7 percent.

Unemployment was the ultimate impact of the recession, but the jobs of many people were affected by the recession short of unemployment. Many people were employed in sectors of the economy where the impact of the recession was particularly great, and they were very worried about losing their jobs. Those who were in the labor force were asked how worried they were about losing their jobs, and some 7 percent said they were very worried, and an additional 19 percent said they were somewhat worried. The 26 percent who manifested some worry about losing their job were thus experiencing some impact of the recession. The respondents were also asked whether they were forced to work a shorter week because of the recession, and 12 percent answered affirmatively. Still another way in which the recession affected jobs was to curtail the amount of overtime work. Some 14 percent of the workers told us that they were forced to work less overtime because of the recession. Yet another way in which the recession impacted on jobs was to force people to work harder because of layoffs. The respondents were asked whether this had happened to them, and almost a quarter of the chief wage earners, 24 percent, said that they had to work harder because of layoffs. The respondents were also asked how many workers were laid off at their place of work because of the recession. Some 27 percent said a lot were, 29 percent said some were, and 44 percent said hardly any layoffs had occurred. These various measures of the recession's impact provide the basis for an index of this concept. In constructing this index we have assigned a high score to the unemployed, as well as those who answered at least three of the remaining five questions positively (a "yes" response to a

shorter work week, less overtime, working harder, worrying
about losing a job, and having a lot of coworkers laid off). This
high impact category comprise some 23 percent of the sample.
The medium impact category is made up of those who were
employed but answered one or two of the remaining five
questions positively, a group consisting of 37 percent of the
sample, and the low or no impact category, the employed who
answered none of these questions positively, comprise 40 percent of the sample.

THE RECESSION VICTIMS

Who are the people most likely to be victims of the recession? Are they evenly distributed through the various segments
of society or does the recession have an impact on certain
groups rather than others? What role does social class play in
recession impact? Table 2.4 shows the connection between
four social class indicators and recession impact, subsample,
income, occupation, and race-ethnicity.

**Table 2.4: Recession Impact by Selected Social Characteristics
(percentages)**

	Recession Impact				
	None	*Some*	*Considerable*		*N*
Subsample					
Poor	20	29	51	100	(323)
Blue collar	32	42	26	100	(581)
White collar	54	36	9	88	(769)
Income					
Under $7,000	17	28	54	100	(261)
$7,000–$12,999	29	40	31	100	(323)
$13,000–$19,999	38	43	18	99	(411)
$20,000 and over	56	36	8	100	(451)
Occupation					
Higher white collar	55	34	10	100	(573)
Lower white collar	47	40	13	100	(241)
Higher blue collar	28	38	34	100	(293)
Lower blue collar	27	37	36	100	(566)
Race-Ethnicity					
White	44	39	17	100	(1,180)
Black	30	33	38	101	(385)
Spanish-speaking	15	33	52	100	(85)

Table 2.4 shows that the recession was much more of a problem for certain social groups than for others. Fully half the poor were hard hit by the recession compared with a one-quarter of the blue collar and less than one-tenth of the white collar groups. Income proves to be a strong determinant of recession impact. More than half of those earning under $7,000 were hard hit by the recession, a figure that steadily declines as income increases, reaching only 8 percent of those with incomes above $20,000. Conversely, those who managed to escape completely from the recession steadily increases with income, from a low of 17 percent in the lowest income group to a high of 56 percent in the highest income group. The poor tend to have semiskilled and unskilled jobs, and, as the third part of Table 2.4 shows, it is precisely those in the lower blue collar occupations who are hardest hit by the recession. But it is also possible that for some people the causal connection between income and recession runs in the other direction. Some people undoubtedly became poor because they lost their jobs due to the recession.

The data for occupation in the third part of the table show that the critical distinction is between white collar and blue collar employment regardless of level. Blue collar workers, whether they are skilled or unskilled, are equally vulnerable to recessions and white collar workers, whether professionals and managers or clerical and sales, are relatively immune to the ravages of recessions. Thus, only about one in ten of the white collar workers compared with one in three of the blue collar experienced a considerable impact of the recession on their jobs. Finally, as can be seen from Table 2.4, the blacks and Spanish-speaking suffered much more from the recession than the whites. Although not shown in the table, education too, is strongly related to recession impact, as the poorly educated were much harder hit than the well educated. Just as inflation had its greatest impact on the least powerful and the under-privileged, so these same groups are most vulnerable to recession.

Those who were touched by the recession, especially the unemployed, but those who had to work shorter weeks and less overtime as well, undoubtedly suffered more from inflation than those who were not affected by the recession. After all, not only did their income not keep up with rising prices, but it actually declined because of the recession. The recession victims were thus in a double bind. At the same time that prices were rising, their incomes were decreasing. The data show that they indeed had more difficulty keeping up with rising prices. Among those who were untouched by the recession, 28 percent said they were better off financially and 33 percent had stayed even. Thirty percent were a little worse off, and only 9 percent were a lot worse off. Among those who experienced some impact of the recession, the better off declined to 14 percent, those who had stayed even, to 21 percent, those a little worse off had climbed to 43 percent and those a lot worse off to 25 percent. Those who were especially hard hit by the recession had most difficulty with inflation. Only 21 percent of them stayed even or moved ahead, whereas 39 percent were a little worse off and fully 40 percent a lot worse off. In spite of this strong relationship, it would seem that one's financial situation is affected by factors other than security of employment, inasmuch as 21 percent of those hardest hit by the recession were able to stay even with rising prices, and some 39 percent of those who were not affected by the recession said their financial situation was worse than it had been.

A major finding of the analysis so far has been the sharp difference between whites and minority groups with regard to unemployment and other facets of the recession. The recession would appear to concentrate on the minorities, leaving the dominant white group relatively untouched. To what extent is this racial-ethnic difference a consequence of other factors, such as income and occupation? The blacks and Spanish-speaking tend to have much lower status occupations than the whites and to earn less money. Do these factors explain the ethnic difference? Table 2.5, which examines ethnicity in the context of first income and then occupation, provides the answer.

From the top half of Table 2.5 we see that income does not explain the differences between the ethnic groups. On the lower income levels the blacks were more likely to have been hit hard by the recession than the whites, and on those income levels where there were sufficient numbers of Spanish-speaking to percentage, they turned out to be the hardest hit group. Nor does occupation wash out the race-ethnicity differences. Even though blacks tend to be on the lower rungs of the occupational ladder, they still suffered more from the recession than the whites in every occupational group. Only among the higher blue collar occupations do the whites approximate the blacks in recession impact. But among the higher and lower white collar groups and the lower blue collar, whites clearly fared better than blacks during the recession.

Earlier we saw that blacks and the Spanish-speaking were affected by inflation more so than whites even when income was taken into account and Table 2.5 shows that these minority groups suffered more from the recession than the whites for reasons unrelated to their income or occupation. These findings provide convincing proof of the second class status of the blacks and Spanish-speaking in America. Even when they match the whites in terms of income and occupation, they still lose out by being the victims of inflation and recession much more so than the whites. Their being victims of the recession might be understood in terms of the principle of last hired first fired. But why should they experience inflation more than the whites? Clearly, their incomes have not kept up with rising prices to the same extent that the incomes of the whites have. Could this mean

Table 2.5: **Percentage Experiencing Considerable Impact of the Recession by Ethnicity Holding Constant Income and Occupation**

			Race-Ethnicity			
	Whites		*Blacks*		*Spanish-Speaking*	
Income						
Under $7,000	44	(71)	58	(141)	65	(45)
$7,000–$12,999	28	(185)	34	(107)	41	(29)
$13,000–$19,999	18	(350)	16	(50)	*	(5)
$20,000 and over	8	(403)	8	(39)	*	(3)
Occupation						
Higher white collar	9	(501)	21	(57)	*	(6)
Lower white collar	9	(185)	18	(43)	20	(10)
Higher blue collar	30	(224)	33	(48)	75	(16)
Lower blue collar	25	(270)	44	(237)	55	(53)

that minorities have fewer chances for promotion and salary increases than whites?

The tables presented above make clear that unemployment and the other negative facets of the recession, such as reduced income and fear of job loss, are primarily a problem of minority groups and the poor, even more so than inflation. Perhaps it is for this reason that no dramatic effort has been made by the government to combat unemployment. For all the hue and cry about unemployment and the recession, relatively little has been done about it, and these data suggest that the reason for this is that the people who suffer from the recession are the powerless—the people who don't count.

This chapter has examined the kinds of people vulnerable to inflation and recession. We have seen that both of these economic ills have their impact on the same kinds of people, the poor, the poorly skilled, the poorly educated, and members of minority groups. The haves in society are much more successful than the have nots in avoiding the scourges of inflation and recession. Of the two evils, inflation and recession, we found that the effects of inflation were more pervasive than those of recession. Thus, even among the well-off, significant minorities said that they had been hurt by rising prices. In contrast, unemployment and the recession generally are almost exclusively a problem of the downtrodden, the poor, the unskilled, and the blacks and Spanish-speaking. These findings provide some insight into the policies of the key decision-makers in society. For all the evils of recession, inflation seems to be even more feared by governmental policy-makers, probably because it has some impact on the powerful middle classes, whereas unemployment is a problem that besets the powerless. By affecting the have nots much more than the haves, the economic calamities of inflation and recession exacerbate the basic cleavage in society between the two groups. In times of prosperity, the differences between the privileged and the underprivileged tend to be muted; when the economy goes awry, the have nots are so disproportionately the victims that society runs the risk of being torn asunder.

Chapter 3

SUBJECTIVE INFLATION CRUNCH

The previous chapter dealt with the extent to which family resources were able to keep up with the rising cost of living. The unemployed of course were worst off, but many others fell behind as their incomes failed to keep pace with inflation. As noted, the discrepancy between income and rising prices can be viewed as "objective inflation crunch," and the kinds of people who were the victims of objective inflation crunch were described in the previous chapter. But families in the same objective circumstances frequently respond differently. Some families who managed to stay even with rising prices but failed to have their economic situation improve dramatically may have been deeply disappointed and on a subjective level suffered a good deal. Conversely, other families whose incomes failed to keep up may have developed stoic attitudes and while tightening their belts, not experienced any deprivations. In short, the subjective dimension of inflation crunch is by no means the mirror image of the objective dimension. Some families in similar circumstances undoubtedly suffered much more from inflation than others. The task of this chapter is to explore this subjective dimension of inflation crunch.

The respondents were presented with a series of statements with which they could agree or disagree, that tapped their experiences with inflation and the degree to which they were hurting. Table 3.1 presents these statements and the frequency of responses to them.

The eleven statements cover a wide range of responses to inflationary pressures. The item most widely accepted, by 58 percent of the respondents, is that inflation is depressing. The item endorsed by the fewest number, only 15 percent of the sample, is that inflation has brought the family to the brink of poverty. Only four of the statements were endorsed by at least half the sample; in addition to inflation being depressing, these

Table 3.1: Impact of Inflation

Q. I'm going to read to you a list of statements about inflation that might apply to you. For each one, tell me whether you agree or disagree.

Statement	Agree	Disagree	DK/NA
(1) Inflation is depressing to me; it's as if it will never end	58%	38%	4%
(2) The money we earn is becoming worthless	57	36	8
(3) We've stopped buying any luxury items	55	41	4
(4) We now repair a lot of things we used to throw away	51	45	4
(5) Because of inflation, we are scrimping and doing without	47	51	2
(6) We're earning more than we ever did and can't save a penny	38	52	10
(7) Things are so bad that we've had to go into our savings	36	55	9
(8) We've even stopped buying many things we need	34	64	2
(9) Things have gotten so bad that many people have to do illegal things in order to survive	31	61	7
(10) We've never been hurt so hard before, everything is turning into a hardship	27	69	4
(11) We are on the brink of poverty	15	81	4

are that money is becoming worthless, the exclusion of luxury items from the family budget and repairing items rather than throwing them away. Almost half the respondents said they were scrimping and doing without and more than a third have been unable to save money and have had to dip into their savings in order to get by. Nine of these eleven items have been combined into an index of subjective inflation crunch, that is, how much the family is hurting because of inflation. (The two excluded items are "we are on the brink of poverty" because so few people accepted it and "we've stopped buying any luxury items" because this item would not seem to reflect much pain.) The distribution of cases on this measure is as follows:

Index Score	N	Percentage
0 low	239	12
1	218	11
2	255	13
3	230	12
4	220	11
5	214	11
6	215	11
7	224	11
8	125	6
9 high	42	2
	1,982	100

Some 12 percent of the sample felt no pain at all as a result of inflation in that they rejected all nine of these symptoms of suffering, and an additional 11 percent felt virtually no pain in that they endorsed but one of the nine items. At the other extreme, 8 percent were particularly crushed by inflation in that they answered affirmatively to eight or nine of the symptoms. For the purposes of the subsequent analysis we shall distinguish four groups on this index: those who scored low (0 or 1) consisting of 23 percent of the sample; those who had a medium low score (2 or 3), 25 percent; those with a medium high score (4 or 5), 22 percent; and those with a very high score (6 or more), a group constituting 30 percent of the sample.

Just as New York scored higher on objective inflation crunch than the other cities, so it leads the others in subjective inflation crunch with 59 percent scoring in the high categories. Atlanta was the next hardest hit city with 52 percent high, followed by San Francisco, 50 percent, and Detroit, 49 percent. In all, relatively little variation occurs across cities, as was the case with objective inflation crunch. The inflation crisis of the past few years has been very much a national rather than regional problem.

In the previous chapter we saw that the underprivileged were much more likely to be victims of inflation than the more privileged social groupings. Will this be true of subjective inflation crunch, the degree of suffering caused by inflation? Table

Table 3.2: Subjective Inflation Crunch by Selected Social Characteristics (percentages)

| | Subjective Inflation Crunch | | | | | |
	Low	Medium Low	Medium High	High		N
Subsample						
Poor	6	11	26	58	100	(323)
Blue collar	14	26	23	37	101	(581)
White collar	34	29	19	18	100	(769)
Retired	31	24	24	21	100	(309)
Income						
Under $7,000	9	14	26	51	100	(395)
$7,000–$12,999	14	21	24	41	100	(390)
$13,000–$19,999	20	27	24	29	100	(435)
$20,000 and over	38	33	18	11	100	(462)
Occupation						
Higher white collar	33	30	18	18	99	(680)
Lower white collar	34	23	22	21	100	(296)
Higher blue collar	14	26	24	36	100	(344)
Lower blue collar	12	18	25	45	100	(662)
Race-Ethnicity						
White	28	27	21	24	100	(1,464)
Black	10	15	26	49	100	(407)
Spanish-speaking	3	17	18	61	99	(88)

3.2 presents the data on four measures of privilege, the sub-samples, income, occupation, and race-ethnicity.

The patterns in Table 3.2 are very much like those in the previous chapter with one critical exception. The lower the privilege of the social group, the more likely is it to suffer from inflation. The exception is the retired. From the top part of the table we see that the poor were much more likely to suffer from inflation than the other groups as more than half of them were in the highest category and 84 percent of them in the two high categories. But rather than the retired being in second place, it is the blue collar sample that occupies that position. The retired, in spite of having their income fall behind rising prices to almost the same extent as the poor, were not nearly as likely as the poor to be hurting. On the contrary, the retired were almost as free of pain from inflation as the white collar group. When these results are compared with those for objective inflation crunch, we find that the poor and the blue collar were as likely to be hurting as they were to have fallen behind rising prices, but the white collar and the retired were much more likely to be high on objective inflation crunch than on subjective crunch. The white collar group presumably has more resources than the other groups that allow it to adjust better to inflation. But the retired are not likely to have financial resources, and their ability to adjust to inflation must come from different sources. Perhaps the retired experience less pain from inflation than the poor and the blue collar families because they are relatively inactive as consumers. They are at the stage of life where their wants tend to be minimal, and this might make it easier for them to adjust to rising prices.

The patterns for income shown in Table 3.2 are as expected. Those earning under $7,000 were five times more likely to be in the high category than the most well-to-do families. Comparing these results with those found for objective inflation crunch shows that the higher income families, like the white collar families, were more likely to experience inflation than suffer from it. Thus, 56 percent of those in the $13,000-$19,999 range said their incomes had fallen behind rising prices, compared with 47 percent who said they were hurting from inflation (at least medium high). In the highest income group these figures are 38 and 30 percent. In contrast, among those earning under $15,000 almost as many were suffering from inflation as were experiencing it.

The occupational patterns are much the same as those for income. The higher the occupation, the less likely were people to be suffering from inflation. Finally, the blacks and Spanish-speaking were much more likely to be suffering from inflation than the whites. As can be seen, only a minority of the whites, a smaller proportion than those who experienced inflation, were suffering from it. In contrast, three out of every four black families (medium high and high) were hurting because of infla-tion, and the Spanish-speaking were even harder hit than the blacks. Just as the objective experience of falling behind rising prices is much more likely to be a problem of the poor and the underprivileged, so the pain of inflation is even more likely to be an affliction of the poor and minority groups.

When education is taken into account, the results are much the same as those for income and occupation. The more edu-cated the family head, the less likely is the family to be suffering because of inflation. Of those who failed to complete high school, fully 69 percent were in the high categories on subjective inflation crunch, a figure that steadily declines to 29 percent of those who graduated from college. Income, occupa-tion, and education are traditionally viewed as the key dimen-sions of social class. It is clear then, that social class is a key determinant of a family's vulnerability to or immunity from the ravages of inflation. Those who are favored in social life are relatively immune to inflation; those who are underprivileged are especially likely to be victims of economic ills.

As we saw in the previous chapter, those most vulnerable to rising prices were the people who suffered a sharp decline in income because they were unemployed. Table 3.3 shows how unemployment specifically and the recession impact index generally are related to subjective inflation crunch.

The unemployed were twice as likely as the employed to be in the highest category of subjective inflation crunch. All told, more than four out of every five unemployed families were

Table 3.3: Subjective Inflation Crunch by Unemployment and Recession
            Impact (percentages)

| | Subjective Inflation Crunch | | | | | |
	Low	Medium Low	Medium High	High		N
Employment Status						
Employed	23	26	21	29	99	(1,503)
Unemployed	8	10	24	59	101	(169)
Recession Impact						
None	37	32	15	16	100	(666)
Some	15	23	28	34	100	(617)
Considerable	7	15	22	56	100	(390)

suffering from inflation (the two highest categories) compared
with only half of the employed families. From the second half
of Table 3.3 we see that suffering from inflation is strongly
related to recession impact. Among those who were hard hit by
the recession, including many who did not lose their jobs, a
majority were in the highest category on subjective crunch
compared to only 16 percent of those who were not at all
touched by the recession. Table 3.3 dramatizes the evils of the
twin aberration of inflation and recession. Those who are
affected by the recesssion are people whose earnings powers
have been impaired by the economic slowdown. And it is
precisely these people who are unable to cope with rising prices.
In short, those who suffer from recession are the same people
who suffer from inflation.

In the previous chapter we saw that family size was related to
objective inflation crunch once income was held constant and
we saw that the race-ethnicity differences persisted even when
income, a major determinant of inflation crunch, was taken into
account. Table 3.4 presents these relationships for subjective
inflation crunch.

From the top half of the table we see that with one slight
reversal, family size is related to subjective inflation crunch
once income is held constant. The reversal occurs in the under
$7,000 group, where the medium sized families were slightly

Table 3.4: Percentage High on Subjective Inflation Crunch by Family
            Size and Race-Ethnicity Holding Income Constant

	Income			
	Under *$7,000*	*$7,000-* *$12,999*	*$13,000-* *$19,999*	*$20,000* *and Over*
Family Size				
1, 2 persons	68 (200)	48 (151)	43 (122)	23 (114)
3, 4 persons	87 (131)	71 (157)	51 (211)	28 (220)
5 or more persons	83 (64)	82 (82)	67 (102)	39 (128)
Race-Ethnicity				
White	64 (192)	58 (247)	50 (301)	27 (414)
Black	89 (152)	75 (112)	60 (50)	51 (39)
Spanish-speaking	83 (47)	79 (29)	* (5)	* (3)

more likely to be hurting than the large families. It turns out
that family size is even more strongly related to subjective
crunch than to objective crunch shown in the previous chapter.
Small families suffer less from inflation than large families even
when their incomes fall behind rising prices. Or put another
way, the same degree of inflation is more costly to large than to
small families. The second part of the table shows that income
does not explain the difference between whites and the minorities on subjective crunch. Even when income is held constant,
the blacks and Spanish-speaking were much more likely to
suffer from inflation than the whites. Apart from income,
blacks and Spanish-speaking families would seem to lack the
resources that would allow them to adjust to inflation. Perhaps
their families are larger and hence their needs are greater on
each level of income. Or perhaps they are more removed from
the patterns of adjustment to be explored in a later chapter.
Whatever the reasons, the data clearly show that the minority
groups are not only more likely to be victims of inflation but
they are also more likely to suffer from it than the dominant
white group.

Objective v. Subjective Inflation Crunch

Families which claimed that they were worse off financially
than a few years earlier (those who experienced objective infla-

tion crunch) were of course much more likely than those who had kept up with rising prices to be suffering from inflation. Thus, among those who said that their financial situation had improved, only 19 percent were hurting, a figure that rises to 26 percent of those who managed to stay even with rising prices. Among those who said they were a little worse off financially, the percentage hurting soars to 61 and among those who said they were a lot worse off financially, the rate of suffering is 83 percent, an overall difference of 64 percentage points. The strong correlation between objective and subjective inflation crunch notwithstanding, an equally important finding is that some of those who stayed even or got ahead of rising prices still reported to be suffering from inflation, and some of those who failed to keep up with rising prices nonetheless had no complaints and were not suffering. These deviant cases are deserving of closer examination. Table 3.5 identifies the frequency of the different types based on the objective and subjective dimensions of inflation crunch.

The largest group, consisting of 41 percent of the sample, are the victims of inflation who fell behind rising prices and suffered as a result. The next largest group, 29 percent of the sample, consists of those who escaped completely from the stresses of inflation. Not only were they able to keep up with rising prices but they suffered no inconveniences because of inflation. Of particular interest are the two deviant groups, those with a number of complaints about inflation even though their income had kept up with rising prices, a group we call the complainers, and those who say they have not suffered even though their income has fallen behind rising prices, a group we

Table 3.5: Typology Based on Objective and Subjective Inflation Crunch

Inflation Crunch				
Objective	Subjective	N	Percentages	Type
Low	Low	565	29	Untouched
High	Low	361	18	Stoics
Low	High	236	12	Complainers
High	High	794	41	Suffering victims
		1,956	100%	

call the stoics. The subsequent analysis is devoted to an examination of these social types.

Table 3.6 shows how the various measures of social privilege—subsample, income, occupation, and race-ethnicity—are related to this typology of inflation crunch.

The capacity of the middle classes to escape the ravages of inflation is documented by Table 3.6 as the white collar subsample has by far the largest percentage of "untouched" families, as is true of the high income families, the families at the top of the occupational hierarchy, and the white families. In contrast, the poor, the low income, the lower blue collar workers, and the blacks and Spanish-speaking lead all others in being "suffering victims," people who not only experienced inflation but were suffering from it. As the earlier data suggested, the retired lead all the other subsamples in being stoics. Those in the highest income group were also more likely to be stoics than those of lower income, as was true of white collar compared with blue collar occupations and whites compared with blacks. In short, even when the more privileged groups do experience inflation, they are likely to absorb the shocks without suffering. The critical significance of income in immunizing families from the ravages of inflation is shown by the income patterns in Table 3.6. The single group most immune to inflation consists of those earning over $20,000. Had we broken out the truly high income group, say those earning over $40,000, we would have found that almost all of them were members of the "untouched" type. The race-ethnicity differences are especially sharp in Table 3.6. Whereas more than one-third of the whites were untouched by inflation, only tiny fractions of the blacks and Spanish-speaking were in this group. In fact, whites were as likely to be untouched as suffering victims, as 34 percent of them were in the latter category. In contrast, about two-thirds of the minority groups were suffering victims. The complainers are fairly evenly distributed in the various groups, although complaining is somewhat more typical of the blue collar, especially the higher blue collar workers.

Just as education served to protect families from the costs of inflation, so the better educated were much more likely to be in

Table 3.6: Inflation Crunch Typology by Selected Social Characteristics (percentages)

			Inflation Crunch Typology			
	Untouched	Stoics	Complainers	Suffering Victims		N
Subsample						
Poor	6	10	14	70	100	(318)
Blue collar	26	14	16	44	100	(575)
White collar	41	22	11	26	100	(758)
Retired	28	27	7	39	101	(305)
Income						
Under $7,000	9	14	10	66	99	(389)
$7,000-$12,999	19	16	12	53	100	(385)
$13,000-$19,999	28	19	15	38	100	(431)
$20,000 and over	50	21	12	17	100	(462)
Occupation						
Higher white collar	41	22	9	28	100	(670)
Lower white collar	34	23	11	32	100	(292)
Higher blue collar	23	16	16	45	100	(341)
Lower blue collar	17	14	14	55	100	(653)
Race-Ethnicity						
White	35	20	11	34	100	(1,446)
Black	12	13	13	62	100	(400)
Spanish-speaking	5	16	13	67	100	(87)

47

the untouched category, than the poorly educated. Some 44 percent of the college graduates belong to the untouched type in contrast with 35 percent of those who had some college, 28 percent of the high school graduates and 17 percent of those who had less than a high school education. At the other extreme, only 23 percent of the college graduates were suffering victims compared with 56 percent of those who did not graduate from high school. The better educated no doubt have more resources to tide them over bad times.

Table 3.7 shows how unemployment and recession impact are related to the inflation crunch typology.

The great majority of the unemployed are suffering victims, whereas only a little more than a third of the employed are in this category. The employed are more likely to be stoics than the unemployed, but they are also more likely to be complainers. One would think that none of the unemployed could have escaped inflation, but this is not quite true as 8 percent of the unemployed, some thirteen families, fall into the untouched type. No doubt some unusual circumstances such as inherited wealth explain these deviant cases. As for the recession impact index, the patterns are the expected ones: the greater the impact of the recession, the more likely the family is found among the suffering victims, and the less the recession impact, the greater the likelihood of being untouched by inflation.

We have seen that income does not explain why the minority groups are more likely to experience inflation and the recession than whites and are more likely to hurt when they do feel inflation. Inasmuch as income was a powerful determinant of inflation impact and the blacks and Spanish-speaking earn much less than the whites, it was reasonable to assume that income was the critical link in the race-ethnicity findings. That it is not poses somewhat of a mystery. To make sure that income has no bearing on the race-ethnicity findings, we submit it to a fourth test, its role in the relationship between race-ethnicity and the inflation crunch typology. This is done in Table 3.8.

As can be seen from the table, the differences between whites and the minority groups persist when income is taken into account. On each income level whites are more likely to be

•

Table 3.7: Inflation Crunch Typology by Employment Status and Recession Impact (percentages)

	Untouched	Stoics	Complainers	Suffering Victims		N
Employment Status						
Employed	32	18	13	37	100	(1,484)
Unemployed	8	10	10	72	100	(166)
Recession Impact						
None	48	20	13	19	100	(655)
Some	20	17	15	47	100	(609)
Considerable	11	11	10	68	100	(387)

Table 3.8:   Inflation Crunch Typology by Income and Ethnicity
(percentages)

Inflation Crunch Typology	Under $7,000			$7,000–$12,999		
	White	Black	Spanish-Speaking	White	Black	Spanish-Speaking
Untouched	17	1	2	23	14	10
Stoics	19	9	15	18	12	10
Complainers	4	11	13	11	13	3
Victims	57	79	70	47	59	76
	100	100	100	99	100	99
N	(190)	(149)	(46)	(245)	(109)	(29)

Inflation Crunch Typology	$13,000–$19,999			$20,000 and Over		
	White	Black	Spanish-Speaking	White	Black	Spanish-Speaking
Untouched	30	22	*	52	28	*
Stoics	20	16	*	21	21	*
Complainers	14	12	*	11	18	*
Victims	36	49	*	16	33	*
	100	100		100	100	
N	(371)	(49)	(5)	(414)	(39)	(2)

untouched by inflation than blacks or Spanish-speaking families, and conversely, on each income level blacks much more
often than whites are suffering victims of inflation. These differences are especially pronounced in the lowest income group,
where 79 percent of the blacks compared with 57 percent of
the whites were suffering victims, and where virtually no blacks
were untouched by inflation compared with 17 percent of the
whites. As income increases, the number in each ethnic group
that was untouched by inflation steadily increases. But the
whites benefit most from income as a majority (52 percent) of
the whites in the highest income group were untouched by
inflation compared with only 28 percent of the blacks on this
high income level. Clearly, there is something about the life
circumstances of blacks that makes them more vulnerable than
whites to inflation even when income is held constant. As noted
in the previous chapter, the race-ethnicity differences are not
explained by differences in the number of wage earners in white

and black families nor by the small differences in the size of white families compared with minority families. Since the race-ethnicity differences in inflation impact cannot be explained by income or other factors, race-ethnicity joins income as a major determinant of vulnerability to inflation and recession. It is almost as if the impersonal forces of inflation and recession were somehow engaging in discrimination.

The inflation crunch typology that we have been examining has real consequences for the styles of life of the families interviewed. At one point in the interview, the respondents were asked whether they were prepared to lower their standard of living in order to make ends meet. Oddly enough, in spite of the large numbers who were hurting from inflation, only 35 percent of the respondents said they were willing to lower their standard of living. The readiness to make such a sharp change in life style is strongly related to the inflation crunch typology. Only 9 percent of the untouched said they were ready to lower their standard of living compared with 22 percent of the stoics, 35 percent of the complainers, and fully 59 percent of the suffering victims.

This chapter has reviewed the subjective component of inflation crunch. A measure was developed of how much families have been hurt by rising prices, and we saw that the same social characteristics that were linked to objective inflation crunch were related to the subjective component. Thus, the poor, the blacks and Spanish-speaking families, the blue collar workers, and the poorly educated were much more likely to be suffering from inflation than the well-to-do, the whites, white collar workers, and the well-educated. The unemployed in particular suffered from inflation. Although strongly related, these two dimensions of inflation crunch were somewhat independent of each other, as we found that some families found themselves falling behind rising prices but did not suffer (the stoics) and others managed to stay even with rising prices but still reported hurting from inflation (the complainers). We found that the retired were more likely than the others to be stoics. The stoics were also more common on the higher income levels. Finally, we saw that the typology of inflation crunch was strongly related to willingness to lower one's standard of living. Those who were untouched by inflation were virtually unamimous in rejecting the idea whereas a majority of those who were suffering victims of inflation said they would lower their standard of living to make ends meet.

Chapter 4

THE VOICE OF THE PEOPLE: INFLATION'S IMPACT

IN THE VARIOUS SUBSAMPLES

Chapters 2 and 3 have identified the kinds of people whose incomes failed to keep up with rising prices, the kinds who were affected by the recession, and the kinds who were hurting because of inflation. These facts emerged from the statistical analysis of the data from the survey of 1,982 households. In this chapter we shall hear the voices of the people behind these statistics. Drawing on the depth interviews that were conducted at the beginning of the research, we shall see how families in the different subsamples experienced inflation and recession. We shall present such qualitative data on poor families, blue collar families, white collar families, and the few retired families that were interviewed in depth.

Impact of Inflation on the Poor

About twenty poor families, most of whom were living on welfare, were interviewed intensively in the early stages of the research. They ranged from complete families to broken families, from families with very young heads to families headed by elderly women. A very young head, an eighteen-year-old black woman, an unwed mother of a six-month-old child, living with her mother and being supported by welfare while she tried to complete high school had this to say:

> It's been very bad for me. Between clothes and the baby's food, it's been very high. My check runs out in the middle of the month. I then borrow from my mother and my friends. I've had to give up a lot of things like clothes, shoes and coats.

Like so many poor people, this woman is dependent on her relatives and friends to help her meet the basic needs of life.

A fifty-year-old black woman whose husband lost his job, forcing the family to turn to welfare, gave this account of the impact of inflation:

> It's been very bad for us. We never have enough money. I can't afford clothes for myself. We can't even eat the type of food we want. I'm a nature food fan but it costs more than regular food. The food is terrible now; you don't know what you're eating. . . . Last time I went to the doctor he told me to get some vitamins but I couldn't—I didn't have the money. I buy the cheapest meats. We're eating more rice, potatoes and beans. My daughter shouldn't be eating that type of stuff because she's already overweight. I'm even letting her eat the free food lunches at school even though I know the food is terrible. My husband says I have to because it's free. I would like a sewing machine and I want a piano for my daughter. My family has told me that my daughter has a real talent for the piano. This is important to me and I feel terrible because I can't have these things.

When the poor are hit by inflation, they must, like this woman, forego health aids like vitamins and sacrifice the proper diet for their children to say nothing of having such luxuries as a sewing machine or piano.

A middle-aged black woman with five children ranging in age from eight to eighteen, living on welfare, said:

Oh, goodness, everything is going up so high. I was getting a check for $249 and they cut it back to $207 when my oldest daughter graduated high school in June. They put her on her own budget. After I pay the rent and buy the food stamps, there's nothing left. I just got a check today and all I got left is a dollar. My son came in today and told me his things were stolen out of his gym locker in school. Now I have to buy all that stuff again. . . . Only way to make it is go to the supermarket when they have a sale on. Social service says they're going to give a raise, but everytime they give a raise they take it back. Food stamps have gone from $55 to $66 for the same amount. It's very hard when I get the check. I got to get the kids sneakers or something but I can't get all the things at once. I've got to let something go. I wish I could get a good job and tell welfare where to go.

Not only must the poor cope with rising prices, but all too often they are the victims of crime which adds to their expenses as in the case of this woman's son whose locker was broken into and looted. Also, the poor with limited resources, like this woman, must constantly make hard choices about which of their many needs they will currently satisfy since they cannot satisfy all of their needs at once. The constant confrontation of such hard choices is part of the life style of the poor and differentiates them sharply from the more affluent classes, which do not have to face those choices with any frequency. Finally, note should be taken of this woman's attitude toward welfare. Later on, we shall confront a number of welfare mothers who express their bitterness toward the humiliating welfare system.

A twenty-six-year-old white woman on welfare with a son born out of wedlock now married to an ex-addict with psychiatric problems, who is undergoing treatment in the outpatient department of a mental hospital, gave this account of how they are surviving:

We now buy less food. We eat a lot less meat. I used to buy London broil steak but now it's chicken and franks. We only get food stamps for me and my son. My husband gets a good meal at the hospital. When we eat in the evening, it's chicken or ground meat. Stewart [the husband] gets unlimited lunch. He sticks a couple of extra sandwiches in his pocket and brings them home. The recession has turned us into thieves. But it is not really stealing since he's entitled to unlimited lunch.

The husband's psychiatric treatment turns out to be an important subsidy to the family's food budget.

A fifty-eight-year-old black woman with an elderly retired husband had worked in factories for over thirty years and was recently laid off by General Motors in a New Jersey automobile plant. At the time of the interview she was receiving unemployment insurance that was about to run out:

It's been extremely difficult for us. We've had many troubles and it's going to get worse when my unemployment insurance runs out next month. I *always* was careful with money. I always cut expenses. But we used to go on trips. Not any more. I was always scrimping on food, so that hasn't changed much. No big expenses were ever considered. But our financial situation is much worse now. It's hard to get any worse but it looks like it will get worse anyway. . . . We don't have a standard of living. We buy food and that's all. My oldest was glad to get enough part-time work to buy himself a pair of shoes. . . . It's been very rough making payments on the car and when the unemployment insurance runs out, I won't be able to pay at all. I worry a lot about paying my bills. People see me smile but I'm crying on the inside. But it's my problem. Nobody's going to give me anything, so I do my best.

This woman's story is a reminder that poor families are always struggling whatever the state of the economy. They live in a world of constant inflation. As she points out, she has always scrimped on food, and big expenses were always out of the question. What sharply rising prices and recession do is to make a bad situation worse. In the face of inflation, this woman lost her job; her unemployment benefits were about to expire and her family was in deep trouble. "We don't have a standard of living," she said, a telling commentary on life at the margin.

A forty-year-old black widow with six children living at home, worked part time as a school aide but depended primarily on social security. Her home was in a slum tenement that the interviewer described as falling apart, with big holes in the hallways, many broken windows and no heat. When asked how she was experiencing rising prices, she said:

I always buy a lot of chicken. The kids like steak, but I can't afford that. I've been cooking less. I'll fix sandwiches and soup now. I used to buy cakes and cookies for the kids once in a while but now I make my own sweets. We used to drink a lot of soda; now we drink Koolaid or tea. I buy less milk now that the kids are big. . . . I bought some eggs the other day for 89¢. The man in the store told me to buy the ones for a dollar because they're bigger, but I told him it didn't matter. My kids are going to fix themselves two eggs no matter how big they are. . . . I need some boots but I just can't afford them. I need some flooring for the kitchen and bedroom suites but I can't get anything now. The kids need new coats but I can't get them. I told the kids before Christmas that I couldn't get them nothing. They told me they understood. I used to have a gift for everyone under the tree. This year nobody had anything. Things are worse now than last year. The price of everything goes up but the money doesn't. There should be a law against cutting poor people back. What makes it so bad is I was getting food stamps and social security before. Then they cut me off food stamps and cut my social security check back. Then they cut my Medicaid. Thank God nobody got sick. This week I'm going to apply for the Medicaid care and food stamps again. I went down there when they were cut. But they asked me so many questions and treated me so bad, I just stopped going down to them.

The economy had actually improved from the peak of inflation and recession when this woman was interviewed, but with shrinking benefits, she only felt that things were getting worse. Not only did she economize on food expenditures, but she could not buy any of the things that she and her children needed. And the Christmas holiday was an empty one for this home full of children. And like the woman quoted earlier, this woman was so humiliated by the welfare system that she turned away from it without getting the benefits she felt she was entitled to.

A thirty-four-year-old Puerto Rican man with four children had worked six years in a General Motors plant as an assembly line worker only to be laid off. At the time of the interview he was living on welfare:

> Everything is too high. Every week things go up another 25 or 30 cents. I can't make it at all. I can't even afford a week's groceries. We're falling way behind. I was on unemployment for one and a half years and that ran out. I've just applied for welfare. But there's no cost of living on welfare. People are gonna die 'cause they can't buy nothing. They got to steal. I liked my job on the assembly line. Now I have nothing. I can't even buy a toy for the kids. This is the most difficult period I have ever seen or known of. It's much worse than my childhood in Puerto Rico. I used to have $4,000 in savings. It's all gone now, for rent, for the doctor for the kid, hospital bills. If I had some of it now, I could buy toys for Christmas and make my kids happy. My kid has been sick, pneumonia and other lung things. We have to keep him in the house all the time and the hospital bills have been terrible.

The devastation of unemployment is evident in this man's account. And on top of all his other troubles he had to cope with a sick child and the costly medical bills arising from this. The failure of our society to develop a national health insurance system is a grotesque tragedy for the millions of underprivileged families. And the empty Christmas theme is echoed in his account as well. Among its many evils, poverty deprives a man of the opportunity to play the role of the loving father.

A thirty-one-year-old black woman with five young children was officially separated from her husband so that she could get welfare, but unofficially, her husband was in the house. He was unemployed and collecting unemployment insurance. She gave this account of her experience with inflation:

> It's been terrible. It's not enough money. It's not enough for food and clothes and rent. I want to get things for my kids but I can't. I have to compromise. If I get something for one, another one is going to have to do without. The kids need things for school, like a little money for this or that. There's always something—a school trip or

school pictures. What am I supposed to do? Pull it out of a hat?
Lucky my baby ain't in school yet 'cause I don't have no money to
get a wardrobe for him.

The hard choices of how to allocate their limited resources that
constantly confront the poor are aptly illustrated in this account. It is not merely a matter of buying one thing or another,
but also choosing which child's needs to satisfy first. In such a
fashion, poverty tends to generate guilt in parents who in
meeting one child's needs must neglect another child.

The next two cases of poor women trying to cope with
inflation are quite similar. Both women are white, in their
twenties, mothers of young children, living on welfare, and
attending the same college. The first of these women is twenty-
nine years old, with a two and a-half-year-old child, living with a
man who is not the father of her child:

> Out of necessity, I've learned how to budget. I had to learn to shop
> differently. I'm just barely making it. It's the side effects, the nerves
> and aggravation that make it so bad. I rarely use meat. I buy all the
> cheapest cuts. Once in a while I buy a good cut and make three
> meals out of it. I cook completely differently now. I use beans,
> lentils, mix a little of everything, throw in little pieces of meat. I
> throw it all together and make a stew. . . . I stopped buying records
> and books. I don't buy toys. I don't buy clothes and cosmetics I
> would like. . . . Two years ago it was terrible too. We were living in a
> one room apartment and working. The major difference is that
> today I don't feel that things are going to get better soon like I did
> two years ago. . . . The unemployment lines are around the block;
> the welfare office is packed when you go for your face to face
> interview. It used to be half empty. I don't think things are going to
> get better soon.

This woman was a junior in college and presumably she hoped
that in the long run her education would allow her to substantially improve her life. But her account is filled with pessimism
rather than optimism as she is convinced that the hard times
will be with us for some time. It should be noted that this

interview was conducted in the winter of 1976 when the economy was presumably improving.

The other white welfare mother of two young children
attending college gave this account:

> I guess you fall behind and you can't help it, because prices keep
> rising. I've been on welfare for two years and it's never increased.
> They never increase it and because of that you're always falling
> behind. It's always been hard for me and so I'm used to the pressures
> of inflation. It's really been hard. Take buying Pampers. When I was
> buying Pampers for my older daughter, it was $1.25 a box. Now it's
> $2.49. Buying clothes for the kids is rough. My son keeps out-
> growing his clothes and they're expensive. I don't buy clothes for
> myself because I can't afford them. Every week it seems that things
> are going up. It's ridiculous. The problems that affect me right now
> are the city's bankruptcy. It could screw everything up if the day
> care center closes or they start charging tuition [at the City Univer-
> sity of New York]. If they charge tuition it would screw up my
> personal finances worse than they already are. . . . I can't do a lot of
> things because I can't afford baby sitters. I can't afford to go to
> movies. I'd like to go to plays and I'd like to go to the ballet, but I
> can't. It's impossible. Even a bottle of wine is an extravagance.

Of course, the City University did charge tuition the next year.
This woman's comments make clear how even relatively trivial
expenses, such as the price of a movie, are luxuries forbidden to
the poor.

The neglect of health needs by the poor under inflationary
pressure is shown by this twenty-eight-year-old black woman
whose husband earned under $10,000 as a medical technician:

> I haven't gone to the dentist because of the cost. I won't go until my
> teeth really hurt. I'm not taking any preventive steps. I haven't been
> to the doctor for a thorough examination since the baby came. I
> haven't felt well but I feel he'd tell me what I already think anyway,
> that the symptoms are psychosomatic. If it cost $10 instead of $25,
> I would have gone.

A twenty-one-year-old black woman living with her sister has
a five-year-old son living with his grandmother. She is in a

special college program which gives her a stipend and she cuts hair on the side, earning forty to fifty dollars a month off the books. This woman has developed ways to maintain her equilibrium in spite of the economic pressures:

> I'm not really worried about my life. It's always been hard. Nothing in my life has been easy. Everyone is facing something. What keeps me together is meditation and yoga. I do plenty of exercise. I have a whole lot of faith. And I'm a vegetarian. My being a vegetarian has to do with my having problems with low blood pressure. My food budget is now lower and I also get into a lot of fasting. It's always been hard on me. This inflation doesn't strike me as something I can't see my way through. I'm not really concerned with material things. It doesn't bother me as much as it should. I think most people in my shoes would get frantic and hit someone on the head, but I just wait for a better day and it usually comes.

In spite of the hard times confronting this young woman, she has maintained her good spirits through various self-help measures and is optimistic about the future. In this respect she seems markedly different from her counterparts who sound exhausted from their struggle to survive.

A thirty-nine-year-old black woman with five children at home, separated from her husband, is employed as a nursing assistant, earning $8,000 a year, but because of her large family, she also receives supplementary welfare:

> I stinch on food. I buy a large piece of meat and cut it up and have it for three meals. Since the kids are getting big, I don't buy much milk. I buy a lot of chicken and fish. . . . We eat a lot of leftovers. I don't make breakfast and for lunch it's just a sandwich. My thing is to have one meal in the evening.

Her story of her shrinking food budget is in keeping with the accounts of the other poor women we interviewed. The idea of three square meals a day is quite likely a middle class phenomenon; for the poor, one square meal a day would seem more typical. When asked how her financial situation today compared with what it was two years earlier, she said:

We're better off now, because I'm making more money now, but you've got more places to spend it and everything costs more.

In Chpater 2 we saw that a tiny fraction of the poor (4 percent) felt that they were financially better off than previously and this woman's story provides some clue to who these people are. This woman felt she was better off because she had been in even worse shape financially two years earlier. In short, this response is a comparative one, and it would be a mistake to interpret it as meaning that the family was well-off. This woman was still struggling with rising prices even though she felt her situation had improved.

A forty-two-year-old black woman separated from her husband, living with five of her children and one of her grandchildren and being supported by welfare, told of her efforts to manage:

> I write out a list and try to budget it. If you don't make it, no one will help you. God will help only if a person first helps himself. If it's just a neckbone and some rice, we'll eat something. I got to walk a mile for a sale and then when you get there, you often find it is not on sale. I can't tell you how I make it. As long as the meat ain't sick, I buy it. It will fill you up and keep you alive. . . . Inflation is a bitch. If you don't have the money it's your problem. It happened to me last month. I just had to borrow and do the best I could. That was around Thanksgiving. I was going to have a dinner even if I had to go out and steal something but things haven't got that bad yet.

Again we find a case of the poor turning to friends to borrow money to tide them over. And we hear this woman even entertaining the idea of theft to insure that she would have a Thanksgiving dinner for her family.

Illegal activities are not uncommon in low income communities, and a thorough study might well disclose that various forms of crime play a significant role in sustaining the poor. A twenty-eight-year-old Puerto Rican woman with three children receiving welfare was living with a boy friend who had various businesses including a numbers game.

My boy friend takes me shopping when he sees me doing without too much. He'll buy me $40 shoes. I get upset because I know I can buy three pair for that money. But he says these will last and he's right. He buys me coats. You see he's a bookie and sometimes people have to do illegal things. Without my boy friend, I'd have to crawl to my husband and I would never do that. We broke up two years ago.

Not only did this woman benefit from the largesse of her bookmaker boy friend, but she was also able to earn money helping him out with his numbers business:

I'm working for my boy friend. I do some of the numbers for him. I put the kids to bed early and sit down here and take the numbers out of the books. It took me three days working many hours a day to do the numbers for last month. Sometimes I wonder if it's worth it. But I make about $150 a week this way. I look at other women around me and I don't feel so bad. Many don't have enough to buy their children clothes.

As a result of her illegal income and benefactor boy friend, this woman had little difficulty coping and considered herself rather well-off in comparison with her less fortunate friends.

A forty-nine-year-old black woman with a sixteen-year-old son who was being supported by welfare gave a long account of the various ways in which she tries to cope including trafficking in stolen goods:

I shop at the major supermarkets, not the little stores around here. You get better products and they're cheaper. My son likes grits so I go around and find where they are cheapest and stock up. In stores around here, eggs are 99¢ but I go to the meat house and get them fresh from New Jersey for 75¢. That store is open only two days a week but you get real bargains there. . . . It's been pretty rough. But it's harder on my son. He wants a lot of things I can't give him. He's a growing boy. He needs nice jackets and sweaters. I go to the Salvation Army for things I need. I got this sweater there. I paid only 50¢ for it. I put these buttons on it and it was like new. I've gotten a lot of things there.

This woman then went on to describe the "bargains" available in the streets, bargains that stem from stolen goods:

> If you are out on the streets with some money you can get almost anything. This is something I found out. Last week four boys came through with TV sets for $40. And they came through with shopping carts full of steaks. You've just got to be there at the right time and have some money. Fellows come straight from the slaughterhouse. You can get a side of beef for 4 or 5 dollars. You got to trim the fat yourself but who cares at that price.

From her account, it would seem that shopping in the marketplace of stolen goods is rather prevalent in low income communities and is another facet of how poor families are able to manage in the face of rising prices.

The stories of the poor people we have interviewed provide a good idea of how hard life is for people trapped in poverty. They find themselves unable to meet many of their basic needs. They must make hard choices of which of many needs to satisfy for they cannot come close to satisfying them all. Often this means choosing which child will have to go without. We have also encountered many examples of ingenuity in stretching the family budget, especially in the area of food. And finally, we have seen that at least some poor people, and perhaps many, engage in illegal activities in order to survive. Inasmuch as life in poverty has always been hard, the rampent inflation of the mid-seventies probably did not upset the poor as much as it did the working and middle classes. They have always had to tighten their belts and struggle to make ends meet, and inflation only meant increasing these economizing efforts one step further, like tightening the belt one more notch.

Impact of Inflation on Blue Collar Families

The twenty-five or so blue collar families that were interviewed intensively presented a more varied picture than the poor families. Almost all of the poor families were suffering a good deal and struggling to get by. But among the blue collar families some were hurting a good deal because of economic conditions, but others had little difficulty maintaining their way of life, while still others made relatively minor concessions to the economic hard times.

Even those who claimed to be hard hit by inflation still managed to get by with less difficulty than the poor. Typical of the blue collar families that were suffering from inflation is a white family with four children. The thirty-six-year old husband worked as a letter carrier for the post office, and the wife worked as a waitress, giving them a family income of $20,000.

> It's been very difficult. We do a lot less and my wife works now for the first time and whenever possible I take a second job. We're struggling to stay even and sometimes we fall behind. We never really get ahead. It's just that sometimes we almost catch up. I haven't bought any new things for quite a while. . . . I've lost some of my second jobs. Like I was teaching part-time for a while and I lost that job because of budget cuts. I used to work on my day off at a food wholesale house and there's no work there now. . . . It's been pretty difficult in that it's caused a lot of disruption in the home life. I have to work two jobs and my wife has to be away from the house and that's caused a lot of problems with the children. And there's the worry about paying the bills. There's been a few bills that we just couldn't pay. We have no luxuries. The kids would love to take piano or art lessons and you know, we got the same old car since 1966. In the house, we have no rugs, no storm windows, nothing but the basic essentials. . . . We're really just making it and thank God we have no really bad health problems. Our house at least is not falling apart.

The need to raise income through extra jobs has caused some problems for this family, presumably because they are away from the children too much and they have had to sacrifice all luxuries. But nonetheless, they seem to be maintaining their way of life without too many modifications.

Another working class person who was struggling to manage is a twenty-nine-year-old black woman with two children and no husband who used to be on welfare but found a job as a teacher in a day care center and was earning $8,500. When asked how she was coping with rising prices, she responded:

> By scraping pennies and trying to get as much as I can for a dollar. I pass down my older son's clothes to the younger one. As for clothes for myself, I just buy jeans. I don't need elaborate clothes for work. . . . I think I may be staying even because I budget my money. When I see bargains at the supermarket, I'll buy huge quantities. . . . We can't do a lot of things we would like to do. Sometimes I might want to take the kids to the show but I don't have the money. I try to take them ice skating when the weather gets cold enough and when the weather is warm enough I like to take them to nice places in the city. I myself would like to have a little more in the house and I would like to have more clothes than I do, but I can't because I don't have the money.

Clearly this woman has had to restrict her shopping scope and not buy many things that she would like, but at the same time she seems to manage quite well in providing her family with the essentials. Unlike the poor, she is not pressed to make hard choices about which of many needs to satisfy now and which to forego.

Another woman who had climbed out of poverty to a marginal position in the working class was a forty-four-year-old black widow with seven children at home who had been on welfare but was now working as a teacher's aide, earning $6,000 and also receiving social security:

> We just manage. We just learn to do without a lot. I changed the way I shopped a long time ago. I used to have steaks and pork chops once a week. Now it's once every three weeks. Now I boil a pot so there'll be something left over the next day. I try to buy in large quantities. Like this week the supermarket had chickens for 43¢ a pound. I'll by 12 chickens and put them in the freezer so that I won't have to buy them when they go back to 69¢. . . . We're worse off today than we were a few years ago. My income is a couple of pennies more, but prices are up. The kids are older and they eat more now, much more. Bread used to be 43¢ and now it's 69¢ and I need twice as much now. The kids are older and the things cost more. I can't say to the older kids, here's a quarter; I've got to give them a dollar and what

can you buy for a dollar? And the price of shoes. There's no more
$5.95 shoes. Even the ten dollar shoes fall apart. You've got to
spend $20 if you want them to last more than a month.

This woman's story is similar to those of the poor families
considered earlier. Like them she must cut corners and struggle
to get by. But at the same time there are subtle differences
suggesting that she has somewhat more resources than the
mothers on welfare. For example, she has enough money to buy
twelve chickens at a time, even if the price is somewhat lower,
and she has a freezer in which to store the chickens.

A black family, the husband and wife in their thirties, with
two young children, the husband a motorman with the Transit
Authority, earning $18,000, owned their own home and many
of their financial problems had to do with maintaining their
house:

Moneywise, it's been terrible. You can't spend the way you used to.
Everything has gone up except salaries. The kids' clothes and what
not; you can't do like you want to. You can't go out to dinner or a
good movie even. You have to neglect a lot of things. With a house
we really have bills. I can't get things for the house the way I would
like to. The cost of maintaining a house has gone up. The mortgage,
taxes, gas, electricity, the telephone too, have all gone up. Even the
cost of the fertilizers to do the lawn have gone up.

This woman went on to complain about the cost of meat, the
high cost of clothes and the fact that she and her husband go
out less often than they used to, and they are unable to have
people over because of the cost of entertaining them. This
family has obviously tightened its belt and sharply curtailed its
expenditures but at the same time there is no note of despera-
tion in her account, and it seems they will have no difficulty in
riding out the economic storms.

Another working class family struggling a great deal because
of inflation consists of a twenty-one-year-old Puerto Rican who
works as a computer coding clerk for the city. His wife works,
and their combined income is $12,000. They have just had their
first child:

In general, it's been very hard. The new baby means a lot of responsibility for me. We've stopped going to movies, and we've given up all outings except visits to our families. There's no money involved in visiting. . . . It gets worse every month. We just lost our telephone. They took it out. I need a phone. Nobody lives near us and so without the phone it's hard. Also, there used to be "munchies" in the fridge, but not any more. We've been losing the luxuries of life one by one. . . . Things are worse now than a few years ago. I had no money at that time but I had no debts either. Now I have terrible debts. We just moved and have almost no furniture and can't afford none. Luckily, because of my job, I have good medical and dental coverage or else I would never go to the doctor.

When asked to assess the difficulty of this period in his life, this man made a revealing statement:

I've known worse. When I was a baby, we had a large family and we frequently went without enough to eat. That was really the worse. I've never seen anything like that since. But this is the worst that's happened to me since then. This is the worst shape I've been in since I started working at the age of 12.

This family is obviously struggling in much the same manner as the poor families that have been reviewed. Again we find an interesting comparative perspective. This man grew up in abject poverty and knew starvation as a youngster, and however bad off he is now, he still appreciates being better off than he had been as a child.

These cases typify the blue collar families that were hard hit by inflation. However much they were tightening their belts they were typically better off than the poor. The other blue collar families that were interviewed were affected by inflation even less than these families.

A middle-aged couple with their twenty-nine-year-old son living at home provides an example of a working class family that was only moderately affected by the economic problem. The husband was a sheet metal worker, earning $19,000, who had been laid off only two weeks prior to the interview, and the

son was a cable splicer for the telephone company, earning
$16,000:

> If I were working now, we'd be staying even [with rising prices].
> (How difficult has this period of inflation been for you?) Well, it
> hasn't been a hardship, but we're a family used to going out more
> often, doing what we want. We'd eat out once a month. Now we
> have to buckle down. No vacation. As far as food, I spend the same.
> I haven't cut down on my family.

This man was not too worried about having been laid off.
Apparently, layoffs are not uncommon in his line of work.

A thirty-three-year-old man with two children earned
$14,500 from the gas company, did odd moving jobs with his
father-in-law and began college with the aid of the GI Bill. When
asked about the impact of inflation on his family, he said:

> Because of the GI Bill, I'm staying even, but before that I was falling
> behind; things were starting to squeeze. The GI Bill stops in June
> and then the shit hits the fan. I'm getting less overtime now. I used
> to get as much overtime as I wanted; no more. It's not as secure as it
> was. They keep threatening us. I've been there 13 years so I'm not
> really afraid. (Have you cut down your expenditures?) Not really.
> We're spending more for the same amount of things. My wife looks
> for sales. She cuts coupons and shops at more than one store so she
> can pick up what's on sale.

This man was able to manage because of the additional income
deriving from the GI Bill, and he was worried what would
happen when that ran out. Also he experienced the recession in
that he could not work overtime as he had done previously.
And his wife had learned to shop for bargains, but on balance,
he felt that his family was not affected much by inflation.

A middle-aged Italian couple with three children also was
managing fairly well in spite of inflation. The husband was a
former baker, now on a disability pension, earning $8,000 a
year:

> It's been bad, but we're living just like we were. We haven't suffered
> too much. We've cut down a little. Like, we don't go any place.

> Never take vacations, never eat out. There must be people who suffer a lot, who have to do without a lot, but we don't. We're happy. As for saving, I guess everybody has a different method. I guess the Italian people have their method, you know, the way we live. We can't cut down on food so we buy cheaper foods. Two, three times a week we have macaroni and meat balls. We don't have steak too often and we've cut down on buying clothes.

This family has made some accommodations to rising prices but by its own estimate it is living pretty much as it had before and is not experiencing inflation as a serious problem.

A middle-aged longshoreman with grown children, earning $14,000, also felt that his family was staying even with inflation:

> Before we had a little more freedom of money, but now I'm not as free with money as before, because you never know what's going to happen. You have to hold on to it and spend it wisely. I used to just go out and buy it but not any more. Now you got to think twice before you spend a dollar. (How are you coping with rising prices?) We're doing away with the most expensive things. We try not to buy things that are expensive. We try to shop from store to store where we can get products cheaper. The difficult part is to buy food. Food is very expensive so we've got to stay away from a lot of things. You've got to buy cheaper cuts of meat.

In spite of these accommodations to rising prices, this man believed that his family was holding its own and was not too affected by inflation.

A childless couple, the husband a twenty-year-old cab driver earning $8,000 and the wife a recently employed store clerk, also felt they were managing without too much difficulty:

> We've cut down on certain food items and household items. We make do with what we have. But otherwise there has been little effect. We don't go out as often as we used to, but we're holding our own. My wife just started to work in a department store. We could make ends meet without her working but it will help. I can work extra days or hours whenever I want and I occasionally do.

Without the expense of children, this couple was able to manage on their modest income, and they did not experience any difficulty with rising prices or the recession.

A fifty-five-year-old brewery worker, earning $14,000, had two grown children and lived only with his wife. When asked about the impact of inflation on his family, he replied:

> It didn't affect us as much as it did some other people. I still have my job. I'm working the same amount of hours. I'm getting the same amount of pay. We've cut back on some things: on food, on certain kinds of meats. We used to eat steaks. Now we buy cheaper cuts of meats. We're falling behind a little bit. We aren't able to save any money the way we used to.

Again we find minor accommodations, but no sense of woe; rather quiet confidence that they will manage. In fact, this man takes comfort from the fact that unlike some people he knows, his job is secure.

A third group of blue collar families that was interviewed consists of those who were hardly bothered at all by the inflation or recession. An example is a middle-aged black couple who owned their own home. The husband works for the post office and has a second job as a school aide and the wife works as a saleswoman in a department store. Their joint income is over $20,000:

> I think that people in the middle income aren't suffering. It's the poor who are hurting. Go down this block, these people have got what they want. They complain but they are living just as well as they ever did. Everyone we know is doing well. . . . We complain but things haven't gotten worse, they've gotten better. . . . In case of illness, we can get by because we're well insured. Even our prescriptions are paid for. . . . Having our own home, we don't have to worry about where we're going to live. You can say we have a sense of security. (Have you been able to save money?) Oh, yes. We've been able to save more than ever before. Of course, our food is more but our income has increased. We save as much with high prices as before. Most people complain so we complain with them. We couldn't say to the people who are complaining that we are saving.

This is a good example of a family that has been untouched by inflation. Their income has more than kept up with rising prices and their way of life has not changed at all. Note should be taken of the great security provided this family by adequate health insurance, in contrast with the Puerto Rican man presented earlier who was being wiped out by all the medical bills stemming from his sick child. Finally, this woman's perception of her neighbors as being well-off in spite of their complaints is noteworthy. The phenomenon of rising prices touches off complaints and makes complaining fashionable, and, as this woman admits, she too joins in the complaining. But in reality, she is not suffering, nor does she believe her neighbors are.

Another example of a working class family that was not hurting because of inflation consists of a 29-year-old policeman, whose wife also works and their four-year-old son. The family has an annual income of $28,000:

> We seem to be managing very well simply because my wife is working also. We have two incomes, although most of my wife's income we put in the bank. Whenever we run short on my salary, we have hers to fall back on. We are staying even; we are definitely not falling behind. (Have you had to cut down on expenditures?) No, we are spending more money on the same items but I'm not cutting down on the items I buy.

The chief reason why this family has been able to weather the inflation storm is that both wife and husband are working. The enormous growth in the number of working wives in America may be the critical factor in how families have managed to cope with rampant inflation.

Another longshoreman with a working wife and a family income of $28,000 had little difficulty coping with rising prices:

> Oh, we're managing. We used to go to New York shows and plays and now we don't go too often. We used to eat in better restaurants and now we don't too often. But we're staying even. I'm working and I get my full salary. . . . We pay higher prices and higher taxes. Everything goes up. We're keeping up but we should have more than

we do. . . . I just bought a car and I would have liked to buy a better one, but I couldn't afford it. I bought a Dodge Cornet, but I really wanted a Cadillac.

This blue collar worker has made some accommodations to inflation, such as not eating out in expensive restaurants as often as he would like and settling for a Dodge rather than a Cadillac, but he is certainly not hurting and all in all is managing well. It should be noted that he too has a working wife, which places his family in a high income bracket.

A fifty-three-year-old black woman with grown children whose husband worked for the Transit Authority and earned $15,000 also had few complaints:

I haven't had to pinch too much. We tried to cut down a little on everything. We don't buy as much clothes because they're expensive now. We do our own repairs. My husband is good in that department. . . . Every Sunday I go through the newspaper and find out where the best bargains are. I have a turkey in the oven that I got for 48¢ a pound. It's much more than we need but it will be good for my husband's lunches and I'll make different dishes out of the left-overs.

A young couple in their late twenties with various sources of income told us that they had little difficulty managing. The husband worked as a truck driver but had a number of off-the-books jobs. His wife worked as well, and they had no children:

We're doing rather well. I got a raise in salary and I'm making more money. I've never felt the effects of inflation. I read about it in the paper but it has nothing to do with me. We still spend the same money and we still eat the same way. We don't save any money but we never saved any money, so it doesn't affect me. I know when I go in the supermarket the prices are higher, but that's all. I mean I still pay it. We're keeping up with inflation.

This man is only aware of inflation because he reads about it in the newspapers.

The final example of a blue collar family having no difficulty coping with inflation is a couple in their twenties of which the husband does not have a regular job:

Do you want to know the truth? I'm not hassling at all. I'm home, I do anything I want. A couple of years ago, I imagine I was doing better because I was working then. But I'm doing the same thing now. In fact, I'm planning to open a business. I managed to save some money from working and my wife is working. I do a lot of work off the books. I wash windows. I shampoo rugs. But only when I want to. I do this work on the side at my convenience. I have no regular occupation. But I plan to open a bagel store. This is now my main concern and when I have time to do a floor, I'll do a floor and if I don't feel like doing a floor, I won't do a floor.

This man is accustomed to working at his convenience, and he is completely confident in his ability to pick up enough work whenever he wants. And his entrepreneurial spirit will soon impel him into a business of his own.

In sum, the blue collar families we have reviewed range from those who were suffering a good deal from rising prices and the recession to those who were not hurting at all.

Impact of Inflation on White Collar Families

As we saw in the previous chapters, white collar families were least likely to have been affected by inflation and recession, and this is borne out by the depth interviews. Only a minority of the white collar families interviewed were hard hit by inflation; the rest were either completely untouched or only moderately affected by rising prices. Included in the minority who claimed they were suffering from inflation was a twenty-five-year old woman, the mother of three children, whose husband was a civil servant earning $23,000:

We're more in debt than ever before. It's a very bad situation. We use credit cards sometimes just because there is no other money. We're falling way behind. Bills, bills, bills. I'm paying bills all the time. I think we're catching up and something happens and we fall behind

again. . . . My husband's wages are frozen at the 1973 level. He's a
managerial civil servant and they are threatening to freeze his wages
for the next three years. This means that he will be earning 1973
wages in 1978. Since we were expecting the raise he didn't get, he
had to take a second job to pay the bills and meet the mortgage.
We've cut down on food, clothing, doctor visits and the dentist.
Furniture for the house and entertainment are now dead issues.
We've wiped out our savings in the past 12 months.

This family was hurting from inflation because its expectations
for a better life had not fully materialized. They had recently
bought a house but because of the financial squeeze were
unable to furnish it satisfactorily and their expenses were such
as to wipe out their savings.

A young couple in their late twenties and their two young
children were also hurting from inflation. The husband is a
systems programmer earning $16,000.

Our expenses are going up at a faster rate than our salaries can keep
up with. Also our family expenses are going up. The children are
getting older and it costs more to feed them. Of course, part of the
problem is not wanting to adjust our life style. I've had to change. I
no longer have a cleaning woman. I really needed her. This apartment is big. But I can't afford that if I want a baby sitter. The
cheapest baby sitter is around $2-$3 an hour. . . . We're far behind
where we envisioned we would be. We wanted to be in a house at
this point. But they're too expensive. We went to see a house last
night and they want a $20,000 down payment. All this upsets us a
lot. The house isn't the only thing. I'd like a cleaning woman. I'd
like not to scrimp. My husband needs a new coat. Last year, he
couldn't get the clothes he needed. Plus, I'd like not to shop around
so much just to find what I can afford. Also, I'd like to be more
generous to other people. It makes me feel bad to be so skimpy.

This family provides a good example of the frustrations of the
middle class trapped by rising prices. There is no question of
this family's being able to survive as was true of some of the
poor families, but it finds itself unable to realize its aspirations
for a home of its own and to maintain the style of life to which

it had been accustomed, complete with domestic help and entertaining others.

Another young couple in their mid-twenties with a young child was hurting. The husband was a school teacher, and when the wife worked, their family income was $18,000:

> It's been tough. We have to give up a lot of what we'd like to do and have. We try to cut down on extravagances like going out and buying a house and other things. . . . A lot of things you need, you make do with what you have. I look for bargains and coupons. We eat a lot of chicken. . . . Our parents help out with gifts, like a winter overcoat for our son. Almost all our furniture, they bought for us. Both sets of parents have helped. We do a lot of things for ourselves. For example, we painted the apartment ourselves rather than hiring someone.

This young couple too has had to defer its plans for a house. As the wife points out, they have had the good fortune of being subsidized by their parents or else their situation would be much worse than it is.

A thirty-nine-year-old systems analyst for a large corporation earning $19,000 with three children gave this account of inflation's impact:

> It's aggravating, but we're doing O.K. We're struggling and doing without the luxuries that we used to indulge in. We used to go out every Saturday night. We would eat out a great deal. Now eating out is a big deal. There's been a big change in our entertainment. We use to take the children out for dinner every week or so and now we virtually never take the children out. Now it's once a month at the most and then it's McDonald's. . . . My wife now takes advantage of specials at the supermarkets and she uses coupons. And she now gets the kids clothes out of the Sears catalogue instead of the fancy stores.

Whereas inflation for the poor is a battle for survival, for the middle class, like this family, it is more a matter of giving up luxuries, like eating out and shopping at expensive stores. But whatever the level of deprivation, middle class families like this one consider themselves hurting from inflation.

A middle-aged couple with grown children living in a luxury apartment building in Manhattan also complained about inflation. The husband is a musician earning $25,000 a year:

> (How are you coping with inflation?) Very badly. No, that's not really true; it hasn't been that bad. But we have been buying less, going out less, eating out less, and entertaining less. We're falling behind. My husband's salary doesn't cover what it did before and his salary increases haven't been enough to compensate for the rising cost of living. He has had to take a second job. He is now a substitute at the ballet. He's working during the rest weeks and vacations. . . . When I go out shopping, I get P.O.'d at the prices. I'm doing more things for myself now rather than paying other people. For example, rather than dry-cleaning, I'll wash. I take fewer taxis and more public transportation. I'm cutting down on electric bills and I use the phone less often.

This middle-class housewife has been forced to economize in a variety of areas because of the financial squeeze on her family. As in the previous cases, this family has had to forego a number of luxuries.

A thirty-year-old stockbroker, married without children and earning $45,000, also complained about the high cost of living:

> (How are you coping with inflation?) With a lot of arguments. We are definitely more selective now, especially in shopping. For instance, we don't buy bacon anymore. It's too expensive. We buy house brands of food, eat more tuna fish and less roast beef. We don't take taxis anymore or if we do, it leads to arguments. (How difficult has this period been for you?) It's been argumentatively difficult. We fight much more over money. Also, I don't like paying exorbitant prices. It makes me angry. We've cut down on food, clothing, transportation, and dental care. My wife needs expensive dental work and we can't afford it.

Even this young couple with an income well above average and without any children finds itself suffering from inflation and forced to forego many things they need including dental care.

The largest number of the white collar families interviewed at the beginning of the research were affected to some extent by inflation but they themselves did not consider the situation serious. An example is provided by a twenty-eight-year-old new father employed as a social researcher by the city and earning $17,500:

> We are managing O.K. although we're not saving any more. Until last year or so, we always managed to save at least a little. I really know when it is the end of the pay period now. I run out of money before the new check comes in. I think we're slowly falling behind rising prices. (Forced to give up buying certain things you want?) Yes, like a movie camera and projector and other luxuries. We're now dipping into our savings for the first time. Fortunately my work doesn't require me to wear expensive suits. If it did, we'd have to cut back sharply on other things.

This man mentions a theme that shows up frequently in the interviews with middle class families, the inability to save. Even if they are able to maintain their standard of living within limits, many white collar families find for the first time that they are unable to save money, which they find rather disturbing.

A musician who gives piano lessons and coaches singers and whose wife works as an editor has a family income of $50,000, and yet he too was complaining about inflation:

> We are managing not to cope [with inflation]. Everything is fantastically expensive even with the money we both make. When we used to make a lot less we were living better than we are today. Money keeps disappearing. Everything is extravagant.... We've cut down on entertainment. We used to have some very nice parties and that's terribly needed for my work. Now we haven't had a party in more than a year.... We live from day to day and can't put anything aside.

This couple too, was unable to save in spite of their high income.

In another middle class family with two children, the husband, a business executive with a family income of $65,000, at first claimed that he was not affected by inflation, but then his wife proceeded to list the various ways in which they had cut back their expenditures because of inflation:

> (Husband) We're coping very well. Our income keeps going up and we will be able to afford a standard of living that we haven't been able to afford in the past. (When asked if they had cut back, the wife replied.) We didn't get that desk for the bedroom and we've cut down on clothes, travel, and expensive food such as steak and veal. We don't do as much eating out or go to the theater as we used to. Normally, we would have bought a new car by now but we haven't so far. (Husband) I used to buy four suits a year. Now I just buy underwear and shirts. (Wife) I haven't bought a coat. We used to figure we would spend $1,000 each for clothes a year and now we spend less than $100.

When first asked about inflation, this man was ready to say they were not affected by it, pointing to the steady growth of his income. But as the interview progressed, first his wife and then he too pointed out the various ways in which they had been forced to economize.

One family had experienced a hard time because the husband had been struggling trying to make it as a contractor. But he finally found a job and since he has been working, his family has been managing rather well:

> We've become more stable financially since my husband recently got a job. When he was struggling as a contractor in the recession it was a rather harrowing experience. But now we're holding our own, although I have been cutting back more and more, on food, clothes and things for the house.

Compared to the insecurity they experienced when the husband was self-employed, the wife felt that they were now doing rather well even though inflation was forcing them to cut back in many areas.

A twenty-five-year-old engineer earning $16,000, whose wife was pregnant for the first time, did not feel that he was being hurt much by inflation although a number of the signs were present:

At this stage in my career, raises come quickly so we're staying ahead, but not as far ahead as we should be. . . . We go out less, go away less, and buy less clothing. Also we're unable to save any money. We wanted to buy a house but we had to put that off when we bought a car, a compact. . . . I never used to think how much money was in the checking account before writing a check. Now I have to. Sometimes I have to plan which bills to pay first.

Like the previous interviewee, this man was impressed by his rising income but he too spelled out the symptoms of an inflation impact, such as having to postpone plans for major purchases, and cutting back on entertainment, travel, and clothing.

A business executive, earning $35,000, listed minor adjustments his family had made to inflation:

We're keeping even with rising prices but we've cut down on some luxury food items which we buy less often, like smoked salmon. We won't go out and buy lobster tails. But those are luxury items. We don't pay much attention to inflation. (Have you been forced to give up buying things?) Well, just delaying buying. For example, I had a small car I didn't like but I put off buying a new one. We would like to take a ski trip with the children, but we didn't because of the lift costs and everything. We didn't decorate the house upstairs.

Again we find some ambivalence in the respondent. On the one hand, he is prepared to say they are keeping up with rising prices and are not hurting from inflation, and on the other, he can list a number of ways in which his family has tightened its belt to accommodate to higher prices.

A forty-three-year-old divorced woman with two adolescent children currently living with a man was the executive director of a nonprofit organization and with her boy friend had an income of $35,000:

We're staying even, just about. What used to be a substantial amount of money no longer is. . . . We manage but we can't buy what we used to. We've cut back on food expenses and entertainment but that's about all. What's really happened is that we can't meet our rising expectations.

This woman makes quite explicit a significant way in which middle class families are affected by inflation. It is not so much that they must cut back and reduce their standard of living as that they are unable to realize their aspirations for a substantially better way of life. As we have seen, a number of middle class families have had to put off their plans for owning their own home.

A forty-six-year-old night manager of a supermarket whose wife works and has a family income of $20,000, said:

> I think we're staying even because my wife is working now. But everything is so high. Our utility bills are very high, $95 a month in the summer when we use the air conditioner. In the winter it's from $50 to $60 a month and that's with hardly any major appliances. As far as food goes, we try to get large quantities that are on sale in the supermarket. If chickens are on sale, we'll buy maybe ten of them and freeze them. I only buy clothes when they are on sale. I bought a smaller car to save money on gas.

Although this man thought he was staying even with inflation, he related a number of ways in which his family was adjusting to rising prices.

A third group of white collar families, a rather large one, consists of those who felt they had completely escaped the ravages of inflation.

A twenty-eight-year-old real estate lawyer with an income of $30,000, a two-year old child, and a pregnant wife was in this category. As his wife told the interviewer:

> We're managing. My husband's income is rising faster than the cost of living. Right now, we're moving ahead. My husband's not on a fixed income. In the last three years his income has increased a lot. We're not as tight as we used to be. We spend money more freely now.

The director of data processing for a research firm, earning $27,000, also felt unaffected by inflation:

> We may be falling behind rising prices, but we manage O.K. This

hasn't been a difficult period for us. We've been better off than some
of our friends and neighbors who have been hit by unemployment.

This man provides one clue to why those who feel they have
escaped economic hard times feel this way: they have friends
and neighbors who are much worse off.

A young couple, the husband an industrial psychologist and
the wife a college professor, with a joint income of $38,000,
reported that they were not feeling inflation:

> We're not feeling inflation. We've been able to keep up with rising
> prices. We've managed to struggle through. Compared to our friends,
> things are much better for us because we are both employed as
> professionals. Of course our expenses have increased along with our
> salaries. This house has trebled our expenditures every month. We
> bought it three months ago. Buying a house is a tremendous increase
> in expenses, but it is an investment.

This couple has not had to defer their aspirations for a house
and as the husband observes, they are acquiring equity as a
result.

A young school teacher with a working wife and a family
income of $16,000 had no complaints about the cost of living:

> We've been managing with enough to save some too. Since we've
> been married it's been about the same. We've been a little ahead. Our
> friends are complaining more than we are. We are doing better than
> they are. As soon as my wife gets paid, we put the money in the
> bank. Then when something goes wrong, like with the car, we'll take
> some money out, but we try to keep a certain amount in the bank at
> all times.

This young couple reveals a sure sign of escaping inflation:
being able to save. Unlike many of the other young couples who
just manage to get by without saving, this couple was able to
put money in the bank.

A thirty-year-old study director for a major opinion research
firm, earning $43,000, with two young children also was not
affected by inflation:

We're doing quite well. My income is variable. Generally, I'm moving ahead of inflation. . . . Prices increase and it makes you more careful of what you buy. Last time we bought a car, we took about a week to look around before we bought one. Now we need another car, and we've been looking for two months. . . . I feel guilty about spending money, like taking a vacation when my parents are struggling for necessities. I have a great deal more guilt. My father has been out of work twice in one year. It's hit older people and it's put pressure on kids in college. My sister had to drop out of college—the cost couldn't be justified. It's difficult to be happy even when you feel prosperous when people in your family are having tough times. We've laid out a great deal of money to support some of these people.

This young man's success story is marred by the financial misfortunes of his close relatives. Not only has he provided for his own family but he has had to contribute to the support of his relatives as well. Through his relatives, even this financially successful man has been touched by the economy.

A thirty-three-year-old editor of a trade journal with a working wife and a family income of $23,000 reported:

We haven't felt it much at all. I see my bills doubled since we've owned this house, but our income has too. And some expenses have gone down, like our boy was in private school and he is now in parochial school. Five years ago we bought the house and the car and we incurred expenses then. We don't have any real big ones now. We live pretty simply. . . . We've been able to save $3,000 this year.

A sure sign of the economic well-being of this family is that in spite of inflation, they have been able to save a substantial amount of money.

A young couple (mid-twenties) have set up their own jewelry business which has been quite successful:

Before we started this business, we were taking home a lot less and couldn't do much. Now we don't feel it. We are jewelry designers and manufacturers. Jewelry has done very well the past five years. It's been on the upswing. Our income has increased, but it's hard to tell by how much. We take out about $15,000 but the business is worth $40,000. . . . We've done really well. We've saved a lot. We're waiting to decide where we want to live, what we want to do. We can afford to do a lot now.

This young couple feels that their lives are expanding as a result of their new found affluence and neither inflation nor the recession has gotten in their way.

Another musician with a wife working as a school teacher had a family income of $43,000 and had few complaints about inflation:

We're managing. Our income is such that even though inflation cuts in, we can still manage. We're staying even in that our income is sufficient. The only difficulty is the nagging feeling that two of us have to work and we see what we get being eroded by inflation. . . . In some ways we are spending more than we used to. You have a certain feeling that money is worthless now. So we have a tendency to be freer with it now. When you see it disappear so fast, you say what the hell. You don't know how long it will last anyway.

This couple provides a new twist to the impact of inflation. Since money is losing its value under inflationary pressure, they are inclined to spend it rather than save it, a logic that makes good sense in times of rampant inflation.

A final example of a middle class couple not hurting from inflation provides some not so hidden costs of inflationary pressures. The husband, in his late fifties, is a merchandising manager for a major department store and his wife works part-time, giving them a joint income of $23,000:

I'm a little ahead now because my income has gone up. But we can't take the prices going up. We watch carefully what we buy. I'm lucky to have a job with all the lay-offs. . . . It hasn't been difficult but it has been annoying. We'd like to save and we can't. We'd like to have a lot of money and it doesn't happen. At least if prices reflected quality, things wouldn't be so bad, but that's what bothers me more than anything—nothing's good anymore. . . . The financial squeeze has affected my whole life planning. It's lengthened the number of years I have to work, which in turn delays my retirement.

Although this couple was maintaining its standard of living, it was unable to save any money and this in turn was forcing the husband to stay in the labor market longer than he wanted to. Note should also be taken of his profound observation about prices and quality of goods. Usually when one pays more for something, he expects it to be of higher quality. But the tragedy of inflation is that the prices of goods go up at the same time as quality goes down. This is a true violation of the economic laws one learns in school and is an important clue to the anger that people feel in the face of rising prices.

As we have seen, a number of white collar families were able to keep up with rising prices and were experiencing no pain from inflation, but many others did find themselves falling behind and were forced to economize on their budgets, turning to less expensive food, buying fewer clothes, and giving up vacations. These middle class families were forced to emulate the poor in cutting corners in order to make ends meet. In this respect, rampant inflation contributes to the proletarianization or impoverishment of the middle class.

Impact of Inflation on the Retired

Only a few of the eighty depth interviews conducted at the beginning of the study were with retired people mainly because of the difficulty of finding retired people in the metropolitan area of New York City. Although three or four retired people were in fact interviewed, only two of these interviews have managed to survive. Both are examples of more well-to-do people. One of these is an eighty-three-year-old former lawyer living with his wife in a small apartment in a suburban community. They are living comfortably on a combination of their savings, stocks and bonds, and social security. Both the husband and wife were ready to share their impressions of inflation with the interviewer:

> We took this small apartment five years ago so that we can be near our youngest daughter. Before that we had this 12 room house in Scarsdale. . . . We don't shop the way we used to. I keep my eyes

open. I went through the depression and in that time it was easier to get along. If you couldn't afford steak, you had beef stew or lamb stew which was much cheaper. Now they're all high. The butcher used to give you bones for soup. . . . The families that have been hardest hit are the families with children. What do people do with five or six kids with the cost of milk today? Things are not bad for us partly because our needs are less and we're spending less. (Husband) I used to have a car and don't have one now. It's not for financial reasons. I wanted a car but my son dissuaded me. I discovered that once you're over 80, you can't get insurance. We walk into town all the time and our neighbors give us rides.

This couple has escaped the hardships of inflation in large part because of their wealth. But it should also be noted that in keeping with the elderly, their needs have diminished and they see themselves as spending less than formerly. The fact that the elderly cannot obtain automobile insurance has led this couple to manage without a car, a further symbol of their diminishing consumer activity.

The other retired couple that was interviewed at length also lives in a suburban community. The husband is a retired army colonel who had obtained a position as athletic director at a local college, from which he had subsequently retired. This couple was making a number of accommodations to rising prices:

We notice the much higher cost of everything. We've had to cut down on our demands and purchases. We're not typical in that my husband is a retired colonel. We can still shop at the commissary. We make the 40-minute drive to Fort Dix once a month. Without that privilege, I'd be having a very hard time. . . . It's sort of frustrating and annoying. I definitely do not buy the clothes I used to. I've cut back on food. I think twice before I take something off the shelf. . . . I'm a big gardener but I don't spend the money on the garden I used to for fancy bulbs. I've denied myself that. We deny ourselves entertainment. We don't go to the theater as often as we used to in New York. I love the opera but I don't go very often.

Like so many of the middle class families still in the labor force, this wife of a retired man has made many accommodations to rising prices, accommodations that have reduced the luxuries in her life. But it is equally clear from her account that she and her husband are managing rather well and are not hurting very much from inflation. In the previous chapter we saw that the retired were apt to be stoics, the people whose income had not kept up with rising prices but were not hurting much from inflation. The lowering of needs among the elderly and the reduction of consumer activity might well be one reason for this stoicism. Unfortunately, we have no cases of retired poor people or working class people, and it may well be that retired people from these strata have quite different experiences with inflation.

In this chapter we have presented a picture of how people in the different social strata, the poor, the working class, and the middle class, have experienced inflation. We have seen that inflation and recession hit the poor the hardest, as the statistical data of the previous chapters indicated. The working class was not as hard hit as the poor, but some working class families suffered a good deal while some others managed to escape the burdens of inflation. The middle class white collar families made out much better than the poor and blue collar families, as many of the middle class families were untouched by inflation. But many from the middle class suffered as well. Of particular interest was the differences in the ways inflation affected the poor and the more well-to-do. For the poor inflation meant a struggle to survive, to feed and clothe the family. For the middle class inflation meant the frustration of ambitions, such as aspirations for a home of their own. For the poor inflation meant finding enough money to feed the family; for the middle class it meant not being able to save money. It is as if inflation impaired the present lives of the poor, whereas the middle class resented it because it impaired their future lives. But for a number of the middle class people, inflation also meant lowering their standard of living, foregoing expensive meats, new clothes, new cars, and vacations. As we have noted, these middle class families were experiencing a process of proletarianization.

PART II

CONSEQUENCES OF INFLATION AND RECESSION

Chapter 5

COPING PATTERNS

Families that suffered from inflation were required to make adjustments to this debilitating situation. They had at their disposal a limited number of strategies for closing the gap between their resources and rising prices. To use an energy analogy, they could try to tap new sources of power, i.e., new sources of income; they could curtail their use of power, i.e., reduce their expenditures; and they could try to increase efficiency, i.e., get more value from the power (income) available to them. This chapter examines in some detail the various strategies employed, their frequency and their correlates.

Five strategies or patterns for coping with inflation will be examined: efforts to raise income, reduction of expenditures, and three forms of increasing efficiency: bargain hunting, greater self-reliance, and sharing with others. To these might be added a sixth strategy, trying to maintain one's standard of living by going into debt. We shall consider this strategy as well.

Income-Raising Strategies

One way of trying to maintain one's standard of living in the face of rising prices is to increase one's income. Most people experience a rise in income as a result of progress in their jobs, promotions and raises in salaries as a consequence of tenure on the job. But these normal channels of improving income are inadequate in times of rampant inflation. It is precisely because they are inadequate that families fall behind rising prices and suffer from inflation. To combat rising prices by increasing income, families must resort to extraordinary measures. The survey inquired about three: whether the chief wage earner had taken a second job, whether he worked more overtime, and whether an additional member of the family, typically the wife, went to work to help make ends meet. Only 60 of the more than 1,600 chief wage earners in the sample held two jobs, a mere 4 percent of the sample. Working more overtime was a much more popular strategy, engaged in by 26 percent of the wage earners, and having an additional member of the family enter the labor force was reported by 16 percent of the sample. In all, some 38 percent of the families engaged in one or more of these strategies for increasing income.

The depth interviews provide a number of clues as to how families went about raising their income. The survey inquired about second jobs but what this question failed to distinguish is between work that is above board, that is, work that is regulated by such laws as withholding taxes, employer contributions to unemployment insurance, and so forth, and work that is "off the books" and consequently part of the underground economy. Recently, considerable attention has been given to the underground economy, and it has been estimated that at least 10 percent of all income is tied to this off the books economy. The depth interviews indicated that off the books employment is quite common. A woman in her mid-twenties, the mother of two children, married to a school teacher earning $23,000 gave this report:

I took my present job stringing jewelry for the money. I worked out an agreement with my boss; she's a friend, and I'm working off the books. So I get my salary and unemployment too.

This woman is blithely involved in two illegal activities, working off the books, and collecting unemployment insurance while she is working.

A thirty-four-year-old black woman, married to an employee of the Transit Authority in New York, told how her husband earns extra income:

My husband now simonizes cars in the yard to make extra money under the table. Otherwise we would be up the creek. You've got to save for a rainy day.

As this woman notes, the under the table income can make the difference between getting by or going under.

A night manager of a supermarket earning $19,000 from that job said in response to a question about how he was managing:

My wife got a job and I do TV repair work on the side. Just what I can pick up.

Although he did not specify that the TV repair work represented unreported income the chances are that it did.

A thirty-four-year-old Puerto Rican who was laid off by General Motors and was supported by welfare gave this account:

I help people move or stuff like that when it comes up which is not too often. Also my wife is on welfare now, using her mother's address. We get $100 a month extra that way.

This unemployed man not only hustled part time jobs but he saw nothing wrong with his wife circumventing the welfare rules to give his family some income.

A woman in her early thirties married to a programmer reported her plans for setting up what would seem to be an off the books business:

I look for second jobs. I've been going to school and because of school, I can sometimes get part time teaching jobs. Also my wife has had to go to work. She's working as a waitress now for the first time. We need more money now for the essentials, mortgage, fuel, medical and dental bills.

Some relatively affluent respondents were able to use their financial resources to insure still further income. A twenty-nine-year-old real estate lawyer earning $30,000 a year bought some property according to his wife:

My husband bought a loft building in Manhattan which will increase our income in a few years by $4,000. That will help us get over the hump when we buy a house.

Under the table income is only marginally illegal compared to what some people will do to make ends meet. A thirty-four-year-old white man who is employed as a personnel director at a hospital earning $14,000 a year, told the interviewer that he has become a fence. When asked how he was doing compared with his friends, he replied:

We're all drowning in the mudhole together, but they're taking no initiative, but I am. I've become a fence and I wouldn't be doing that if things weren't tough. I sell illegally things like cigarettes, TVs, stereos and so forth. I make $200 to $275 a month, but I've just started and I expect to earn a lot more.

None of the other respondents confessed to such illegal activity but it might well be that the pressures of inflation and recession have pushed some people into a life of crime. It is well known that crimes of theft increase sharply during periods of recession, documenting that there is a connection between economic ills and crime.

Curtailment of Expenditures

The most prevalent response to rising prices is to curtail expenditures. Families that find themselves victims of inflation generally respond by tightening their belts and lowering their standard of living. First luxuries are dispensed with and then in time adjustments are made even in the necessities of life. Such adjustments have already been captured by the subjective inflation crunch index. In addition to those items that measured hurting, the respondents were asked whether they had made changes in their spending patterns in a variety of areas of consumption in order to save money. The specific areas dealt with and the number who said they had cut back to save money are shown in Table 5.1.

The list of consumption areas ranges from essentials, such as health care, food, and clothing, to nonessentials, such as entertainment and vacations. Accommodations to save money were most likely to occur in the area of food, as fully half the respondents reported cutbacks in expenditures on food. This, of course, does not mean that people were eating less, or were losing out on nutrition, but rather that they were shifting from more expensive to less expensive foods, symbolized by eating more hamburger and less steak. Spending less on entertainment and eating out less in restaurants were as common adaptations as cutting down on food expenditures. Another common area of cutting back was on expenditures for clothes. As people felt the pinch of inflation, they presumably decided to do without new clothes or shifted from expensive to less expensive clothes. These four areas were most often involved in expenditure cutbacks. Inflation had much less impact on expenditures for vacations, as only about one-third of the families reported that

Table 5.1: **Frequency of Economizing
in Designated Areas**

Areas of Economizing	Percentage
Food	50
Entertainment	49
Restaurants	49
Clothes	45
Vacations	34
Transportation	28
Dental care	20
Medical care	15

they had economized on their vacation spending. One reason
for this seemingly low figure is that many families, especially
the poor, never have vacations. A little more than a quarter of
the families reported cutting back on their transportation
expenses. Presumably, included here are people who joined car
pools or began using public transportation rather than driving to
work. Of some significance is the evidence that inflation has had
some impact on health care. Some 20 percent of the families
were forced to put off dental care to save money and 15
percent had to postpone medical care. Inflation not only eats
away at the good life but even at life itself.

These various items have been combined into an index measuring curtailment of expenditures. The distribution of cases on
this index shows that 22 percent of the families did not have to
make any adjustments to inflation in that they did not economize on expenditures in any of these areas. Another 24 percent made cutbacks in only one or two of these eight areas, 25
percent made cutbacks in three or four areas, and 29 percent,
particularly hard hit by inflation, spent less in five or more
areas. Some 5 percent of the sample economized in seven of the
eight areas, and 2 percent of the sample, some forty-seven
families, reported making cutbacks in all eight areas.

An example of a household that cut expenditures in many
areas is that of a thirty-nine-year-old business executive earning
$25,000:

> My wife shops more for specials. We don't buy as many expensive
> foods. We grow our own vegetables. During the energy crisis, I
> carpooled. We didn't buy a new car because the present one gets 25
> miles per gallon. We buy less clothes and make do with what we
> have. My wife makes clothes for the children. I will paint the house
> myself rather than pay $3,500 to have it painted.

A thirty-seven-year-old school teacher with a working wife
and a family income of $37,000 told us:

> We eat less meat. We have a smaller car. We buy less clothes and wear
> them longer. We don't take vacations. We put the thermostat down
> and we don't use the air conditioners.

These respondents are typical of the many who have tightened their belts and sharply curtailed their consumption. A retired man who had been a blue collar worker gave an account in the same vein:

> I buy very little. I don't take vacations. I haven't been to a movie in six years. I've tried to cut down on my light and gas bill. I eat very little meat.

A thirty-four-year-old maintenance man working for an airline gave this account of cutting down on expenditures:

> We quit buying sweet snacks. We buy a lot of vegetables and less meat. We use additives to the meat and we buy less prepared foods. My wife makes more of the children's clothes and we quit taking vacations.

A twenty-eight-year-old blue collar worker earning $15,000 also took similar actions to cope with the inflationary pinch:

> We buy cheaper food now. I share rides to work. We don't buy anything we don't need. We go without vacations.

These respondents and many others who could be cited developed similar strategies for coping with inflation. They shifted to less expensive foods, they changed their transportation habits, they went without vacations, and their wives were likely to make their children's clothing.

Self-Reliance and Bargain Hunting

Apart from adaptations based on supply and demand, increasing the supply of resources or reducing the demand on resources, are those aimed at increasing efficiency, that is, getting more mileage out of the resources on hand. Information was obtained on several techniques for increasing efficiency, including greater self-reliance. Growth in self-reliance was measured by three items. At one point respondents were asked whether they now repair a lot of things that they used to throw away, and 53 percent answered affirmatively. They were asked whether they have surprised themselves by being able to save money and cope with things and 46 percent answered yes to this question, and finally they were asked whether the economic squeeze has led them to discover certain talents that they did not know they had, like fixing things themselves, and 40 percent of the sample responded affirmatively. These three items were, of course, highly correlated with each other, and they have been combined into an index of self-reliance that divides the sample roughly into quarters. Thus, 28 percent of the respondents showed no sign of increased self-reliance; 28 percent responded affirmatively to one of the three questions; 23 percent to two of the questions; and 21 percent to all three questions.

Bargain hunting proved to be a more elusive concept, and only two questions in the survey bear on this notion. Some 70 percent of the respondents said that they mostly buy the things that are on sale, indicating that inflation has sensitized people to shopping more wisely, and 42 percent of the sample said that as a result of inflation they now buy lower quality items. When combined into an index, these items yield the following distribution: 26 percent scored zero on "bargain hunting," 36 percent answered one of the questions positively, and 38 percent answered both questions positively.

Typical of the bargain-hunting mentality are these comments: A black woman in her thirties whose husband earns $18,000 as a motorman:

I shop for bargains. If it is marked the regular price, I don't buy it.

The wife of an airline skycap earning $10,000 told how her food shopping had changed:

I just don't buy as much. If something is too high I don't buy it. I shop around and get a better deal if I can find it.

The forty-nine-year-old wife of a school teacher earning $23,000 said:

I take more advantage of sales and coupon discounts and I use leftovers more efficiently.

The thirty-one-year-old wife of a county official earning $19,000 said:

I check prices carefully. I buy the cheapest things keeping nutrition in mind. I don't buy name brands. I buy store brands.

A thirty-nine-year-old wife of an appliance service manager earning $15,000 gave this account:

I look for bargains. I bought one half of a beef to save costs on meat. I grow my own vegetables.

The sixty-two-year-old wife of an athletic club masseur earning $6,000 said:

I almost always buy the items on sale. We shop around for the best prices.

A twenty-nine-year-old social worker earning $7,000 told how his family copes:

We compare prices and look for bargains. Cook only what is necessary. Cutting down on sugar, cereals and sweets. We eat chicken and luncheon meat instead of expensive meats.

We have already encountered a number of instances of bargain hunting in Chapter 4 and as these quotes suggest, this strategy was quite prevalent.

Sharing with Others

The sixties saw the development of a new life style based on sharing and living together, the whole communal social movement. Under the inflationary pressures of the seventies, this movement has attracted a number of new adherents, people who are not likely to run off and join a commune, but are nevertheless deeply concerned with saving money and see the economic advantage of sharing with others. The respondents were asked a series of questions about whether they have received help from friends in a number of areas and whether they have given help to their friends in these areas. The areas covered were repairs, baby sitting, lending money, sharing food, exchanging clothes, and sharing transportation. The responses to these questions ranged from a low of 9 percent for receiving money from friends to a high of 18 percent for sharing transportation with friends. Oddly enough, the respondents saw themselves as more generous than their friends. In every instance (except transportation where the percentages were identical) more respondents said they helped their friends than received help from their friends. For example, 13 percent said they had lent money to their friends, but only 9 percent said their friends had lent them money; for baby sitting the comparable percentages are 15 and 10; and helping on repairs, 21 and 17 percent. When these twelve items are combined in an index, we find that more than half of the respondents, 55 percent, did not engage in any sharing activities, 26 percent gave one to three positive responses, and 19 percent gave four or more positive responses.

Several of the depth interviews provided information on sharing. When asked whether she and her neighbors help each other out, a nineteen-year-old black woman, an unwed mother of a six-month-old child, living on welfare said:

> Yes, we help each other out. Like if they need to borrow something, we give it to them and if we need something and they have it, they let us have it.

A thirty-six-year-old mailman earning $20,000 said:

> When things need to be done, I either do them myself or get a friend to help me. We have a group of fellows and we help each other. When I need something done, two or three fellows will help me, and when they need something done, I go over and help them. It's a mutual aid society, but it's not formally organized or anything, but we've done a lot of helping each other out. Without them, there

would be less done around the house and the car would have been gone a long time ago.

A twenty-nine-year-old mother attending college and living on welfare gave a detailed account of how the people in her building help each other out:

> Everyone living in this building is working or on welfare. They struggle to survive. We've been helping each other. I have a close friend downstairs. I use her hammer. Her husband borrows my paint brushes. We share food, like milk if we run out, a cup of sugar. Sometimes when we bake, we'll bring it up or down without asking if the other person wants it. We share cigarettes. Others in the building also share and borrow, but not to the same extent. . . . We even share medicines. You know how it started, the kids would come and borrow. The adults followed. Some families are new to the building and they fell in the pattern. When people open their door to you, you have to open yours to them. We pass kids' toys and clothes around. We also support each other emotionally. We're all in the same condition. When we don't have cigarettes, we all laugh about it. I have a friend who can laugh at the worst situations. It helps.

From this woman's comment, it is clear that the pattern of sharing can play an important part in how families, especially poor ones, manage to survive.

Do families put all their eggs in one basket when developing strategies for coping with inflation or do they try everything in an effort to make ends meet? At stake here is whether the strategies are positively or negatively related to each other. Negative relationships would be evidence for specialization in coping with inflation, whereas positive relationships would signify families pulling out all the stops in their effort to cope. Table 5.2 presents a matrix of gamma correlation coefficients showing the relationships among these strategies.

As can be seen from the table, all the coping strategies are strongly correlated with each other indicating that families suffering from inflation will try everything in their efforts to make ends meet. The coefficients range from a low of .34 (bargain hunting and sharing) to a high of .58 (bargain hunting

Table 5.2: The Correlations of the Coping Strategies with Each Other

	Income Raising	Curtailing Expenditures	More Self-Reliance	Bargain Hunting	Sharing
Income raising	–	.48	.42	.36	.47
Curtailing expenditures	.48	–	.51	.58	.49
More self-reliance	.42	.51	–	.52	.41
Bargain hunting	.36	.58	.52	–	.34
Sharing	.47	.49	.41	.34	–

and curtailing expenditures). Curtailing expenditures yields the highest correlations with the other coping strategies, suggesting that it is the core response to inflation. Oddly enough, bargain hunting generates the highest and lowest correlations. It is very strongly related to curtailing expenditures and self-reliance but only moderately related to income-raising and sharing.

Inflation Crunch and Coping Strategies

The families that experienced the greatest impact of inflation and recession should be the very ones developing strategies for coping, and the data show this to be so. Table 5.3 relates coping strategies to objective and subjective inflation crunch, the inflation typology based on the two dimensions and recession impact.

By reading down the columns of each part of the table we see that the measures of inflation impact and recession are strongly related to the coping strategies. The percentage adopting each strategy sharply increases, the greater the impact of inflation and recession. Curtailing expenditures turns out to be the coping strategy most sensitive to inflationary pressures and the recession, closely followed by bargain hunting. Sharing is the strategy with the weakest relationships to these measures, although it too is fairly strongly related to inflationary pressures. Subjective inflation crunch is more strongly related to coping strategies than objective crunch. On the crunch typology we find that the stoics are close to the untouched in avoiding these strategies, whereas the complainers are more like the suffering

Table 5.3: Strategies for Coping with Inflation by Measures of Inflation Crunch, and Recession Impact (percentage high on strategy)

	Coping Strategy					
	Income Raising	Curtailing Expenditures	Greater Self-Reliance	Bargain Hunting	Sharing	N
Objective Crunch						
Better off now	27	27	31	11	37	(308)
Stayed even	31	38	35	26	37	(493)
Little worse off	44	65	50	44	47	(733)
Lot worse off	56	74	53	64	56	(422)
Subjective Crunch						
Low	19	18	18	5	28	(457)
Medium low	31	41	34	17	41	(485)
Medium high	43	66	51	47	47	(434)
High	55	82	66	74	60	(606)
Crunch Typology						
Untouched	22	22	25	8	34	(565)
Stoics	30	42	29	17	37	(361)
Complainers	47	61	54	49	44	(236)
Suffering victims	51	80	61	67	57	(794)
Recession Impact						
None	17	34	30	22	33	(666)
Some	62	64	50	43	50	(617)
Considerable	63	79	68	64	64	(390)

The percentages in this table do not total to 100 percent. They report the percentage high on each strategy according to position on the various crunch variables.

victims in adopting the strategies. This is further evidence that the subjective dimension, measuring how much families are hurting because of inflation, is more important than the objective one. Table 5.3 shows that it is the families hardest hit by the economic calamities of inflation and recession that develop strategies for fighting back.

Social Correlates of Coping Patterns

Inasmuch as the strategies for coping with inflation are very much related to inflation crunch, particularly the subjective dimension of hurting, we might expect that the social correlates related to inflation impact are related to coping patterns. But although related, the coping strategies are not completely interchangeable, and those in certain social situations might find certain strategies more attractive or feasible than others.

Table 5.4 shows how the coping strategies are related to the subsamples, income and race-ethnicity.

The patterns for the strategy of income raising are quite different from those for the other strategies. From the top part of the table we see that the poor are substantially below the blue collar families in employing this strategy, and the lowest income group is below the other income groups. Unlike the other strategies, income raising is not simply a matter of choice, but is influenced by opportunity as well. The head of a poor family may be unable to find any job much less a second one and he may not have the opportunity to work more overtime, and his spouse may be unable to find a job even though she is willing to work. Income raising is most frequently adopted by blue collar families and the families of middle income and, not surprisingly, is least frequently employed by the retired who are out of the labor force. Thus, hardly any of the retired resorted to income-raising devices. The white collar group, not nearly as pressed by inflation as the poor and blue collar, resorted to income-raising strategies less frequently, as was true of the families in the highest income group.

With respect to the other four strategies for coping with inflation, the pattern follows that for inflation crunch. The

Table 5.4: Strategies for Coping with Inflation by Selected Social Characteristics (percentage high on strategy)

			Coping Strategy			
	Income Raising	Curtailing Expenditures	Greater Self-Reliance	Bargain Hunting	Sharing	N
Subsample						
Poor	42	69	66	74	57	(323)
Blue collar	56	61	51	45	51	(581)
White collar	37	46	34	21	39	(769)
Retired	4	43	33	31	35	(309)
Income						
Under $7,000	28	66	61	67	52	(389)
$7,000—$12,999	45	62	48	48	49	(380)
$13,000—$19,999	51	59	46	34	52	(435)
$20,000 and over	37	40	32	16	37	(462)
Race-Ethnicity						
White	36	51	38	31	43	(1,464)
Black	43	61	59	63	47	(407)
Spanish-speaking	43	63	68	60	60	(88)

poor and the blacks and Spanish-speaking, hardest hit by inflation, were most likely to curtail consumption, hunt for bargains, rely on themselves to do things, and share with others.
The blue collar families, next hardest hit by inflation, were next
most likely to use these strategies. Oddly enough, the retired,
who were second only to the poor in falling behind rising prices,
were least likely to employ any of these strategies, with the
exception of bargain hunting, where they replace the white
collar group in third place. We have seen that the retired were
most likely to be stoics, that is, fall behind rising prices without
complaining, and we now see that this stoicism extends to
accepting inflation without making efforts to overcome it. The
difference between the poor and the white collar group is
greatest for the strategy of bargain hunting, where the gap is 53
percentage points, and the poor are also much more likely to
become self-reliant than the white collar families. The idea of
sharing to save money does not differentiate the poor from the
blue collar families, and the gap between the poor and white
collar group on this strategy is only 18 percentage points.
Previous sociological studies have suggested that sharing is quite
common among the poor, but these data lend little support to
this expectation.

The data on income also show the greatest differences for
self-reliance and bargain hunting with many more of the low
income families employing these strategies than the high income
families. These would seem to be the poor man's way of coping
with inflation. From the last column in the income part of the
table we see the almost complete absence of a relationship
between sharing and income. The frequency of sharing is relatively constant through the first three income categories and
falls off only among the well-to-do earning over $20,000. The
retired, who were least inclined toward sharing, are spread
among the lowest and next lowest income groups, and they no
doubt are the reason for the absence of a relationship between
income and sharing. Inasmuch as blacks and Spanish-speaking
families were more vulnerable to inflation, it is not surprising
that they resorted to coping strategies more often than the
whites. Sharing is especially popular among the Spanish-

speaking, who outdistance both blacks and whites in this respect.

The findings presented in Table 5.4 are in keeping with what we would expect from the findings on inflation crunch. By and large, the families that were hurting the most from inflation were the ones who employed strategies for coping with it. The same patterns hold for the other social characteristics found to be related to inflation crunch. Thus families headed by blue collar workers, whether skilled or unskilled, were more likely to employ coping patterns than either higher white collar or lower white collar families, the unemployed were much more likely to resort to coping strategies than the employed, and larger families more so than smaller families. Finally, the more poorly educated family heads used these coping strategies more often than the well-educated family heads. But all of these findings may be a mere relfection of the greater inflationary pressure felt by the more underprivileged families, the poor, the minorities, the unemployed, blue collar workers, and the poorly educated. It may well be that inflation crunch is what leads to the developing of coping strategies irrespective of social characteristics. But it is 'also possible that the underprivileged have been forced by the circumstances of their lives to develop survival strategies that stand them in good stead in times of rampant inflation. Even in good times, the poor and minorities may be bargain hunters and self-reliant and engage in sharing. Whether the underprivileged are more prone to coping strategies than the more privileged can only be determined by taking inflation crunch, particularly the subjective dimension which measures degree of hurting, into account. This is done in the subsequent analysis. Table 5.5 shows how the subsamples are related to coping when hurting is held constant.

Table 5.5 presents the results of five separate three variable tables, one for each coping strategy. The top row in each part of the table shows the percentage who engage in the strategy among those who did not experience any pain or suffering from inflation while the second row shows the percentage employing the strategy among those who did suffer from inflation. Needless to say, in every case those who were hurting because of

**Table 5.5: Strategies for Coping with Inflation by Subsample and
Subjective Crunch (percentage high on strategy)**

		Subsample			
		Poor	Blue Collar	White Collar	Retired
Coping Strategy					
(1)	Income Raising				
	Low crunch	24	43	25	1
	High crunch	46	65	58	7
(2)	Curtailed Expenditures				
	Low crunch	39	35	28	24
	High crunch	75	78	78	66
(3)	Self-Reliance				
	Low crunch	39	37	22	19
	High crunch	71	60	53	50
(4)	Bargain Hunting				
	Low crunch	28	16	7	12
	High crunch	83	65	45	55
(5)	Sharing				
	Low crunch	52	44	31	26
	High crunch	58	55	53	45
N	Low crunch	(54)	(232)	(487)	(169)
	High crunch	(269)	(349)	(282)	(140)

inflation were much more likely to employ the coping strategy
in every sample than those who were not. The differences
between those hurting and not hurting are especially pronounced for curtailing expenditures, self-reliance and bargain
hunting, and are smallest for sharing. For our present purposes,
the differences shown by reading across the rows, that is, the
differences between the subsamples, when subjective inflation
crunch is controlled, are more important. If the poor are more
resourceful in coping with inflation than the other groups, we
should find them more prone to these strategies even when
inflation crunch is held constant. But by reading across the
rows, we find that this is certainly not true of income raising.
This strategy is dominated by the blue collar group and among
those in high pain; and the white collar group is more likely to
engage in income raising than the poor. When it comes to

curtailing expenditures, we find no differences between the poor, blue collar, and white collar groups who were hurting because of inflation. (Among those not hurting, the poor were somewhat more likely to curtail consumption than white collar workers.) Only on self-reliance and bargain hunting do the poor score higher than the blue collar workers, who score higher than the white collar workers when inflation crunch is taken into account. If the poor have a propensity for survival tactics independent of inflation crunch, it is apparent only in their greater readiness to do things for themselves and spend time shopping for bargains. Sharing is just as popular among the white collar families who experience inflation crunch as it is among the poor. The passive stoicism of the retired is indicated by their being least likely to engage in coping strategies, even when subjective crunch is taken into account. The only exception to this rule is found for bargain hunting, where among those both low and high on inflation crunch, the retired are somewhat more likely to hunt for bargains than the white collar families.

Whether family income is related to coping strategies when subjective inflation crunch is held constant is shown in Table 5.6.

The economic plight of the poor is shown quite vividly by their inability to employ the strategies that would raise their income. Even when suffering a great deal from inflation, the poor are not nearly as likely as those of higher income to do the things that would raise family income. This strategy proves to be most popular in the second highest income group, those earning between $13,000 and $20,000. It may well be that many families are able to be in this fairly high category because they have more than one wage earner. Belt tightening by cutting down on consumption is quite prevalent on all income levels when inflation becomes painful. Even those in the highest income group are as likely to cut back on spending as those in the lowest category. Sharing also fails to differentiate the low income from those better off. Only in the highest income group does sharing fall off, but even here it is not too far below the level in the lowest income category, and this strategy, like

income raising, is most popular in the second highest income
group. Only self-reliance and bargain hunting have greater pro-
portions of low income than high income people. These strategies are most popular in the lowest income group and fall off as
income rises. Of the five strategies, it would seem that self-
reliance and bargain hunting, the two on which the poor are
dominant, are the ones least dependent on outside circumstances and most subject to the free choice of the family. Low
income families probably never buy luxuries, and there is a limit
to how much they can curtail their expenditures; sharing
depends on other people, and income raising, as we have noted,
depends on a host of circumstances beyond the family's control. But to rely on oneself to do things and shop around for
bargains are things that the poor can do, and, as Table 5.6
shows, they rely on these tactics more frequently than higher
income families.

Table 5.6: Strategies for Coping with Inflation by Income and Subjective
Crunch (percentage high on strategy)

	Income			
Coping Strategy	Under $7,000	$7,000-$12,999	$13,000-$19,999	$20,000 and Over
(1) Income Raising				
Low crunch	7	27	35	29
High crunch	35	55	65	56
(2) Curtailed Expenditures				
Low crunch	32	36	37	26
High crunch	77	76	79	73
(3) Self-Reliance				
Low crunch	32	30	32	25
High crunch	70	58	58	49
(4) Bargain Hunting				
Low crunch	26	16	13	6
High crunch	80	66	53	41
(5) Sharing				
Low crunch	42	40	43	33
High crunch	55	54	60	46
N Low crunch	(93)	(139)	(207)	(325)
High crunch	(302)	(251)	(228)	(137)

Table 5.4 showed the minorities leading the whites in the employment of all these coping strategies, even income raising, but as Table 5.7 indicates, much of this was due to their greater vulnerability to inflation crunch.

As in the previous tables, we find that in every group, those who suffered from inflation were more likely than those who did not to employ coping strategies. But the apparent greater propensity of the minorities to employ these strategies turns out to be largely a function of inflation crunch. Thus, the blacks are not more likely than the whites to engage in income-raising activities, and they are not more likely to curtail consumption or engage in sharing once subjective crunch is taken into account. But like the poor, they do rely more than the whites on self-reliance and bargain hunting, even when subjective crunch is held constant. Contrary to the view that sharing is a popular adaptation among the low income, the blacks, who

Table 5.7: Strategies for Coping with Inflation by Race-Ethnicity and Subjective Crunch (percentage high on strategy)

			Race-Ethnicity	
	Coping Strategy	Whites	Blacks	Spanish-Speaking
(1)	Income Raising			
	Low crunch	25	21	39
	High crunch	51	51	44
(2)	Curtailed Expenditures			
	Low crunch	30	28	39
	High crunch	78	72	68
(3)	Self-Reliance			
	Low crunch	25	39	33
	High crunch	55	67	77
(4)	Bargain Hunting			
	Low crunch	11	18	17
	High crunch	55	78	71
(5)	Sharing			
	Low crunch	35	30	61
	High crunch	54	52	60
N	Low crunch	(812)	(102)	(18)
	High crunch	(652)	(305)	(70)

tend to earn much less than the whites, actually engage in sharing slightly less often than the whites, both among those who do and those who do not suffer from inflation. Sharing would seem to be very popular in the culture of the Spanish-speaking for they far outdistance both blacks and whites in this respect and, oddly enough, sharing by the Spanish-speaking is not influenced by inflation in that those who are not hurting are just as likely to engage in sharing as those who are hurting.

Occupation, as we noted, was another social characteristic associated with coping strategies. Those lower down the occupational scale suffered more from inflation and they were more prone to these strategies. But just as in the matter of race-ethnicity, these differences are largely due to inflation crunch. When subjective crunch is held constant, the occupation groupings differ only on those strategies free of outside restraints: self-reliance and bargain hunting. Employing strategies for raising income is predominantly a blue collar, especially higher blue collar, tactic. But when inflation becomes painful for the family, white collar workers, even those at the top of the hierarchy, turn to this strategy with almost the same frequency as the blue collar workers (48 and 50 percent v. 55 and 50). And when it comes to belt tightening, white collar workers more than match the blue collar workers in curtailing consumption when inflation hurts (77 percent compared to 76 percent), and the white collar groups engage in sharing with others as often as the blue collar groups do (54 and 56 percent v. 48 and 51 percent). Only with respect to those strategies that seem to be specialties of the less fortunate, self-reliance and bargain hunting, do the less prestigious blue collar workers, particularly the semiskilled and unskilled, outshine the white collar workers, especially the higher white collar group. Thus, whereas 43 percent of the higher white collar respondents suffering from inflation engage in bargain hunting, 76 percent of the lower blue collar workers who are hurting do. And for self-reliance, the comparable figures are 51 and 64 percent.

We have seen that coping strategies are responsive not only to inflation crunch but to the recession as well. Families that suffered from unemployment or a shorter work week or having to work harder because of layoffs were more likely to develop coping strategies than families that were not affected by the recession. Table 5.8 shows the joint impact of inflation and recession on coping patterns.

Much of the variance in coping strategies can be explained by the joint impact of inflation and recession. As inflation crunch increases, so do the rates of each coping strategy whatever the recession impact, and conversely, as recession impact increases, so do the coping strategy rates among those both low and high on subjective inflation crunch. The only exception to the pattern occurs for income raising among those high on inflation crunch. Here we find that those who suffered most from the recession were not quite as likely to employ this strategy as those who suffered only somewhat. But this group contains a large number of the unemployed, who by virtue of being without a job, are cut off from a number of income-raising

Table 5.8: Strategies for Coping with Inflation by Recession Impact and Subjective Crunch (percentage high on strategy)

		Recession Impact		
	Coping Strategy	None	Some	Considerdble
(1)	Income Raising			
	Low crunch	11	55	64
	High crunch	31	67	63
(2)	Curtailed Expenditures			
	Low crunch	23	42	47
	High crunch	61	78	87
(3)	Self-Reliance			
	Low crunch	22	35	44
	High crunch	48	59	74
(4)	Bargain Hunting			
	Low crunch	9	13	20
	High crunch	51	61	76
(5)	Sharing			
	Low crunch	29	44	58
	High crunch	41	54	66
N	Low crunch	(456)	(232)	(85)
	High crunch	(210)	(385)	(305)

strategies, such as working overtime or taking a second job. Table 5.8 makes clear that the people most moved to try to combat inflation are the people who are suffering from the twin evils of inflation and recession. Given their desperate situation, the unemployed are likely to take whatever action they can to make their lot more tolerable.

Reliance on Credit

In considering strategies for coping with inflation, we have dealt with a three part model: increasing resources, i.e., income, reducing consumption, and improving efficiency. Each of these strategies contributes to a closing of the gap between rising prices and family income. But there is still another tactic families might employ to cope with rising prices: going into debt. Given the widespread availability of consumer credit, it is conceivable that families will turn to credit to finance their consumption in a period of rising prices. They are likely to rely on credit only if they think that the economy will soon turn around and things will get better. If indeed inflation should slow down considerably and income gradually improve, then families who use credit would have little difficulty maintaining their credit obligations. But if inflation should continue at a high rate, then families who use credit will only get deeper into trouble as time passes. Thus readiness to use credit should depend on the degree of confidence people have in the economy. At one point in the interview the respondents were asked whether they were now using credit more, less, or about the same as in the past. Almost one-third of the families told us that they never used credit,[1] 34 percent said there was no change in their credit practices, 26 percent said they were using credit less than formerly, and only 8 percent said they were using credit more. Clearly, most people were pessimistic rather than optimistic about the economy, as many more people cut down on

1. This is much higher than the national average. Previous research indicates that at least 90 percent of American households have used consumer credit. Perhaps the retired who seldom use credit are responsible for this high figure.

credit use than increased it. To go deeper into debt was not an inflation remedy for most people. Table 5.9 shows how use of credit is related to objective and subjective inflation crunch.

From the last column of each part of the table we see that avoidance of credit varied little with objective or subjective inflation crunch. (Those who said their financial situation had actually improved were more likely than the others to use credit.) It is clear from these data that those who were hardest hit by inflation, both objectively and subjectively, were most likely to change their credit practices, but the direction of change is by no means consistent. Those who suffered the most from inflation were both more likely to use credit *more* and use credit *less* than formerly. The tendency to reduce credit exceeds the tendency to use it more for those who were hard hit by inflation.

It turns out that the people most likely to change their credit practices are the same types of people who suffered most from inflation. Thus the poor were more likely than the well-to-do to reduce their use of credit, as were the blacks and Spanish-speaking and those of blue collar occupations and the poorly educated. The unemployed also cut down on their use of credit to a greater degree than the employed. But to a large extent

Table 5.9: Use of Credit by Objective and Subjective Inflation Crunch (percentages)

| | Use of Credit | | | | | |
	More Now	Less Now	Same	Never Use Credit		
Objective Crunch						
Better off now	7	24	44	25	100	(308)
Same	6	18	44	32	100	(491)
Little worse off	9	28	31	32	100	(730)
Lot worse off	10	34	23	34	100	(422)
Subjective Crunch						
Low	3	18	42	37	100	(456)
Medium low	6	26	41	28	100	(482)
Medium high	9	28	34	29	100	(433)
High	10	31	25	31	100	(606)

these social differences are a result of inflation crunch. When inflation crunch is taken into account, the social differences in credit usage tend to be reduced.

Patterns of change in credit use turn out to be related to the other strategies for coping with inflation. Thus both an increase and decrease in credit use is related to a high score on income raising, curtailment of consumption, self-reliance, bargain hunting and sharing. Changing one's use of credit would seem to be yet another strategy for coping with inflation. But, oddly enough, how one changes his use of credit is by no means clear. For some families, the pressures of inflation result in greater reliance on credit, and for even more, inflationary pressures mean reducing reliance on credit. One thing is clear from the data: reliance on credit is not a device for maintaining a standard of living in spite of inflationary pressures. Not only did more people reduce their reliance on credit than used credit more, but reliance on credit was positively related to curtailing consumption. The more areas in which families curtailed consumption, the more likely they were to rely on credit. This is true for those low and high on subjective inflation crunch. For example, of those high on inflation crunch, only 1 percent of those who did not curtail consumption in any area relied more on credit, a figure that climbs to 17 percent among those who curtailed consumption in five or more areas. Clearly, families did not turn to credit as a way of maintaining their standard of living, for the more they lowered their standard of living, the more they relied on credit.

This chapter has examined the responses that families make to the crush of inflation. We have seen that they can try to cope with inflation by raising their income through extraordinary measures, by curtailing consumption, and by increasing the efficiency with which they apply their resources to meet their consumer needs. Whether families employ any of these strategies is very much dependent upon whether they are hurting from inflation. Thus, we saw that families whose incomes have fallen behind rising prices but who are not suffering are not nearly as likely to engage in coping strategies as families that are suffering from inflation even though their incomes have kept up with rising prices. Although the less fortunate or more under-privileged in terms of income, ethnicity, occupation, education, and employment status were more likely to employ these strategies, we found that in most instances this was so simply because they were suffering more from inflation. When inflation became a burden, even the better off—such as those in higher white collar occupations, the higher income brackets, whites and the better educated—sought to raise their incomes, curtailed their consumption, and resorted to sharing to about the same degree as the less fortunate. Only the strategies of greater self-reliance and bargain hunting continued to be used more frequently by the less fortunate when inflation crunch was held constant. Finally, we saw that reliance on credit was also a strategy for coping with inflation. For some families, inflation crunch led to more reliance on credit and for even more, inflation meant curtailing use of credit.

That the better off came to adopt some of the same strategies as the worse off under the pressure of inflation would indicate that inflation is a great leveler among those affected by it. As we saw in previous chapters, those in more privileged statuses are more successful than the less fortunate in avoiding the ravages of inflation altogether, but when they do suffer from inflation, they come to behave like their less fortunate brethren in keeping with the process we have identified as the proletarianization of the middle class.

Chapter 6

IMPACT OF INFLATION-RECESSION ON THE FAMILY

Rampant inflation and unemployment are traumatic events for the families that are affected by them. Familial stability can be badly shaken by the discovery that the family's resources are suddenly incapable of maintaining the standard of living to which the family has grown accustomed. When confronted by such a calamity, some families may grow stronger as the spouses are drawn closer together to combat the common enemy. But in other families strains are likely to occur as a result of economic pressures. As the ambitions and aspirations of family members become frustrated, the danger exists that they will take out their frustrations on each other. It is even possible that one spouse might blame the other for the hard times that have befallen the family. How inflation and recession affect the relations of family members to each other is the subject of this chapter. We shall consider the degree to which strengths and weaknesses in the family have been generated by the economy and the correlates of such impacts.

Precisely because we were interested in the impact of the economy on the family, we limited the sample of white collar and blue collar households to complete families, that is, families in which both the husband and wife were present. By and large, this plan was carried out, as more than 99 percent of the white collar and blue collar families were complete. In a handful of instances, a divorced or separated parent with children was included in these samples. In sampling poor families the rule was extended to include broken families, that is, a mother or father with children. Among the poor families sampled, 81 percent had both a husband and wife present, the remaining 19 percent consisting of broken families as a result of divorce, separation, or death. In sampling retired persons, the rule of inclusion was extended still further to include single persons as well. Among the sample of retired persons, 53 percent were married, 37 percent were widowed, 4 percent were separated or divorced, and 6 percent were single. This chapter deals only with the households in which both a husband and wife were present, a group that constitutes 89 percent of the entire sample. The retired are substantially undersampled in this group.

The respondents were asked a number of questions about the quality of their marriages and how their marriage had been affected by the economy. When asked directly whether the economic pressures confronting their family had made their marriage better, worse, or had had no effect on their marriage, the great majority (84 percent) claimed that their marriage was unaffected by the economy. Oddly enough, economic pressures were likely to have a more positive than negative effect on marriage in that 9 percent of the sample said that the pressures had made their marriages better while 7 percent said they had made the marriage worse.

Four other questions were asked dealing with the impact of economic pressures on the marriage, two tapping a positive effect and two a negative effect. On the positive side, the respondents were asked whether the financial pressures had drawn them closer to their spouse. Almost one-third, 32 percent, answered this question affirmatively. Also on the positive side, the respondents were asked whether financial pressures had led "you and your husband/wife to understand each other better," and even more, 39 percent, answered this question affirmatively. When these two positive questions are combined, we find that 26 percent of the sample claimed that economic pressures had made their marriage better in both respects, 20 percent said things were better in one respect, and 54 percent answered both questions negatively, signifying that economic pressures had not had a beneficial effect on their marriage.

On the negative side of the ledger, the respondents were asked whether financial pressures had contributed to tensions in their marriage and quarrels over money. Some 28 percent said that such pressures had contributed to tensions in their marriage, and 18 percent said that they were quarreling more with their spouse over money matters than they used to. It should be noted that the two questions tapping favorable outcomes received more affirmative responses than the two questions tapping negative ones. On this basis it would seem that economic hard times may contribute more to strengthening families than to weakening them. When the two negative outcome questions are combined, we find that 14 percent of the sample felt that their marriages had deteriorated in two respects, 18 percent felt they had in one respect, and 68 percent reported that economic pressures had had no negative impact on their marriages.

By combining the positive and negative dimensions we arrive at an overall index measuring the extent and direction of change in the marriage induced by the economy. This index yields four types of people: those who claim that the economy has had no impact on their marriage one way or the other, those who claim that it has had a positive impact, those who claim it has had a negative impact, and finally, those who mention both positive and negative consequences for their marriage, a group that we label as "mixed impact." The distribution of cases according to these types is shown below:

Impact of Economic Pressures on the Marriage

No change	40%
Has made marriage better	28

| Has had mixed effect | 19 |
| Has made marriage worse | 14 |

$$101\%$$

$$(1,739)$$

This distribution makes clear what the responses to the individual items indicated, i.e., economic pressures are more likely to have a favorable than an unfavorable impact on marriage, as 28 percent said that their marriage had improved as a result of economic pressures, and only 14 percent said that it had gotten worse. Some 19 percent of the sample mentioned both good and bad effects of the economy on their marriage. By far the largest category consists of those who said that the economy had had no effect on their marriage—fully 40 percent of the sample.

That this index does indeed measure the impact of the economy on the quality of the marriage is shown by its relationships to other questions about the quality of the marriage. The direct question about whether economic pressures had made their marriage better or worse is, of course, related to this index. Only 1 percent of those who are in the "no change" category said that economic pressures had made their marriage worse, 2 percent of the "marriage better" group gave this response, 9 percent in the "mixed" group, and 32 percent of the "marriage worse" group. The respondents were also asked how happy their marriages were: very happy, pretty happy, or not too happy. Again, the percentage who rate their marriages as very happy steadily declines across the marital impact index, from a high of 65 percent of those in the "no change" group, to 63 percent in the "marriage better" group, to 47 percent of the "mixed" group, and 24 percent of the "marriage worse" category. Another attribute of the marriage is strongly related to the marital impact index. The respondents were asked whether they and their spouses were now spending more time at home than they used to. Some 65 percent reported that they were, and only 35 percent said no. Staying home more is no doubt one consequence of inflation and recession for as we have seen, many families cut back on their entertainment budget. It turns out that staying home more is strongly related to strain in the marriage. Only 44 percent of those who said their marriage had not changed reported staying home more. This figure jumps to 76 percent of those who said that their marriage had gotten better and 85 percent of those who reported that the economic pressures have had a mixed impact on their marriage. Among those who said their marriage had gotten worse, the stay more at home rate falls back to 73 percent. Presumably, the change in life style resulting in couples staying at home is symptomatic of strains in the marriage.

The depth interviews conducted at the beginning of the research uncovered a number of instances of changes in the marital relationship as a result of inflationary pressures. The young wife of a mechanical engineer whose income declined because he decided to go back to school for his Ph.D. expressed some ambivalence about the impact of the economy on her marriage:

It has put a strain on the marriage. We both want things. My husband feels he is not providing, and there is strain once in a while. But in a sense it's bringing us closer. We're going through a hardship together. . . . We talk a lot more about money. . . . We used to be very free with money. Spend without care. Now every cent counts. We're not happier because of lack of money, but it's brought us closer. It points up what is really important in life. We're more into each other. It's not important that we are not in a fancy place. In a sense it's given us a deeper relationship.

This woman's account is an example of how inflationary pressures can actually make a marriage better, for in her judgment, the money problems have drawn her closer to her husband.

The damage that money troubles can cause a marriage is illustrated by the comments of a fifty-year-old black woman whose husband had lost his job:

My husband has changed since he lost his job. He's so quarrelsome now. I can't do anything right according to him. He doesn't trust me

with any money. He even does the clothes shopping for our daughter. I asked him for some money to get her some socks and he gave
me a dollar.

Her husband did not realize that in these inflationary times
socks cannot be bought with a dollar.

A twenty-nine-year old white woman with a two-year-old
child living on welfare broke up with her common-law husband
because of money problems:

> I don't think we would have had any problem if money wasn't a
> problem. We are actually very compatible. Money broke us up. We
> had so many financial arguments. Each of us felt that the other was
> spending foolishly. We would be arguing about other things but the
> undercurrent would be money. . . . We had such a good relationship
> to start with. Then the financial situation got bad and it wrecked us.

As marriage counselors are well aware, money problems are a
major cause of marital break-ups.

When asked if the financial situation had led to any fights
with her spouse, the thirty-year-old wife of a systems programmer earning $16,000 said:

> Yes, we've had a couple of real duzzies. We fight about which things
> we must have, like shoes for the kids. But once we decide to buy
> something, we do it right. Money has become more of a topic of
> conversation and it grates more. . . . My husband is frustrated. He's
> not making what he thinks he should.

A twenty-five-year-old mother of three children whose husband is a civil servant earning $23,000 told us:

> Because of his second job, my husband loses sleep. He's away so
> much, I'm very lonely now and we're both more tense with the kids
> when the money pressures build up. . . . We fight more about money
> than we used to. Also, there are some fights I should have been
> having with him about money that I haven't had yet.

This woman is nursing some grievances about money matters
that she thinks she should bring up with her husband even if it
means having a fight.

A twenty-one-year-old Puerto Rican working as a computer coding clerk for the city earning $12,000 gave this account:

> We're happy with each other. But with all the problems, the bills and all that, we don't see the good qualities in each other. Only about one day a month do we have time to enjoy each other. We argue a lot until we get all the tension out. Then we can enjoy each other.

Quarrels with his wife over money have become a more or less standard feature of this man's marriage.

Even the well-to-do do not always escape marital disputes over money. A thirty-year-old stockbroker earning $45,000 said:

> It [the economy] hasn't really affected us except we now have many more arguments. We had a fight just last night about taking a taxi.

These quotations from the depth interviews provide some idea of how financial problems cause strain and tensions in the marriage. We turn now to the survey data to find out what kinds of families experienced marital tensions because of economic pressures.

The respondents' reports of how inflation and recession have affected their marriages are confirmed by the relationships between marital impact and the crunch variables shown in Table 6.1.

On every measure of inflation and recession impact we find a strong relationship to marital strain. The more families were affected by inflation, the more they suffered from it, and the greater the impact of recession, the more their marriages suffered. The strongest relationship is that for subjective inflation crunch. Hardly any of those who scored low on subjective crunch experienced marital difficulties while more than half of those who were high on this attribute had their marriages suffer. And more than half the families that were especially hard hit by the recession had marital troubles compared with only one-fifth of the families that completely escaped the recession. These findings document the broad ramifications of the economic

Table 6.1: Marital Impact by Measures of Inflation Crunch and Recession
           Impact (percentages)

	Marital Impact					
	No Change	Marriage Better	Marriage Mixed	Marriage Worse		N
Objective Crunch						
Better off	55	24	11	10	100	(292)
Stayed even	51	27	14	9	101	(434)
Little worse	35	32	18	15	100	(648)
Lot worse	23	23	33	21	100	(344)
Subjective Crunch						
Low	66	24	5	4	99	(408)
Medium low	50	30	11	9	100	(439)
Medium high	32	31	22	15	100	(369)
High	17	26	33	24	100	(523)
Crunch Typology						
Untouched	62	25	7	6	100	(517)
Stoics	51	31	9	9	100	(317)
Complainers	30	27	26	17	100	(209)
Suffering victims	21	28	29	21	99	(675)
Recession Impact						
None	53	27	11	9	100	(650)
Some	35	28	22	16	100	(591)
Considerable	19	24	35	22	100	(336)

crises of inflation and recession, namely their ability to undermine the family.

The Social Correlates of Marital Strain

Given the strong connection between inflation crunch, particularly subjective inflation crunch, and marital strain resulting
from the economy, it is not surprising that the social characteristics found to be related to inflation crunch are also related to
marital strain. Thus, the poor were more likely to report a
mixed impact or that their marriage had gotten worse than the
blue collar families, who, in turn, experienced more marital
strain than the white collar families. Of the various subsamples,
the retired turn out to have had the least marital strain. Reports
of marital strain steadily declined as the three indicators of

social class, family income, occupational status, and education increased, and finally, blacks and Spanish-speaking families reported more marital strain than white families. To what extent are these relationships a consequence of inflation crunch? To answer this question requires examination of these correlations in light of subjective inflation crunch. Table 6.2 shows how the subsamples, family income and race-ethnicity, are related to marital strain when subjective crunch is taken into account.

As can be seen from the table, the relationships between these social characteristics and marital strain tend to disappear when subjective inflation crunch is taken into account. The ethnic differences disappear entirely, and the differences among the subsamples are sharply reduced, although the retired are far less likely to experience marital strain than the other subsamples whatever the level of inflation crunch. The income differences are reduced considerably among those who did not suffer from inflation, but among those who did suffer from inflation there is still some connection between income and marital strain. Among those hard hit by inflation, the marriages

Table 6.2: **Percentage High on Marital Strain by Selected Social Characteristics and Subjective Inflation Crunch**

	Subjective Crunch			
	Low		High	
Subsample				
Poor	28	(43)	54	(214)
Blue collar	30	(229)	53	(342)
White collar	14	(477)	45	(272)
Retired	4	(98)	23	(64)
Income				
Under $7,000	24	(50)	54	(199)
$7,000–$12,999	17	(122)	56	(236)
$13,000–$19,999	18	(201)	47	(220)
$20,000 and over	16	(320)	37	(135)
Race-Ethnicity				
White	15	(320)	48	(560)
Black	12	(87)	50	(255)
Spanish-speaking	25	(16)	54	(64)

of those of higher income were better able to withstand the pressures than the marriages of those of lower income. Even smaller differences between the groups persist when subjective inflation crunch is taken into account for the other two indicators of social class, occupation and education. Of those low on subjective inflation crunch, the difference between the higher white collar occupations and the lower blue collar occupations is only 6 percentage points, and for those high on crunch, this difference is 11 percentage points, whereas before inflation crunch was taken into account, the difference between higher white collar and lower blue collar was 19 percentage points. For education there is no difference between the low and high groups who are low on subjective crunch, and only a 5 point difference among those high on inflation crunch.

The findings presented so far all show that subjective inflation crunch is a major reason for the differences found on the various social characteristics. True, the poor have more marital strain than the well-to-do, whatever the level of inflation crunch, but this difference is reduced when inflation crunch is taken into account. But there are a few social characteristics that remain significant for marital strain even when inflation crunch is taken into account. One of these is family size. Among those low on subjective inflation crunch, there is little difference in marital strain among families of different size, but among those high on subjective crunch family size has a substantial effect. In the two person families 39 percent reported some marital strain, in the three and four person families 50 percent did, and in the five or more person families the rate of marital strain was 57 percent.

Another factor that continues to be related to marital strain when subjective inflation crunch is taken into account is recession impact. Those who were hard hit by the recession experienced more marital strain regardless of how much they were hurt by inflation. Among those low on subjective crunch, only 11 percent of those who were unaffected by the recession experienced marital strain, a figure that climbs to 24 percent of those who were somewhat affected by the recession and 28 percent of those who experienced a considerable impact of the

recession. Among those who suffered a great deal from inflation, the rates of marital strain range from 41 percent to 65
percent as the impact of recession increases. The devastating
impact of the twin evils of inflation and recession on marriage is
made clear by these figures. When both are absent, the rate of
marital strain is only 11 percent; when both are present, it
climbs to 65 percent.

Marital Strain and Strategies for Coping with Inflation

Just as we found the social characteristics related to inflation
crunch to be related to marital strain, so we find the various
coping strategies which were strongly related to both objective
and subjective inflation crunch to be related to marital strain.
This is not surprising inasmuch as inflation crunch is a cause of
both coping strategies and marital strain. The critical question is
whether marital strain will continue to be related to coping
strategies when inflation crunch is held constant. Should the
relationship persist, then we might conclude that marital strain
is one cause of coping strategies. According to this model,
inflation crunch causes strain on the marriage and to relieve the
marital strain and cope with inflation families develop coping
strategies. But it is conceivable that the relationships between
marital strain and coping strategies will disappear once inflation
crunch is taken into account. Such an outcome would mean
that inflation crunch causes both marital strain and coping
strategies, and that there is no intrinsic connection between the
two. The relative merits of these interpretations can be seen
from Table 6.5, which shows the relationships between marital
strain and the coping strategies when subjective inflation crunch
is held constant.

Inflation crunch by no means explains the relationships between marital strain and coping strategies for even when subjective crunch is held constant, the relationship between marital
strain and coping strategies persists. In every instance, whatever
the level of change, the group whose marriages were not affected by inflation were least likely to engage in the coping strategy. Those whose marriages got better because of the diffi-

culties caused by inflation were more likely to develop coping strategies and those for whom the marital impact of inflation was mixed were even more likely to engage in coping strategies. Of particular interest are the results for the group who said their marriages had gotten worse because of inflation. In some instances they were even more likely than the mixed group to develop the coping strategy, but in other instances they were less likely to do so. In the high crunch group those whose marriages had gotten worse led all the other groups with respect to curtailing consumption and bargain hunting, but they fell behind the mixed group on income raising, sharing and self-reliance. These strategies would seem to require more effort than curtailing consumption and bargain hunting, and those whose marriages had gotten worse were not as likely as those in the mixed group to make this effort. We have assumed that changes in the marital relationship are causes of coping strategies, but it is possible that marriages have gotten worse because

Table 6.3: Coping Strategies by Marital Impact and Subjective Inflation Crunch (percentage high on coping strategy)

		Marital Impact		
Coping Strategy	No Change	Better	Mixed	Worse
(1) *Income Raising*				
Low crunch	22	26	49	59
High crunch	41	49	67	63
(2) *Curtailing Consumption*				
Low crunch	21	36	63	43
High crunch	66	72	83	84
(3) *Self-Reliance*				
Low crunch	15	51	65	31
High crunch	42	65	73	54
(4) *Bargain Hunting*				
Low crunch	7	14	22	17
High crunch	46	64	69	71
(5) *Sharing*				
Low crunch	25	40	60	67
High crunch	40	47	64	62
N Low crunch	(490)	(231)	(68)	(58)
High crunch	(207)	(251)	(256)	(179)

one of the spouses had not made efforts to cope with inflation. In general, the results of Table 6.3 indicate that when inflation does have an impact on marriage, causing the marriage to change, the family is apt to take action to fight the effects of inflation whether it has suffered a little or a lot from inflationary pressures. Conversely, if the marriage has remained unaffected by inflation, then even the families that are suffering a good deal from inflation are not likely to take coping actions. This is yet another reminder that families similarly situated with regard to inflation nonetheless behave quite differently depending on other factors.

Impact of Inflation on the Children

Families with dependent children were asked several questions about how economic pressures had affected their children, for example, whether their children understood the financial pressures they were under, and whether the children "cooperate in trying to save money by being careful about electricity, household supplies and groceries." Approximately half the respondents with children answered affirmatively to these questions (49 percent to the former and 52 percent to the latter). These two items have been combined into a measure of what might be called "child cooperation." It turns out that 45 percent of the families with children received no cooperation from their children, 20 percent scored one on this index and 34 percent, scoring two, were in the high cooperation group.

Child cooperation turns out to be, as expected, strongly related to objective inflation crunch, but somewhat surprisingly, it is only weakly related to subjective inflation crunch. Full cooperation from children increases from 20 percent of those whose financial situation had improved to 32 percent of those whose situation had remained the same to 38 percent of those a little worse off and 40 percent of those a lot worse off financially. But when related to subjective crunch, the overall difference from low to high is only 10 percentage points. When related to the crunch typology, we find, as expected, that families untouched by inflation are least likely to report full cooperation from their children (25 percent) while the suffering victims are most likely to (40 percent), but oddly enough, the stoics report more cooperation than the complainers (37 percent compared with 30 percent). Perhaps one reason why families are able to accept the hardships of inflation gracefully is that their children are apt to pitch in and help out.

Receiving cooperation from children is only weakly related to income and ethnicity and moderately related to occupation and education, with blue collar families reporting more child cooperation than white collar families and the poorly educated more cooperation than the well educated. Of all the social characteristics, child cooperation is most strongly related to family size; the larger the family, the more likely are the children to cooperate in helping the family cope with inflation. One would think that families hard hit by the recession would have more cooperative children, but this turns out not to be the case. Of those who suffered most from the recession, 37 percent said their children were very cooperative, compared with 34 percent of those who avoided the recession entirely. Of the various coping patterns, only one is related to cooperation from children, self-reliance. Parents who are self-reliant and do things for themselves to fight inflation are likely to have children that show signs of self-reliance as well, in that they pitch in to fight inflation. Thus, among those who scored low on self-reliance, only 26 percent reported full cooperation from children, a figure that climbs to 40 percent among the highly self-reliant.

Obtaining cooperation from children in coping with inflation is only one way in which children are involved with inflation. Another way is the degree to which parents have had to deny things for their children or plans for children have had to be changed because of inflation. When asked whether they found it necessary to deny their children things they have wanted because of lack of money, 40 percent of the respondents answered "yes." Three other questions dealing with disappointments for children were asked, but only small fractions of the sample responded to these affirmatively. When asked whether their children had to postpone going to college because of the money pinch, 9 percent of the sample said "yes," but only 2 percent said that their children had to postpone marriage because of the economic situation. It was a much more common experience— shared by some 12 percent of the families with children—for children to stay at home because of the economic situation when ordinarily they would have moved out. These questions dealing with the deprivations of the children generated by the high cost of living have been combined into an index of what might be called "child denial." On the basis of this index, some 43 percent reported some child denial and 57 percent did not.

The depth interviews provided several accounts of child denial. For example, a forty-seven-year-old black woman with three children, living on welfare, reported that her seventeen-year-old son had recently been arrested for having participated in a robbery:

> I used to be able to buy my younger daughter some things. Now I can't. She doesn't believe me. She never had to do without so much before. Now my older daughter who is twenty, she understands. I think that's why my son went out and did what he did [the robbery]. He wanted things I just couldn't get him.

To this woman, her son's crime must be understood in light of the deprivations he experienced because of the family's money problems.

A thirty-six-year-old mailman with a working wife and a family income of $20,000 was also concerned about the effect of the economic pinch on his children:

> It's probably had a bad effect on the family especially in that my wife and I are not home with the kids as much as we would like to be because we have to be out working. I don't mind that the kids have to do without certain things. But there is so much time spent talking about money it must have an effect on the children. There's really a lot of time and effort spent on talking and getting money for essentials. It's hard to measure how it influences the kids because we can make $20,000 and we barely get by. To a child that's a lot of money. Years ago, we didn't talk as much about money. We can't get away together and see things that make a family have good remembrances, like I remember going out with my family when I was a kid.

This man is concerned that the money crunch is depriving his
children of the rich family life he enjoyed when he was young.

A fifty-eight-year-old black woman who lost her job at a
General Motors plant and is now living on unemployment
insurance, said:

> The family gets very depressed. They can't do the things they used
> to. It puts a lot of pressure on you. The kids are all right. It's me, I
> feel the pressure when I can't give them things. The kids ask for
> money, but I can't give it to them. They'll want two dollars for
> something at school or whatever, but I don't have no money for
> nothing.

The measure of child denial is strongly related to both
objective and subjective inflation crunch, with only 14 percent
in the lowest category on objective crunch and 20 percent in
the lowest category on subjective compared with two-thirds in
the highest category on each variable reporting child denial. The
index of child denial is also related to the inflation crunch
typology. The suffering victims were most likely to have their
children affected by inflation (64 percent) followed by the
complainers (44 percent), the stoics (28 percent) and the untouched (19 percent). The need to deny their children gratifica-
tion might well be one reason for the type known as complainers, those who managed to keep up with inflation but still
felt they were hurting because of rising prices. The very fact
that their children were being hurt by inflation might well
explain why these families were complaining even though they
were keeping up.

Those who were hurt by the recession as well as inflation
were much more likely to report child denial (58 percent) than
those who were not affected (30 percent). And child denial is
strongly related to the three indicators of social class, income,
occupation, and education. As income increases, the percentage
reporting child denial declines from 68 percent to 27 percent.
Among lower blue collar workers, the rate of child denial is 56
percent; for higher blue collar workers, it is 46 percent; for
lower white collar, 37 percent; and for the higher white collar

group, only 32 percent. And as education increases, child denial declines from 58 percent to 26 percent. The groups that were high on child denial were also the groups that suffered from inflation crunch and hence these correlations are not surprising.

It is of some interest that child denial is strongly related to the various coping strategies reviewed earlier. In every instance those who reported at least some child denial were much more likely to have tried the various coping strategies. These findings provide one clue as to why families do or do not take action to combat inflation. Apparently, when the crunch is so great that their children are affected, families are likely to be motivated to fight back.

The respondents were asked one final question about the impact of the economy on their family: whether the economic situation had influenced their plans to have more children. When this question was limited to families in which the housewife was under forty-five (older women are not likely to have plans for children whatever the state of the economy), we found that some 18 percent answered affirmatively. Needless to say, those who suffered most from inflation and recession were the ones who felt that they could not afford to have more children (see Table 6.4).

The measure of objective crunch shows a strange curvilinear pattern as those who claim that their economic situation has actually improved are somewhat more likely to say that their plans for children have been affected by the economy than those who say their economic situation has not changed. But those who have fallen behind rising prices are most likely to say their plans were affected. Subjective inflation crunch and reces-

Table 6.4: Economic Situation Affecting Plans for More Children by Inflation Crunch and Recession Impact (percentage "yes")

Objective Crunch		Subjective Crunch		Recession Impact	
Better	18 (158)	Low	8 (219)	None	12 (390)
Same	11 (255)	Medium low	16 (257)	Some	18 (403)
Little worse	20 (369)	Medium high	18 (217)	Considerable	28 (241)
Lot worse	25 (213)	High	26 (341)		

sion impact show clear relationships. As suffering from inflation increases, so does the proportion who say their plans for children have been affected by the economy; the same pattern holds for recession impact. Those most affected by the recession were the ones most likely to have their plans for children affected by the economy.

The various social characteristics bear little relationship to the economy's impact on family planning. Those with incomes below $13,000 were somewhat more likely to answer affirmatively than those of higher income, but there was virtually no relationship to the other two indicators of social class, education and occupation. Nor were there differences between whites and blacks in this respect. Not surprisingly, smaller families were somewhat more likely than large families to say their plans for children were affected inasmuch as small families are not as likely to be complete as large families. Perhaps the most significant finding on this issue is the absolute number of people who said their plans for children were affected by the economy. As we have seen, this number comes to 18 percent of the sample. Roughly one out of every five families of child-bearing age had had their plans for children affected by the state of the economy. Inflation and recession not only cause misery for families affected by them, but they have import for the unborn as well, having an effect on the birth rate of the country.

This chapter has examined the impact of inflation and recession on family life. We have seen that economic pressures have resulted in changes in most marriages. For more than a quarter of the families these pressures have resulted in closer ties between the spouses as they team up to cope with economic adversity. For even more, the economic pressures have produced bad as well as good effects; some 19 percent reported a mixture of good and bad consequences for their marriage and 14 percent reported only bad consequences. Those most vulnerable to inflation crunch and the recession were the ones whose marriages were likely to be affected, and chiefly for the worse. When inflation crunch was held constant, some social characteristics continued to be related to marital strain, particularly income and family size. But other characteristics, such as occupation and ethnicity, were found to have no relationship to marital strain once inflation crunch was taken into account. The recession had a major impact on marital strain even when inflation crunch was taken into account. Those whose marriages suffered the most were the ones who were victims of both the recession and inflation. Marital strain was found to be related to the various coping strategies, suggesting that one reason why people were motivated to fight inflation was that their marriages were being affected by the economy. We saw that inflation also affected the parent-child relationship in the family, as many parents (43 percent of the total) were forced to deny their children things they wanted because of the economic pinch, and finally, we saw that a minority of families (18 percent) were forced to postpone their plans for children because of economic pressures. In sum, the data presented here have shown that inflation and recession do take their toll on family life. While some marriages actually got better under the economic adversity, even more experienced strain. The state of the economy has many ramifications, and as we have seen, it has implications for the societal birth rate and probably the divorce rate as well.

Chapter 7

IMPACT OF INFLATION-RECESSION

ON MENTAL HEALTH

As a source of frustration and anxiety, rampant inflation in combination with a recession might very well affect the mental health of those most vulnerable to these economic pressures. The respondents were asked a series of questions dealing with their state of mind and feelings, questions that will allow us to study the impact of the economy on mental health.

The questions dealing with mental health are of two kinds, a series of questions linking feeling states to economic pressures and a series of questions dealing with positive and negative feelings not tied directly to the economy. From the first set of questions we can measure the extent to which respondents blame the economic pressure for their mental anguish, and from the second set of questions we can assess the state of psychological well-being of the respondents, that is, whether they are in a positive or a negative frame of mind. We can then see whether these feeling states are linked to the measures of economic pressures.

Measuring Mental Health

The respondents were asked five questions about the impact of economic pressures on their mental health. The questions and the percentage answering yes or no appear below:

	Yes	No	Total
(1) Do you find yourself worrying a lot about how you're going to make ends meet?	35%	65	100%
(2) Do you find yourself easily irritated and annoyed these days?	32%	68	100%
(3) Because of the financial pressures do you find yourself frequently depressed?	29%	71	100%
(4) Do the financial pressures ever make you want to scream and shout in anger?	19%	81	100%
(5) Because of financial pressures, do you ever find yourself so mad that you're ready to hit somebody?	11%	89	100%

The positive responses to these questions ranged from a high of 35 percent for the question about worry over making ends meet to a low of 11 percent for the question about being angry enough about financial pressures to almost hit someone. Significantly, none of these questions was answered affirmatively by a majority of the respondents, indicating that most people did not lose their equanimity in the face of rampant inflation and recession. These five questions have been combined into an index of mental strain induced by economic pressures. The distribution of cases on this index is as follows:

Index of Mental Strain

High	Score 0	52%
	Score 1	14
	Score 2	10
	Score 3	10
	Score 4	7
	Score 5	7
		100%

Slightly more than half of the sample (52 percent) scored 0 on this index of mental strain, some 24 percent scored either 1 or 2, constituting a middle group, and 24 percent scored 3 or more, comprising a group high on mental strain. The subsequent analysis will deal with the groups that are low, medium, and high on mental strain.

The measure of psychological well-being based on feeling states is modeled after the work of Norman Bradburn.[1] Bradburn developed a sophisticated measure of well-being, what he considered to be happiness, based on the balance of a series of positive and negative feelings. In Bradburn's research, respondents were asked about five positive and five negative feelings, and their well-being score was simply the resultant of these two measures.

Our measures of positive and negative feelings were borrowed largely from Bradburn. The respondents were asked:

Compared with how you used to feel, during the past few weeks have you frequently felt:

The items and the distribution of responses to them are as follows:

Positive Feelings	Yes	No	Total
(1) Pleased about having accomplished something	68%	32	100%
(2) Proud because someone complimented you on something	60%	40	100%
(3) That things were going your way	49%	51	100%
(4) Particularly excited or interested in something	38%	62	100%
(5) On top of the world	26%	74	100%

1. Norman Bradburn, *The Structure of Psychological Well-Being,* Chicago: Aldine, 1969. See also, Bradburn and Caplovitz, *Reports on Happiness,* Chicago: Aldine, 1965.

Negative Feelings	Yes	No	Total
(1) Nervous and tense	32%	68	100%
(2) Bored	22%	78	100%
(3) Headachy	20%	80	100%
(4) Upset because someone criticized you	16%	84	100%
(5) Lonely and remote	15%	85	100%

It is clear from these distributions that the respondents were much more likely to have positive than negative feelings, indicating on balance a favorable state of mental health in the sampled cities. Satisfaction with personal achievements turns out to be quite common as two-thirds said they were pleased with having accomplished something and three-fifths were proud because they had been complimented on something they had done. Of the various negative feelings, the most common is feeling nervous and tense, reported by one-third of the sample. Table 7.1 shows the distributions when these feeling states are combined into indices of positive and negative feelings.

Only 17 percent of the sample failed to have any positive feelings in the weeks preceding the interview while fully 53 percent had avoided negative feelings. Conversely, 49 percent had had at least three positive feelings, but only 17 percent had had that many negative feelings in the recent past.

One might suppose those who score high on positive feelings would score low on negative feelings and vice versa, that is, that

Table 7.1:   The Distribution of Cases on Positive and
             Negative Feelings (percentages)

Index Score	Positive Feelings	Negative Feelings
0	17	53
1	14	17
2	20	13
3	21	9
4	18	5
5	10	3
	100	100
	(1,982)	(1,982)

there would be a strong negative relationship between positive and negative feelings. And indeed this was pretty much the assumption in the scientific community until Bradburn's pioneering research. When Bradburn first developed his questionnaire for his happiness research, he had included questions measuring only negative feelings. He was advised by a consultant to guard against response set by including a battery of positive feelings as well. This concern with a technical matter, response set, paved the way for Bradburn's startling discovery that contrary to the expected strong negative relationship, there was in fact no relationship between positive and negative feelings. Having positive feelings in no way protected a person from having negative feelings, and what was critically important for psychological well-being was whether one had more positive than negative feelings, not just a high or low score on either index. The absence of a relationship between positive and negative feelings was first detected by Bradburn in a pilot study conducted in 1962 and reaffirmed in the main study on a larger sample in 1964. Will this path-breaking finding that revolutionized social research on psychological well-being be repeated in our study? Table 7.2 shows the relationship between positive and negative feelings in our sample.

Table 7.2 shows that just as in Bradburn's research, positive and negative feelings are largely independent of each other, or at best only weakly related. Those who have many positive feelings are somewhat more likely to have no negative feelings,

Table 7.2: Positive Feelings by Negative Feelings (percentages)

| | Positive Feelings | | | | | |
Negative Feelings	0	1	2	3	4	5
0	53	43	54	53	57	63
1	10	20	15	19	20	19
2	15	15	12	12	13	8
3	12	13	10	7	5	4
4	7	5	6	6	3	4
5	4	4	3	3	2	3
	101	100	100	100	100	101
	(333)	(283)	(402)	(413)	(353)	(198)

but having many negative feelings is as likely to occur among those with many positive feelings as among those with few positive feelings. In fact, as we read across the five rows of Table 7.2, we find that as positive feelings increase, the percentage having any given number of negative feelings changes as much as 10 percentage points in only one instance (those reporting no negative feelings). Our data thus confirm Bradburn's basic finding of the independence of positive and negative feelings.

To arrive at a measure of psychological well-being, we must subtract the negative feeling score from the positive feeling score. Since positive feelings were much more common than negative feelings, we can obtain more refinement at the positive end of the continuum. Combining the two dimensions yields a large number of scores, which we have reduced to five. All those who had more negative feelings than positive feelings have been combined into a single group. The next group consists of those who had as many negative feelings as positive feelings. A third group consists of those who had neither any positive feelings nor any negative feelings, an emotionally flat group that we distinguish from those who had equal numbers of positive and negative feelings. The fourth group consists of those who had, on balance, at least one or two more positive feelings than negative feelings, and the fifth group consists of those who had three, four, or five more positive than negative feelings. The distribution of cases in these five groups is as follows:

Category on Balance of Feelings	Percentage
One to 5 more negative feelings	19%
Equal number of positive and negative feelings	8
Zero positive and zero negative feelings	9
1-2 more positive feelings	30
3-5 more positive feelings	34
	100%
	(1,982)

Having developed two measures of mental health, the question now arises as to how they are related to each other. Not surprisingly, there is a very strong relationship between these measures of mental health. Of those who had a negative balance of feelings, 66 percent were high on mental strain; of those with an equal number of positive and negative feelings, 46 percent were high on mental strain. Those with one or two more positive than negative feelings had only 15 percent high on mental strain, and those with a surplus of three or more positive feelings had only 6 percent high on strain. Quite surprisingly, those with neither positive nor negative feelings were as free of mental strain as those with a large surplus of positive feelings as only 6 percent of them were in the high category. On a priori grounds it was by no means clear whether these emotionally flat people would be more like those showing stress or more like those showing euphoria. But we now see that they are very close to those with the most favorable balance of feelings. This group with no feelings is very different from the group with an equal number of positive and negative feelings. Had we mechanically followed the formula of substracting negative from positive feelings, this zero, zero group would have been combined with those with equal numbers of positive and negative feelings, which would clearly have been a mistake. Those with an equal number of positive and negative feelings turn out to be much closer to those with negative feelings than to those with a surplus of positive feelings and hence in the subsequent analysis, we shall combine the equal with the negative group. But we shall keep the no feelings group separate from the others to see whether it continues to resemble the relatively happy people. Inasmuch as the two measures of mental health are closely related, we shall in the subsequent analysis present the data on each measure in the same table.

Before turning to the statistical data which will shed light on the causes of mental stress, let us first consider the expressions of mental anguish offered by the respondents in the depth interviews. The twenty-one-year-old Puerto Rican computer clerk quoted in the previous chapter was asked how worried he was about paying his bills:

I'm not as worried about the bills as I am about feeding my family. I worry about that a lot. I've lost 15 pounds from all the worrying and cutting down I'm doing. The economic situation has made me very tense. I'm very easily aggravated. I can't sleep. I wake up with a headache. Everything seems to be a rush now. I'm constantly on edge. I'm not very nice to live with lately.

The devastating toll that economic ills take on peace of mind is aptly shown by this man's comments. In his own words, he has become difficult for others to live with.

The wife of a retired army colonel gave this account of the effect of the economy on her state of mind:

It has affected my sense of well-being. I worry terribly about what effect inflation will have on me if my husband passes away. I worry that the kids will have to take care of me. If a five dollar bill won't buy a loaf of bread, I would be dependent on my children. It hangs over me like the sword of Damocles.

Many people experience money worries as depressing. A black woman in her thirties, married to a motorman with the transit system earning $18,000, was frustrated because she could not contribute as much as she wanted to her church:

At church last Sunday we had a woman's day. They asked each woman for $31. I just didn't have it. I gave my regular dollar. I'd love to do more. It makes me feel aggravated. It's like a stumbling block. It's depressing. I'm confined to the house because gas costs so much. My husband feels depressed too. He worries about it. He worries a lot.

A young white couple also worried about bills and experienced depression in this account given by the wife:

We're plenty worried about the bills. We put away to make sure that we have the rent. But sometimes the phone bill and the electric bill have to wait. My husband gets paid only once a month. He gets a check and it disappears in two minutes after we pay the bills. *He gets very depressed by this* but we try to bolster each other up.

A thirty-four-year-old Puerto Rican with four children lost his job at a General Motors plant and was surviving on welfare at the time of the interview. When asked how worried he was about making ends meet, he replied:

> I worry about making a living, that's all. Money makes you sick in your mind. You can't want too much. Only to make a living. I don't want lots of money, but you got to have enough to make a living. The kids are unhappy now because Christmas is coming. But they try to understand. They say, "Popi, we just unhappy because you have all this trouble."

The personal grief that follows upon unemployment is evident in this man's lament that "you got to make a living."

A twenty-eight-year-old black woman whose husband earned $11,000 as a medical technician said:

> We talk about the economic situation more than we should. You talk until you can't stand the sense of helplessness. I feel it's very destructive.

A twenty-nine-year-old woman living on welfare whose common law marriage broke up over money matters, cited in the previous chapter, shared her perceptions of other people with the interviewer:

> This recession can tear down the strongest people. When I ride the bus, the people are more tense than ever before. You can see it in their faces. They are always fighting in supermarkets. Fights between women have increased in all situations. There's no question that the fighting is the result of economic pressures.

Of course there is no clear evidence of the merits of this woman's perceptions, but her hypothesis that economic pressures undermine public civility and order is an interesting one.

Inflation Crunch and Mental Health

The first measure of mental health, what we call "mental strain," is directly linked to economic pressures and therefore should be strongly related to the inflation crunch variables. But will the balance of feelings index, a more general measure of happiness, also be related to inflationary pressures? Table 7.3 shows the relationships of the mental health measures to the inflation-recession variables.

Not only is the measure of mental strain strongly related to the impact of inflation and recession but so is the balance of feelings index. As one's economic situation deteriorates under the pressure of inflation so one's mental health deteriorates. From the top of the table we see that hardly any of the people whose economic situation improved in spite of inflation experienced mental strain or negative feelings, whereas about half of the people whose economic situation had gotten a lot worse suffered mental strain and negative feelings. Both measures of mental health are even more strongly related to subjective inflation crunch than to objective crunch. When inflation is

Table 7.3: **Mental Health Measures by Measures of Inflation Crunch and Recession Impact**

	Mental Strain (percentage high)	Balance of Feelings (percentage negative or equal)	
Objective Crunch			
Better	4	10	(308)
Same	14	17	(493)
Little worse	25	25	(733)
Lot worse	46	53	(422)
Subjective Crunch			
Low	2	6	(451)
Medium low	5	11	(485)
Medium high	23	29	(434)
High	55	55	(606)
Crunch Typology			
Untouched	2	7	(565)
Stoics	5	9	(361)
Complainers	29	33	(236)
Suffering victims	45	48	(794)
Recession Impact			
None	11	15	(666)
Some	26	26	(617)
Considerable	47	45	(390)

experienced as painful, mental health is especially likely to suffer. The results for the crunch typology show, not surprisingly, that the untouched rarely report any mental strain, whereas almost half of the suffering victims had their mental health suffer. The stoics were almost as free of mental anguish as the untouched, while the other deviant group, the complainers, those who claimed to suffer from inflation even though their incomes kept up with rising prices, were close to the suffering victims in having their mental health impaired. The last part of Table 7.3 shows that as recession impact increased, so did the number experiencing mental strain and negative feelings. Table 7.3 thus documents another horror of economic ills—their capacity to undermine the mental health of the population.

Not surprisingly, mental health is very much related to marital health. Those who claimed that inflation has introduced strain into their marriages were much more likely to have their mental health suffer than those whose marriages were not affected by inflation. Only 6 percent of those who reported no change in their marriages were high on the mental strain index, a figure that rises to 15 percent among those who said that inflation had made their marriages better, and 48 percent of those who said the impact on their marriage was mixed, to 50 percent of those who said that inflation had made their marriages worse. The balance of feelings index shows a comparable pattern from 11 percent of the no change group having negative or equal feelings to 56 percent of those who said their marriage had gotten worse. Of course, a deteriorating marriage is undoubtedly one cause of unhappiness and mental strain, but these findings also suggest that the consequences of rampant inflation and recession go hand in hand. The people whose marriages suffered because of inflation tend to be the same people whose mental health suffered. Although marital strain may cause mental strain, it is likely that both are manifestations of the underlying conditions of inflation and recession.

Social Characteristics and Mental Health

Inasmuch as mental health is strongly related to inflation crunch, we would expect the social groups that were particularly vulnerable to inflation to be the same ones whose mental health has suffered. By and large, this expectation is borne out by the data. The subsamples that were hardest hit by inflation, the poor and the blue collar families, were more likely to score high on mental strain than the white collar and retired groups. Thus, 50 percent of the poor were high on mental strain, compared with 27 percent of the blue collar group, 13 percent of the white collar, and 15 percent of the retired. Balance of feelings shows a similar pattern with one notable exception. The retired are much more likely to have negative feelings than they are to be high on the mental strain index. Some 30 percent of the retired had negative feelings, a figure matching the blue collar group. The poor led all the other groups in negative feelings (50 percent) whereas the white collar group scored lowest (13 percent). Having negative feelings is in part a function of age, and it is because they are old rather than because they are suffering from inflation, that the retired are prone to negative feelings.

Mental health according to both measures is strongly related to income. As income increases, the percentage who are high on mental strain and who have negative feelings sharply decreases, from 44 to 10 percent on one measure and from 51 to 10 percent on the other. To be wealthy is not only to be protected against the hazards of inflation and recession, but it means enjoying good mental health.

Just as black and Spanish-speaking families suffered more than white families from inflation and recession, so their mental health was more likely to suffer. Only 18 percent of the whites scored high on mental strain, compared with 40 percent of the blacks and 39 percent of the Spanish-speaking. On the balance of feelings index, 22 percent of the whites had negative feelings, but 43 percent of the blacks and 42 percent of the Spanish-speaking did.

The other social characteristics found to be related to inflation crunch are also related to mental health. Family heads of lower education are more likely to report mental stress than those of high education, and as occupational prestige declined from higher white collar to lower blue collar, so mental stress increased on both the strain measure and the balance of feelings measure.

In the previous chapter we saw that marital strain was presumably one motive for making efforts to combat inflation by resorting to one or another coping strategy. In a similar fashion, mental stress proves to be another motive for trying to fight back against inflation. As Table 7.4 shows, those who scored high on these measures of mental stress were more likely to resort to the various coping strategies.

Whether the measure is the index of mental strain related to economic pressures (the top half of the table) or the balance of feelings index, we find that as mental stress increases, the family is more ready to fight inflation. Thus, the percentage employing each of the five strategies for coping with inflation steadily increases as mental pressures increase. The striking finding in the second part of the table is that those who experienced neither positive nor negative feelings in the recent past were least likely of all the groups, even those who had a high positive feeling score, to resort to coping strategies. This is yet further proof that those with no feelings are markedly different from those with the same number of positive and negative feelings. Table 7.4 supports the earlier findings. Whether one fights back against inflation depends on how much one is hurting because of inflation, not just on how far one's income has fallen behind rising prices.

Table 7.4: Coping Strategies by Measures of Mental Health (percentage high on strategy)

	Income Raising	Curtailing Consumption	Self-Reliance	Bargain Hunting	Sharing
Mental Strain					
High	56	82	66	72	62
Medium	47	66	53	47	51
Low	26	35	29	19	34
Balance of Feelings					
Negative-equal	47	72	75	67	53
1–2 positive	39	54	42	33	44
3–5 positive	35	45	43	24	44
No feelings	21	31	22	26	25

Controlling for Subjective Crunch

As we have noted, the various social characteristics found to
be related to deterioration of mental health are the same ones
that were related to inflation crunch. It is conceivable then
that the reason why the socially disadvantaged, the poor, those
of low status occupations, minority groups, and the poorly
educated, show more signs of mental strain than the socially
advantaged is that they suffer more from inflation, which we
know causes mental strain. To find out whether these characteristics play a role independent of inflation crunch, we must
reexamine them holding constant the impact of inflation. We do
this by controlling for the degree of suffering caused by inflation, what we have called subjective inflation crunch.

Earlier, when we showed the relationship between the subsamples and the measures of mental health, we discovered for
the first and only time that the two measures of mental health
were no longer interchangeable, as the retired behaved quite
differently on the mental strain index and the balance of
feelings index. Inasmuch as the negative feelings were age-related, the retired were much more likely to have negative
feelings than to manifest strain stemming from economic pressures. The same disparity between the indices holds when we
consider this relationship holding subjective inflation crunch
constant (Table 7.5).

When the suffering from inflation is low, there is little difference among the subsamples on the measures of mental health.
But when inflation does cause suffering, the poor are much
more likely to experience mental strain than the blue collar
workers, who in turn are more likely to have their mental health
suffer than the white collar group. On the measure of mental
strain, the retired behave much like the white collar sample. But
on the balance of feelings index, the retired are much closer to
the poor among those suffering from inflation. Although negative feelings are age-related, it takes inflation crunch to bring
these feelings out among the retired and the poor. On both
measures of mental health, the more privileged white collar
group is least likely to have its mental health affected even
when it is suffering from inflation. We shall see that this

Table 7.5: Measures of Mental Health by Subsamples and Subjective
Inflation Crunch (percentage high on stress)

| | Subsamples | | | |
	Poor	Blue Collar	White Collar	Retired
Mental Strain (percentage high)				
Low crunch	11	2	3	4
High crunch	57	44	29	29
Balance of Feelings (percentage negative and equal)				
Low crunch	13	10	5	13
High crunch	59	33	28	50
N Low crunch	(54)	(33)	(487)	(169)
High crunch	(269)	(232)	(282)	(140)

pattern holds for all the other social characteristics differen-
tiating the more from the less disadvantaged. The more advantaged presumably have more resources to withstand the damaging effects of inflation crunch. These patterns can be detected
in Table 7.6, which shows the impact of family income on
mental health controlling for subjective inflation crunch.

Among those who suffered little from inflation, income
makes relatively little difference in mental health. In this group,
those experiencing mental strain on these measures decline only
slightly as income increases. But among those who were hurt by
inflation, income makes a pronounced difference in mental
health. Those with high income are much more likely to avoid
mental strain even when they are hurt by inflation. High income
presumably provides resources that allow the rich to retain their
mental health in the face of inflationary pressures.

Table 7.6 permits us to compare whites, blacks, and Spanish-
speaking respondents on mental health when subjective inflation crunch is held constant.

Again we find no difference between the advantaged and the
disadvantaged on mental health among those who did not suffer
from inflation. On each mental health measure the minority
groups are as free of mental strain as the whites among those

Table 7.6: Measures of Mental Health by Income and Subjective
            Inflation Crunch (percentage high on stress)

	Income			
	Under $7,000	$7,000-$12,999	$13,000-$19,999	$20,000 and Over
Mental Strain (percentage high)				
Low crunch	11	5	3	2
High crunch	54	47	32	27
Balance of Feelings (percentage negative and equal)				
Low crunch	17	10	7	6
High crunch	61	53	29	19
N Low crunch	(93)	(139)	(207)	(325)
High crunch	(302)	(251)	(228)	(137)

who avoided pain from inflation. But among those who did
suffer from inflation, the mental health of the minorities deteriorated much more than that of the whites. The dominant group
was much better able than the minority groups to absorb the
pains of inflation without having their mental health affected.

Similar patterns show up on two other measures of privilege in
society, occupational prestige and education. When subjective
inflation crunch is low, neither occupation nor education makes
much difference for mental strain or balance of feelings. But
when subjective crunch is high, those of higher occupational
and educational status experience much less mental strain than
those of lower occupational and educational status. In short, in
every instance, the more privileged groups are better able to
retain their mental health when hit hard by inflation.

This chapter has examined the impact of economic crises—
inflation and recession—on mental health. We began by developing two measures of mental health, one closely linked to economic pressures, e.g., worrying about making ends meet and
being depressed because of financial pressures, and the other a
more general and standard measure of mental health based on a
balance of positive and negative feelings. Both measures of

Table 7.7: Measures of Mental Health by Race-Ethnicity and Subjective
            Inflation Crunch (percentage high on stress)

	Race-Ethnicity		
	Whites	*Blacks*	*Spanish-Speaking*
Mental Strain (percentage high)			
Low crunch	3	4	6
High crunch	36	51	47
Balance of Feelings (percentage negative and equal)			
Low crunch	8	11	–
High crunch	39	53	53
N Low crunch	(812)	(102)	(18)
High crunch	(652)	(305)	(78)

mental health were found to be strongly related to inflation and
recession impact. Those whose incomes had fallen behind rising
prices were much more likely to show mental stress on these
measures than those whose incomes kept up with rising prices.
Our measure of subjective inflation crunch, the degree of hurting caused by inflation, was even more strongly related to these
measures of mental stress than the objective fact of keeping up
with or falling behind rising prices. As expected, the typology
of inflation crunch showed that the stoics were much more
likely to retain their mental health than the complainers, with
the suffering victims showing the greatest decline in mental
health. Those who were hit by the recession were also much
more likely to show mental stress than those who were not
affected by the recession. These findings clearly establish a close
connection between the health of the economy and the mental
health of the citizenry.

The social characteristics found to be related to inflation
crunch also proved to be related to mental stress. This the poor,
the blacks, and the Spanish-speaking, the people in low occupational positions and the poorly educated, were much more
likely to manifest mental stress than their opposite numbers. To
find out whether these social characteristics had some relationship to mental health independent of inflation crunch, we

reexamined their relationship to the mental health measures, holding constant subjective inflation crunch. When this was done, we made an important discovery. Among those not hurt by inflation there was little or no relationship between these social statuses and mental health. The disadvantaged were as free of mental stress as the advantaged when they were not suffering from inflation. But among those who were suffering from inflation, these social positions had a marked impact on mental health. In every instance the occupants of the disadvantaged status (e.g., low income, black, or Spanish-speaking rather than white, low occupational prestige, and low education) were much more likely to have their suffering from inflation translated into mental stress. Moreover, we found this to be true on both measures of mental health. It is perhaps not too surprising that mental strain stemming from economic pressures would be much greater among those who said they were hurting from inflation. But the disadvantaged were even more likely to report such strain than the advantaged when they were hurting from inflation. More striking are the findings relating to the second measure of mental health, the balance of feelings index that has been used by a number of researchers to measure mental health. The items that went into this index were not linked to economic pressures. And yet this index too was closely related to subjective inflation crunch. As inflation came to hurt people, so their mental health as measured by this more general index declined. And, most significantly, this connection between subjective inflation crunch and mental stress was most evident among the socially disadvantaged. The privileged in society no doubt have resources stemming from their privileges that enable them to maintain their mental health even when they are hurting from inflation. The underprivileged lack these resources and thus when they are hurt by inflation, their mental health deteriorates. We have seen in earlier chapters that the underprivileged are much more likely to suffer from inflation and recession in the first place. We now have learned that they pay an additional price of mental stress and thus they are double losers. To be privileged means that one is likely to be protected from the crises that beset our economy, but even when the privileged are not protected from these crises, they still avoid paying the same price as the underprivileged. As we have seen in this and the previous chapter, the underprivileged are much more likely than the privileged to have their marriages and mental health suffer when they are hurt by inflation.

PART III

MITIGATING FACTORS: PUBLIC AND PRIVATE ASSETS

Chapter 8

THE ROLE OF THE WELFARE STATE

The deep recession of 1974-1975, coupled with the rampant inflation at that time, constituted the most severe disruption to the economy since the great depression of the thirties. The great depression, with its extremely high unemployment rate, was a time of great turmoil and social unrest. Breadlines were highly visible, the unemployed marched on Washington, riots broke out, and tens of thousands joined radical political parties determined to bring about sweeping transformations in society. In many respects, America was close to a revolutionary *zeitgeist* during the thirties. The second most severe setback to the economy, the recession of 1974-1975 had none of these consequences. In spite of unemployment rates close to 9 percent, there were no marches of the unemployed, there were no riots, and the moribund radical political parties did not experience a resurgence. Why was the public response to the economic hardships of 1974-1975 so different from the response in the thirties? Why was the public calm and almost apathetic in the face of these economic strains? One answer offered by a number of commentators has to do with the development of the welfare state. Since the height of the great depression the government has developed a wide range of programs to deal with the hardships stemming from economic calamities. The unemployed can count on unemployment benefits and public assistance in the form of welfare and food stamps. All these public assistance programs make it possible for families to adjust to economic hardships and presumably reduce the threat to the social fabric of society that was so evident in the great depression.

This theory of the greater social calm and order that occurred in 1975 in spite of the deep recession and rampant inflation implies that the recipients of public assistance would be suffering less from inflation and recession than the nonrecipients. Of course, it would be necessary to take into account the degree to which the family was affected by inflation and recession. Presumably, families affected to the same degree by inflation and recession would respond differently depending on whether they received public assistance or not. The main purpose of this chapter will be to examine the merits of this hypothesis. In the course of dealing with this issue we shall describe the frequency of various welfare benefits in our sample and the types of people who received these benefits.

Frequency of Public Assistance

The respondents were asked about four forms of public assistance: welfare, unemployment benefits, food stamps, and social security. Of the 1,982 families that were interviewed, 130 or 7 percent were receiving welfare and about the same number, 137, again 7 percent, were receiving food stamps. At the time of the interview some 176 chief wage earners in the sample had lost their jobs because of the downturn in the economy. But some of these may have found another job or used up their benefits for only 51 of them were receiving unemployment benefits at the time of the interview, a mere 3 percent of the entire sample. Inasmuch as we deliberately oversampled the retired, social security is by far the most common form of assistance in the sample, as 379 respondents, 19 percent of the total sample, were receiving social security benefits. Of this number, 284, or 75 percent of the social security group, were retired. Of course many people receiving one form of benefit also received another form. It turns out that 72 percent of the sample received none of these benefits, 21 percent received one of them, and a mere 6 percent received two or more. Inasmuch as the retired receive social security as a matter of entitlement regardless of their need it is not clear whether the retired should be included in the test of the basic hypothesis that public assistance eases the pain of economic disruptions. We shall in some instances present data with the retired included and in other instances with the retired excluded. For purposes of describing the recipients of welfare benefits the retired will be included, but when it comes to testing the basic hypothesis of public assistance easing pain, they will be excluded.

Public Assistance, Inflation, and Recession

Table 8.1 shows how receiving public assistance is related to the various measures of inflation and recession: objective inflation crunch, subjective crunch, the crunch typology, and recession impact. The data are presented first with the retired included and then with the retired excluded.

From the top part of the table we see that receiving public assistance is sharply related to objective inflation crunch, whether the retired are included or excluded from the sample. Of course, the percentage receiving benefits on every level of inflation crunch is lower when the retired are excluded since almost all the retired receive social security, and the relationship is somewhat stronger when the retired are included for they were expecially hard hit by inflation. Clearly, those whose incomes fell behind rising prices were more in need of benefits than those who managed to escape the ravages of inflation. The pattern is somewhat different for subjective inflation crunch. When the retired are included, receiving public assistance is only weakly related to subjective inflation crunch, as many of those low on subjective crunch were receiving benefits. We have seen

Table 8.1: Percentage Receiving Public Assistance by Measures of
            Inflation Crunch and Recession Impact

	Entire Sample		Excluding the Retired	
Objective Crunch				
Better	9	(308)	5	(291)
Same	25	(493)	12	(405)
Little worse	28	(733)	14	(609)
Lot worse	42	(422)	32	(346)
Subjective Crunch				
Low	24	(457)	7	(362)
Medium low	23	(485)	10	(411)
Medium high	30	(434)	16	(360)
High	33	(606)	26	(540)
Crunch Typology				
Untouched	20	(565)	7	(480)
Stoics	30	(361)	11	(279)
Complainers	18	(236)	12	(216)
Suffering victims	35	(794)	25	(676)
*Recession Impact**				
None			9	(666)
Some			7	(617)
Considerable			41	(390)

*By definition the retired are excluded from the recession impact index since they
were not in the labor force.

that the retired were much more likely than the nonretired to
be "stoics," people whose income had fallen behind rising prices
but who were not complaining or suffering from inflation. It is
these retired stoics who account for the relatively high proportion of those low on subjective crunch who are receiving benefits. When the retired are excluded, a fairly strong relationship
between subjective crunch and public assistance emerges.
Hardly any of the nonretired who are low on subjective crunch
received benefits (7 percent), a figure that steadily increases as
subjective crunch increases, reaching 26 percent among those
who were high on subjective crunch.

The role of the retired in bringing about a relationship
between stoicism and public assistance can be seen from the
third part of the table where we find that when the retired are
included, the proportion of stoics receiving public assistance

almost matches that of the suffering victims. When the retired are excluded, the rate of public assistance among the stoics sharply declines. As expected, the suffering victims lead all the other groups in obtaining assistance. Of some interest is the fact that the complainers, for the first time, are now closer to the untouched than to the suffering victims. Whether one receives public assistance or not is determined by such objective facts as level of income and not such subjective factors as pain, suffering, and complaints. Inasmuch as the complainers were able to keep up with rising prices, they had little claim to public assistance and in fact did not receive it any more than the stoics or untouched.

From the last part of the table, we see that only those who were hard hit by the recession, a group that includes the unemployed, were likely to receive public assistance. More than two out of every five in this group received some benefits, compared with less than one in every ten of those who felt the recession to some extent or not at all. Table 8.1 demonstrates that it is the victims of economic upheavals who require aid from the government.

The Recipients of Public Assistance

When public assistance is related to the subsamples, we find, not surprisingly, that almost all of the retired (92 percent) were receiving public benefits in the form of social security. The next largest group is, of course, the poor, 48 percent of whom were receiving public assistance. Hardly any of the blue collar and white collar families were—only 9 and 7 percent, respectively. The relatively high rate of public assistance for the poor indicates that public assistance is primarily a benefit of the underprivileged, the people who occupy the lower positions in the various social hierarchies. This is confirmed by Table 8.2, which shows how public assistance is related to various indicators of social privilege, income, occupation, race-ethnicity, and education.

From the top part of Table 8.2 we see that income is strongly related to receiving public assistance. Inasmuch as most of the

Table 8.2: Percentage Receiving Public Assistance by Selected Social
          Characteristics

	Entire Sample		Excluding the Retired	
Income				
Under $7,000	69	(395)	55	(261)
$7,000–$12,999	31	(390)	19	(323)
$13,000–$19,999	9	(435)	4	(411)
$20,000 and over	5	(462)	3	(451)
Occupation				
Higher white collar	20	(680)	7	(573)
Lower white collar	30	(296)	16	(241)
Higher blue collar	24	(344)	12	(293)
Lower blue collar	36	(662)	27	(566)
Race-Ethnicity				
White	25	(1,464)	9	(1,180)
Black	35	(407)	32	(385)
Spanish-speaking	41	(88)	39	(85)
Education				
Less than high school	42	(612)	28	(482)
High school graduate	24	(614)	15	(536)
Some college	22	(401)	11	(349)
College graduate	15	(352)	4	(304)

retired have incomes under $7,000 and almost all of them
receive assistance, the relationship is even stronger when the
retired are included. But the retired have the effect of dampen-
ing the relationship between occupation and public assistance.
Many of the retired had higher and lower white collar jobs when
they were working, and when they are included, the public
assistance rates for these groups increase significantly. When the
table is confined to those currently in the labor force, we find a
rather pronounced pattern with the higher white collar group
hardly ever receiving public assistance while more than a quarter
of the lower blue collar group does. Oddly enough, a slight
reversal occurs between the lower white collar and higher blue
collar groups. The former are slightly more likely to receive
public assistance than the latter.

Most of the retired are whites, and hence the gap between
whites and blacks is not nearly as pronounced when the retired
are included as when they are excluded from the sample.

Among those currently in the labor force, the blacks and Spanish-speaking are much more likely than the whites to be recipients of public assistance. The less privileged in terms of education are also much more likely to get help from the government than the more privileged, and since the retired are not as likely to be as well educated as the younger people still in the labor force, the retired have the effect of strengthening the relationship between education and public assistance. The patterns of Table 8.2 are in keeping with the previous findings. Public assistance tends to go to the underprivileged.

The data presented so far show that the socially disadvantaged are more likely to receive public assistance than the socially advantaged. What about the psychologically disadvantaged, those with personal problems in the form of marital strain and mental strain? Are the psychologically disadvantaged more likely to receive public assistance as well? The data bearing on this question are presented in Table 8.3. When the retired are included, there is little relationship between the quality of the marriage and receiving public assistance, but when the retired are excluded, a moderate relationship emerges. Those whose marriages were under some strain because of inflation were more likely to have received welfare benefits than those whose marriages either got better or were not affected by inflation. A stronger relationship is found between the measures of mental strain and public assistance. Whether the retired are included or excluded, those who reported considerable mental strain because of inflation were more likely to be receiving public assistance. This is not surprising, for those high on mental strain were those who were excessively worried and upset about inflation, and presumably, such people were most in need of public assistance to tide them over. The balance of feelings index shows the same pattern. Those who had more negative than positive feelings, that is, the unhappy people, were much more likely to be receiving public assistance than those who had many more positive than negative feelings (the happy people). Oddly enough, when the retired are included, the affectless people, those with no feelings, are somewhat more likely to receive public assistance than those who had a very favorable balance of feelings, but when the retired are removed, these people without feelings, as in other respects we have examined, are even more extreme than those with many more positive feelings. They have the lowest rate of public assistance of all, just beating out those with many positive feelings.

So far we have examined the frequency of public assistance, the impact of inflation and recession on public assistance, and the kinds of people who are likely to receive public assistance, and we have seen that they tend to be both the socially and psychologically disadvantaged. Remaining to be considered is the central hypothesis of this chapter: that receiving public assistance lessens the pain of inflation and recession. To test this hypothesis we shall compare the responses of recipients of public assistance with those of nonrecipients, holding constant inflation crunch and recession impact. According to the hypothesis, the pain of inflation and recession should be lessened for recipients of public assistance. The measures of the pain caused by inflation and recession include the following: subjective inflation crunch, marital strain, mental strain, and unhappiness as measured by the balance of feelings index. In short, the question we shall consider is whether a given degree of inflation

Table 8.3: Percentage Receiving Public Assistance by Measures of Stress

	Entire Sample		Excluding the Retired	
Marital Strain				
No change	19	(697)	9	(617)
Better	22	(482)	11	(419)
Mixed	24	(324)	22	(314)
Worse	20	(237)	17	(228)
Mental Strain				
None	24	(1,031)	9	(846)
Some	27	(486)	15	(409)
Considerable	36	(465)	30	(418)
Balance of Feelings				
More negative	42	(384)	31	(315)
Equal	34	(149)	22	(126)
1–2 more positive	28	(604)	16	(509)
3–5 more positive	18	(669)	8	(584)
No feelings	25	(176)	7	(139)

crunch or recession impact causes less pain for recipients of public assistance than nonrecipients, with pain being measured by the variables specified above. Inasmuch as the retired almost always receive public assistance in the form of social security and as a group tend to weather the storm of inflation and recession better than the nonretired, we shall exclude them from this analysis for they would bias the data in favor of the hypothesis. The subsequent analysis is thus limited to those who are still in the labor force.

Of course, as we have already seen, receiving public assistance is positively related to each of these measures of pain and suffering. But it might well be that these relationships stem from the underlying connection between inflation and recession and public assistance. The critical issue is whether for any given level of inflation crunch or recession impact, the recipients of welfare suffer less or more than the nonrecipients. Table 8.4

Table 8.4: Percentage High on Measures of Stress by Objective Inflation Crunch and Public Assistance

| | Objective Inflation Crunch | | |
	Better or Same	Little Worse	Lot Worse
Subjective Crunch (percentage very high)			
Receiving assistance	30	52	66
Not receiving assistance	13	33	61
Mental Strain (percentage high)			
Receiving assistance	22	45	65
Not receiving assistance	10	24	43
Balance of Feelings (percentage negative and equal)			
Receiving assistance	27	43	65
Not receiving assistance	13	22	48
Marital Strain (percentage mixed and worse)			
Receiving assistance	42	43	66
Not receiving assistance	30	24	53
N Receiving assistance	(60)	(88)	(110)
Not receiving assistance	(636)	(521)	(236)

shows the relationships between public assistance and the measures of pain when objective inflation crunch is held constant.

By comparing the rows in each part of the table, we see that
in every instance the recipients of public assistance were more
likely to experience stress than the nonrecipients on each level
of objective inflation crunch. Thus, the recipients were more
likely than nonrecipients to suffer from inflation, to experience
mental strain, to feel unhappy as reported by the balance of
feelings index, and to have their marriages suffer. The notion
that receiving public assistance lessens the pain of inflation is
clearly not supported by the data. On the contrary, the data
support a contrary hypothesis, that recipients of public assistance are the greater sufferers because they lack the resources to
be self-reliant. Even though the nonrecipients may find their
financial situation a lot worse than it had been previously, the
very fact that they did not have to turn to public assistance in
order to survive means that they had sufficient resources to
make do, resources that presumably lessened the pain for them
of rampant inflation and recession. Those who had to seek
public assistance when their financial situation declined did not
have the resources to make it on their own and they suffered
more. What welfare benefits may well have done for those who
received them was to tide them over to the extent that they did
not have to take drastic actions such as storming the barricades
in order to survive. But to assume that the welfare benefits are
such a panacea as to remove the pain of those hardest hit by
inflation and recession, those who could not make it on their
own, is no doubt a distortion of the meaning of welfare. The
next test of the significance of welfare supports this second
hypothesis, that the pain and suffering are greater for the
recipients of welfare even when they are compared with nonrecipients who are as hard hit by inflation and recession. Table
8.5 presents these data when recession impact is taken into
account.

Again we find that among those who suffered to the same
extent from the recession, the recipients of public assistance
experienced much more stress than the nonrecipients. They
were more likely to suffer from inflation, to be under mental

Table 8.5: **Percentage High on Measures of Stress by Recession Impact and Public Assistance**

	Recession Impact		
	None	*Some*	*Considerable*
Subjective Crunch (percentage very high)			
Receiving assistance	29	56	60
Not receiving assistance	15	33	54
Mental Strain (percentage high)			
Receiving assistance	17	42	60
Not receiving assistance	11	24	38
Balance of Feelings (percentage negative and equal)			
Receiving assistance	24	49	56
Not receiving assistance	14	25	38
Marital Strain (percentage mixed and worse)			
Receiving assistance	23	46	66
Not receiving assistance	20	37	51
N Receiving assistance	(58)	(45)	(161)
Not receiving assistance	(608)	(572)	(99)

strain, to be unhappy, and to have marital strain. Clearly, receiving public assistance does not make people whole again. Rather than public assistance relieving psychic stress, psychic stress may well be a major reason why people who come upon hard times turn to public assistance. In any event, these findings give pause to those who view the recipients of public welfare as lazy people living off the fat of the land. On the contrary, they are people who are suffering a great deal and are only kept from disaster by the marginal benefits they receive.

Chapter 9

THE ROLE OF HOMEOWNERSHIP

From time to time we have suggested that the more well-to-do must have assets and resources that allow them to absorb inflationary pressures without experiencing much pain, marital or mental strain. Alan Greenspan, the former economic advisor in the Ford Administration, has provided an important clue to what these assets are (New York *Times,* Dec. 18, 1977). Most Americans, some 66 percent of all families, own their own homes, and these homes have appreciated enormously in the past ten years, in large part because of inflation. According to Greenspan, mortgage borrowing has risen to more than 60 billion dollars a year, which is roughly equal to the amount that homes have appreciated in a year. Greenspan feels that many homeowners have made use of their primary asset, their home, to tide them over inflationary pressures. In his view, many homeowners have generated new income by refinancing their homes, but even if people did not borrow on their homes, they could take comfort from the rising value of their homes, knowing that they were far from becoming destitute because of inflation and recession. This chapter explores the role of home-ownership in easing the pain of inflation and recession.

It turns out that homeownership in our four city sample is very close to the national average, as 65 percent of the families interviewed owned their own homes. Had New York not been included in the study, the rate of homeownership in the sample would have exceeded the national average, for homeownership in New York is far below the national average. Only 49 percent of the families in the New York metropolitan area that were interviewed owned their homes, compared with 61 percent of the San Francisco sample, 68 percent of the Atlanta sample, and fully 82 percent of the Detroit sample.

As expected, homeownership is closely related to the various indicators of socioeconomic status. As income increases, so does the rate of homeownership, from a low of 33 percent among those earning under $7,000 to a high of 90 percent among those earning over $20,000. The differences are almost as sharp for occupation, as 80 percent of the higher white collar workers own their own homes compared with 70 percent of the lower white collar, 63 percent of the higher blue collar, and only 49 percent of the lower blue collar. For education, the rates climb from 51 percent of those who failed to finish high school to 79 percent of the college graduates. Extremely sharp differences in homeownership are also found on the race-ethnicity variable, as 73 percent of the whites owned their home compared with 49 percent of the blacks, and only a small fraction, 13 percent of the Spanish-speaking families.

The kinds of people who own their home are also the ones who managed to avoid the strains of inflation and recession. We might expect then that home ownership is related to both objective inflation crunch and the measures of recession, unemployment and recession impact. Table 9.1 shows this to be so.

The greater vulnerability of the nonhomeowners to inflation and recession is clearly shown by these data, as they were much more likely to have their income fall behind rising prices, to be unemployed and to have been hard hit by the recession in general.

Table 9.1:   Percentage High on Measures of Inflation Crunch
             and Recession Impact by Homeownership

	Owners	Nonowners
Objective Crunch		
Percentage worse	52	71
Employment Status		
Percentage unemployed	4	21
Recession Impact		
Percentage considerable	16	38
N	(1,289)	(690)

Table 9.2:   Percentage High on Measures of Stress by
             Homeownership

	Owners	Nonowners
Subjective Crunch		
Percentage very high	23	45
Mental Strain		
Percentage high	16	37
Balance of Feelings		
Percentage negative and equal	19	42
Marital Strain		
Percentage mixed and worse	25	47
	(1,289)	(690)

Just as homeowners were less vulnerable to inflation and the
recession, so we might expect them to be more immune to the
stresses stemming from inflation and recession, subjective inflation crunch, mental strain, unhappiness, and marital strain.
Table 9.2 bears out this expectation. In every instance the
nonhomeowners experienced more stress from inflation and
recession than did the homeowners. They were much more
likely to suffer from inflation, they experienced more mental
strain, they were more likely to be unhappy as measured by the
balance of feelings index, and their marriages were more often
damaged by inflation.

The findings in Table 9.2 follow from the nonhomeowners'
greater vulnerability to inflation and recession. The critical

question is whether homeownership provides greater immunity from these pressures even when the owners are experiencing the same degree of inflation crunch and recession impact as the nonowners. Table 9.3 provides the answer when objective inflation crunch is taken into account.

Comparing the homeowners with the nonowners in each part of the table, we find that even when objective inflation crunch is taken into account, the nonowners experienced much more stress from inflation than the homeowners. Homeownership lessened stress even among those who were able to stay ahead of rising prices (the first column of the table), and it provided more comfort to those whose incomes did fall behind rising prices (those who were a little worse and a lot worse off financially than in preceding years).

Does home ownership ease the pain of unemployment? Table 9.4 provides the answer.

Table 9.3: Measure of Stress by Objective Inflation Crunch and Homeownership

| | Objective Inflation Crunch | | | |
	Better	Some	Little Worse	Lot Worse
Subjective Crunch (percentage very high)				
Owners	5	14	26	54
Nonowners	17	27	47	61
Mental Strain (percentage high)				
Owners	3	11	19	35
Nonowners	8	23	36	56
Balance of Feelings (percentage negative and equal)				
Owners	8	12	20	42
Nonowners	20	31	36	63
Marital Strain (percentage mixed and worse)				
Owners	17	18	28	46
Nonowners	34	37	42	62
N Owners	(248)	(355)	(473)	(192)
Nonowners	(60)	(138)	(259)	(228)

Table 9.4: Measures of Stress by Unemployment and
            Homeownership

	Employed	Unemployed
Subjective Crunch (percentage very high)		
Owners	42	72
Nonowners	70	86
Mental Strain (percentage high)		
Owners	16	43
Nonowners	36	58
Balance of Feelings (percentage negative and equal)		
Owners	16	49
Nonowners	40	54
Marital Strain (percentage mixed and worse)		
Owners	27	36
Nonowners	46	69
N Owners	(1,054)	(43)
Nonowners	(447)	(122)

The base figures, at the bottom of Table 9.4, are of some
interest. The overwhelming majority of the employed were
homeowners, whereas a substantial majority of the unemployed
were not homeowners. This clearly indicates that unemployment is a problem for the less affluent, those who cannot afford
to own their own home. The rows of Table 9.4 tell us what we
already know, that the unemployed suffered much more than
the employed regardless of homeownership. The patterns in the
columns in each part of the table are of greater interest for they
show the extent to which homeownership mitigates the pains of
unemployment. Homeownership does indeed lessen the pain for
the unemployed. In each area of stress, the unemployed who
did not own their homes suffered more than the unemployed
who did own their home. The difference between the two
groups is especially pronounced on the matter of marital strain.
Owning a home makes the unemployed person much less vulnerable to marital tension than his counterpart who does not

own his home. The home is the symbol of the family, and these
data suggest that families that own their home are stronger than
those that only rent. The patterns for the employed are also
noteworthy. Even among those who escaped the worst of the
recession, homeownership makes a considerable difference in
vulnerability to strains induced by the economy. The employed
homeowners were much more likely than the employed nonowners to avoid suffering from inflation, to avoid mental strain,
feelings of unhappiness, and marital strain. In fact, homeownership made an even greater difference for the employed
than for the unemployed, as the percentage differences in the
first column, with one exception, are larger than those in the
second column.

Table 9.5 presents these data when a more general measure of
the recession is taken into account, our index of recession
impact based on more items than just unemployment. Homeownership makes a substantial difference on all levels of recession impact. Even among those who escaped the recession
completely, homeownership substantially reduces the stresses
and strains emanating from the disturbed economy. This holds
for each of the four measures of stress. The same pattern holds
for those who experienced the recession to some extent as well
as for those who were especially hard hit by the recession. In
every instance, the differences between the owners and nonowners are substantial. Tables 9.3, 9.4, and 9.5 clearly establish
the thesis that homeownership was a major buffer from the
deleterious consequences of inflation and recession.

We have seen that homeownership varies considerably with
the social characteristics of the families, with the more affluent
and more advantaged families having much higher rates of
homeownership than the less affluent and more disadvantaged.
To what extent does homeownership explain why certain social
groups suffered more from inflation and recession than others?
To answer this question, we shall reexamine the relationships
between social characteristics and the stress measures in the
light of homeownership. Table 9.6 presents these data for the
subsamples.

Reading across the rows of Table 9.6, we find that homeownership by no means washes out the differences between the

Table 9.5: Measures of Stress by Recession Impact and Homeownership
            (percentages)

	Recession Impact		
	None	*Some*	*Considerable*
Subjective Crunch (percentage very high)			
Owners	11	28	48
Nonowners	34	48	63
Mental Strain (percentage high)			
Owners	8	19	37
Nonowners	22	39	56
Balance of Feelings (percentage negative and equal)			
Owners	11	19	34
Nonowners	30	42	55
Marital Strain (percentage mixed and worse)			
Owners	15	33	49
Nonowners	37	47	64
N Owners	(514)	(411)	(176)
Nonowners	(151)	(205)	(214)

subsamples. Whether they own homes or not, the poor are
much more likely to be hurt by inflation and recession than the
blue collar group, who in turn are more frequently hurt than
the white collar group. The retired are very close to the white
collar sample and in at least one instance they do better than
the white collar group: They are least likely of any group to
experience marital strain. Given the association between age and
negative feelings, the retired score slightly higher than the white
collar sample on negative feelings. In spite of the strong correlations between these measures of stress and the subsamples,
homeownership continues to make a difference within each
subsample. Among the poor, the minority who owned their
own home were better able to withstand the blows of inflation.
Homeownership was especially important to the blue collar
group, as the owners in this group differed markedly from the
nonowners on the various measures of stress. Even in the white

Table 9.6: Measures of Stress by Homeownership and Subsample
            (percentages)

| | Subsample | | | |
	Poor	Blue Collar	White Collar	Retired
Subjective Crunch (percentage very high)				
Owners	45	11	16	21
Nonowners	64	34	25	22
Mental Strain (percentage high)				
Owners	46	19	11	12
Nonowners	51	43	21	21
Balance of Feelings (percentage negative and equal)				
Owners	43	22	11	26
Nonowners	55	45	22	36
Marital Strain (percentage mixed and worse)				
Owners	39	33	22	11
Nonowners	55	53	40	14
N Owners	(101)	(372)	(628)	(188)
Nonowners	(222)	(209)	(139)	(120)

collar group, which was relatively immune to inflation and
recession, homeownership made a substantial difference. White
collar renters were much more likely than owners to suffer from
inflation, to manifest mental strain, to feel unhappy (negative
feelings), and to have strains in their marriages. Homeownership
made the least difference among the retired. The relatively weak
effect of home ownership among the retired no doubt stems
from the special significance of ownership in this group. Many
people when they retire find the one family house in which
they lived most of their lives too large for their needs, and they
are apt to sell their house and move into a small apartment. It is
no accident that the rate of homeownership among the retired
is well below that in the white collar and blue collar samples
and is only higher than that in the poor sample. Given this
tendency to relinquish one family houses among the retired,
homeownership is much less significant for the retired than for

the other groups. As a result, homeownership is much less comforting to the retired and makes only a small difference in the amount of stress they experience from inflation.

We have seen that income is a major factor influencing the degree to which families are affected by inflation and recession and consequently the degree to which they experience the various stresses produced by inflation. Table 9.7 shows how this income relationship is affected by homeownership.

The major role that income plays with regard to the stresses and strains of inflation and recession is shown by the rows of Table 9.7. As income increases, the frequency of stress declines sharply. Marital strain proves to be the exception to this rule. Among homeowners, the amount of marital discord is fairly constant as income rises from $7,000 to $20,000. Only among those earning more than $20,000 does marital strain drop sharply. Among the nonowners, the pattern is irregular, with

Table 9.7: **Measures of Stress by Homeownership and Income (percentages)**

	Income			
	Under $7,000	*$7,000- $12,999*	*$13,000- $19,999*	*$20,000 and Over*
Subjective Crunch (percentage very high)				
Owners	42	32	28	11
Nonowners	55	50	32	15
Mental Strain (percentage high)				
Owners	36	25	15	9
Nonowners	47	40	28	15
Balance of Feelings (percentage negative and equal)				
Owners	45	30	16	9
Nonowners	53	45	26	17
Marital Strain (percentage mixed and worse)				
Owners	35	34	32	19
Nonowners	53	53	37	45
N Owners	(130)	(196)	(325)	(414)
Nonowners	(265)	(192)	(109)	(48)

marital strain increasing in the highest income group. The columns show that homeownership makes some difference as well,
but its effect is not nearly as strong as that of income. Among
the two lower income groups, homeownership has a moderate
effect, especially on the matter of mental strain, but for the two
higher income groups, homeownership makes only a marginal
difference on three of the four strains. For marital strain,
homeownership makes a major difference in the highest income
group. That the highest income groups did not get that much
protection from homeownership when compared with the nonowners of comparable income probably reflects the different
meaning of homeownership among the wealthy. Wealthy people
by definition have the resources to own homes, and if they
choose not to own a home, this no doubt reflects tastes and
values rather than the absence of resources. And their resources
no doubt explain why the rich nonowners do not differ much
from the rich owners when it comes to experiencing strains
from inflation and recession. Presumably, wealth is sufficient to
immunize one from the ravages of inflation and recession and
owning a home contributes little to this privileged group.

We have seen that minority groups are much more vulnerable
than whites to inflation and the costs of inflation, and, as noted
earlier, the minorities are not nearly as likely to be homeowners
as the majority whites. Will the gap between the whites and
blacks be reduced when homeownership is taken into account?
Table 9.8 deals with this.

Homeownership clearly does not explain the differences between whites and the minority groups for even when home
ownership is taken into account, substantial differences between the whites and the others remain. Thus, on every indi-
cator of stress, blacks and Spanish-speaking families suffer more
than whites among homeowners and nonowners alike. The one
exception would seem to be marital strain. Among homeowners, there is very little difference in marital strain between
blacks and whites, and the Spanish-speaking have the lowest
rate of all three groups. But only eleven Spanish-speaking families own their own home, and percentages based on this small
number are unreliable. The critical point in Table 9.8 is that

Table 9.8:   Measures of Stress by Homeownership and Ethnicity
(percentages)

	Ethnicity-Race		
	Whites	*Blacks*	*Spanish-Speaking*
Subjective Crunch (percentage very high)			
Owner	20	36	46
Nonowners	33	60	64
Mental Strain (percentage high)			
Owners	14	27	27
Nonowners	29	52	40
Balance of Feelings (percentage negative and equal)			
Owners	17	30	18
Nonowners	35	54	46
Marital Strain (percentage mixed and worse)			
Owners	25	29	11
Nonowners	42	52	54
N Owners	(1,064)	(198)	(11)
Nonowners	(397)	(209)	(77)

homeownership makes a difference within each ethnic group. Whites who own their home suffer less from inflation than their counterparts who rent, and blacks and Spanish-speaking families who managed to buy their homes are better protected from the damaging fall-out of inflation than their fellows who are not fortunate enough to own their homes.

Findings comparable to the previous tables emerge when occupation and education are taken into account. On each occupational and educational level the homeowners were more successful than the nonowners in avoiding the stresses induced by inflation and recession. This examination of homeownership in the context of inflation crunch and recession impact, on the one hand, and in combination with the various social characteristics found to be related to inflation crunch, such as subsample, income, ethnicity, occupation, and education, on the other, demonstrates conclusively the significant protection from

the burdens of inflation and recession provided by homeownership. For a substantial majority of Americans, the dark cloud of
inflation has a silver lining. Under inflationary pressures, the
value of their major asset, their home, has appreciated significantly. This has provided a new source of income for many, in
the form of remortgaging their homes, and for many others it
has provided important security in the face of rampant inflation
and recession. Widespread homeownership in America today
may well be the key reason why the most severe recession since
the thirties and the most severe inflation in history have been
met with so much tranquility and equanimity. It may well be
that the norm of homeownership is the central reason why the
country has not experienced marches on Washington, riots,
people jumping out of windows, and wide-spread radicalization
of the populace as happened during the great depression. The
public assets reviewed in the previous chapter are only part of
the picture. The major private asset of homeownership may be
even more important. By the same token, if it should ever
happen that the housing market takes a sharp downturn and
homes lose rather than gain in value, then the dire consequences
of inflation and recession that have so far failed to materialize,
might yet come to pass.

PART IV

THE IMPACT OF INFLATION-RECESSION ON THE MIND

Chapter 10

IMPACT OF INFLATION-RECESSION

ON VALUES AND ATTITUDES

The rampant inflation of the mid-seventies coupled with high unemployment jarred a great many Americans out of their normal life routines. The discovery that income no longer went as far as it did to say nothing of losing one's job forced many people to reexamine the basic assumptions under which they had been living. Under the circumstances, it would not be surprising if many people changed their basic value orientations about what was important and unimportant and their attitudes toward life. This chapter explores the impact of inflation and recession on selected value orientations and attitudes of the respondents. A basic assumption to be tested by the data is that those who were hardest hit by inflation and recession were the ones who experienced the most change in their attitudes and values.

Three value-attitude clusters will be examined: the extent to which aspirations have been lowered, commitment to the dominant economic ideology of free enterprise, and confidence in the various branches of the federal government. Both quantitative and qualitative data will be brought to bear on these issues.

Lowering Aspirations

The respondents were provided with several opportunities to express their views on the economy and the country in general and a number of their comments reflect a questioning of the high standard of living people had grown accustomed to. Typical of these responses were the views of a sixty-nine-year-old retired clergyman:

> Everybody must tighten their belts as much as they can. People demand too high a standard of living. They must lower their sights.

And a forty-nine-year-old school teacher earning $23,000 had this view of how to improve the economy:

> We need to be more conscious of waste. We need to accept the fact that we have to get by with less, to lower our standard of living somewhat. I think we are capable of getting away from dependence on automobiles and all the things that go along with that.

To this man, lowering our standard of living was one way of making the economy more effective. A fifty-six-year-old school teacher earning $30,000 also referred to our standard of living in his criticism of our tax structure:

> We are taxed to the point where we can't save enough for the high standard of living that we have grown accustomed to. So we'll have to lower our standard of living.

A fifty-nine-year-old librarian with the comfortable income of $27,000, when asked if he still had confidence in the American dream, responded:

> What American dream? This is the land of liberty and equal opportunity to move up together. But from the beginning some haven't

moved up and that will always be true. And it is getting worse. If we continue to be grasping and selfish there will be widespread disillusionment with promoting the welfare and happiness for all.

Implicit in his criticism of grasping and selfish people is the idea of lowering aspirations.

A thirty-nine-year-old business executive with an income of $29,000, also expressed the sentiment of lowered aspirations when he said:

I've become more realistic and less optimistic about the way we've been able to do things. Education for the children and dreams of travel, the things you want, may not come to pass.

And a thirty-one-year-old white collar worker employed in the District Attorney's office earning $20,000 said:

It's just not easy today to kid yourself into believing you can have a big house, a two car garage and send your kids to college. It's not realistic to me these days.

Further expressions of frustration with getting ahead were offered by a thirty-year-old school teacher and a forty-year-old truck driver:

No matter how hard one drives or works, It's impossible to achieve what one could before.

An enterprising person who wants to work hard and get ahead can't. Absolutely no way.

Although they did not explicitly say they had lowered their aspirations, the school teacher and truck driver were convinced that it was no longer possible to achieve as much as formerly. As we shall soon see, the respondents who made such comments were in the minority, for the questions which permit us to measure more systematically the impact of the economy on aspirations and standard of living show that a majority did not lower their standard of living in spite of inflation and recession. The questions and distributions of responses are as follows:

(1) Have you decided to lower your standard
of living to make ends meet?

Yes	35%
No	65%
	100%

(2) Do you find yourself more interested in
owning expensive things than you used to
be, less interested or has there been no
change?

More	8%
Less	22%
No change	70%
	100%

(3) Do you find that the events of the past
couple of years have led you to lose confidence in the American Dream?

Yes	35%
No	65%
	100%

It can be seen from the responses to these questions that in
every instance, only a minority had opted to lower their standard of living and their aspirations. Some 35 percent said they
would lower their standard of living to make ends meet, but the
great majority were prepared to maintain their standard of
living in spite of inflationary pressures. And a similar number
(35 percent) said they had lost confidence in the American
dream as a result of the events of the past few years, but again
the great majority had retained their confidence in the dream.
As for interest in owning expensive things, hardly any said this
had increased, but in spite of inflationary pressures, only 22
percent said they were less interested in expensive things, and
the great majority (70 percent) said there was no change in their
attitude.

These three items are all related to each other, suggesting that
they are indicators of an underlying dimension—what can be
called lowering of aspirations. When the questions are combined
into an index of this notion, we find the following distribution
of cases:

	Index Score	Percentage
No lowering of aspirations	0	44
Some	1	37
Moderate	2	17
Considerable lowering of aspirations	3	2
		100%

As can be seen from the distribution, the tendency was not to lower aspirations, as fully 44 percent scored zero on this index. The next largest group, 37 percent, scored one on the index, 17 percent scored two, and only 2 percent answered all three questions in such a way as to indicate lowered aspirations. By combining scores 2 and 3 we find that 19 percent of the sample falls into the "high" group, 37 percent in the "medium" category, and 44 percent in the "low" category.

Lowering aspirations should be the response of those who were hardest hit by inflation. Table 10.1, which deals with

Table 10.1: Lowering Aspirations by Measures of Inflation Crunch (percentages)

	Lowering Aspirations				
	Not at All	*Somewhat*	*A Lot*		*N*
Objective Crunch					
Better off	55	36	9	100	(301)
Same	57	32	12	101	(484)
Little worse	39	39	21	99	(717)
Lot worse	27	42	32	101	(415)
Subjective Crunch					
Low	69	27	4	100	(448)
Medium low	54	37	10	101	(470)
Medium high	38	40	22	100	(427)
High	21	43	26	100	(598)
Crunch Typology					
Untouched	64	31	5	100	(551)
Stoics	56	34	10	100	(351)
Complainers	38	38	24	100	(234)
Suffering victims	25	43	32	100	(781)

objective and subjective inflation crunch and the crunch typology, shows this to be so.

On every measure of inflation crunch we find a strong correlation with lowering of aspirations. A majority of those who kept even with rising prices or were actually better off financially did not lower their aspirations whereas only a minority of those who were worse off managed to avoid lowering aspirations. Conversely, only 9 percent of those who were better off lowered their aspirations substantially compared with 32 percent of those who were a lot worse off. On subjective crunch, the relationship is even stronger, as 69 percent of those who did not suffer from inflation maintained their aspirations compared with only 21 percent of those who suffered a great deal. From the crunch typology, we see that the subjective dimension is the more critical one, as the stoics were close to the untouched and the complainers were close to the suffering victims. This table provides an added dimension to our picture of the stoics. Not only do they avoid complaining even though their income has fallen behind rising prices but they are determined to maintain their standard of living in the face of inflationary pressures. This would suggest that the stoics have a rather modest standard of living to begin with, one that they can maintain even as their buying power is diminishing. As we have seen, the stoics include many retired people who generally have modest standards of living.

Although lowering aspirations is strongly related to inflation impact, it is only weakly related to the social characteristics that were strongly connected to inflation crunch. Thus, when the various subsamples are related to lowered aspirations, the poor were most likely to be in the high category (30 percent) and the white collar and retired samples least likely (13 and 14 percent, respectively). And the lower income groups were more likely to lower their aspirations than the higher income groups. But these differences are largely due to subjective inflation crunch, and when that is held constant, the differences are reduced markedly as can be seen from Table 10.2.

From the rows, we see that subjective inflation crunch is a major determinant of lowered aspirations in all the subsamples

Table 10.2:   Percentage Lowering Aspirations to
Some Extent by (A) Subsample and
(B) Income Holding Subjective Crunch
Constant

| | Subjective Crunch | | | |
	Low		High	
Subsample				
Poor	42	(52)	73	(263)
Blue collar	44	(225)	72	(345)
White collar	39	(474)	74	(279)
Retired	29	(167)	65	(138)
Income				
Under $7,000	36	(92)	74	(295)
$7,000–$12,999	37	(137)	74	(247)
$13,000–$19,999	43	(196)	70	(226)
$20,000 and over	42	(317)	74	(136)

and income groups. But neither subsample nor income makes much difference once subjective crunch is controlled. Among those low on crunch, only the retired are substantially different from the other subsamples in that they are less likely to lower aspirations, and the same holds true for those high on crunch. Income has no effect on aspirations within either the low crunch or high crunch groups.

Ethnicity, too, is not related to lowering aspirations once subjective inflation crunch is taken into account. Among those who were not suffering from inflation, whites were somewhat more likely than blacks to lower aspirations (40 v. 32 percent), but among those who were suffering there was no difference (72 v. 74 percent). Comparable results are found for occupation and education. When subjective crunch is held constant, neither occupation nor education has any bearing on lowering aspirations. The import of these findings is that the decision to lower aspirations is entirely a matter of inflation impact and is not related to one's position in society. If families have been hurt by inflation, they are apt to adapt by lowering their aspirations. If they have not been hurt, they maintain their aspirations for a better life. Since lowered aspirations are strongly related to

inflation crunch, it is not surprising that they are also related to
the other consequences of inflation crunch that we have examined, marital strain and mental strain. Those whose marriages
had suffered because of inflation and those whose mental health
had suffered were much more likely than the others to lower
their aspirations. The critical question is whether these relationships will hold once subjective inflation crunch is taken into
account. Does marital and mental strain result in the lowering
of one's sights independent of inflation crunch, or does this
occur only because of inflation crunch? Table 10.3 provides the
answer.

The rows in the various parts of Table 10.3 tell us what we
already know, that subjective inflation crunch is a major determinant of lowered aspirations. But the columns in the table
show that the other inflation-induced troubles, marital strain,
mental strain, and unhappiness as measured by the balance of
feelings index, also contribute to lowered aspirations independent of inflation crunch. Whether inflation crunch is low or
high, those who experienced tensions in their marriage because
of inflation were more likely to lower their aspirations than

Table 10.3: Percentage Lowering Aspirations to
Some Extent by Measures of Stress and
Subjective Inflation Crunch

| | Subjective Crunch | | | |
	Low		High	
Marital Strain				
No change	35	(476)	61	(205)
Better	39	(227)	68	(248)
Mixed	55	(66)	79	(252)
Worse	53	(55)	78	(175)
Mental Strain				
None	34	(731)	61	(282)
Some	56	(156)	68	(317)
Considerable	65	(31)	81	(426)
Balance of Feelings				
Negative or equal	49	(76)	77	(448)
1–2 more positive	37	(299)	71	(290)
3–5 more positive	41	(433)	67	(226)
No feelings	31	(110)	56	(61)

those who reported no change or an improvement in their marriage. The same patterns are found for mental strain and balance of feelings. Only about one-third of those in the low crunch group who were free of mental strain lowered their aspirations compared with two-thirds of those who experienced considerable mental strain because of inflation. On the balance of feelings index, we find that those who reported more negative than positive feelings or an equal number of both, were more likely to lower their aspirations than those who had a net balance of positive feelings. The somewhat odd finding is that the people who reported neither positive nor negative feelings were least likely to lower their aspirations on each level of inflation crunch. These emotionally flat people not only tended to avoid the pressures of inflation, but they resisted any accommodations to inflation, such as lowering their standard of living.

Commitment to Free Enterprise

Among the values and attitudes explored in this research was commitment to the American capitalistic economy of free enterprise. Three questions dealt with this commitment:

(1) Do you think our free enterprise economy is the best economic system or do you think that some other system is better?
(2) Do you think a socialist kind of system would be better or worse than what we have now?
(3) Do you think that the government is obligated to find a job for everyone who wants to work?

The last question asks about government intruding into the labor market, something that is anathema to the free enterprise purists.

In spite of the fact that a majority of the respondents were buffeted by inflation and that a substantial minority experienced the recession as well, an overwhelming majority of the respondents registered their faith in the free enterprise system. In response to the first question, 64 percent said they felt that free enterprise was the best economic system, only 12 percent said no, and the remainder were not sure. As for socialism being a better system, only 10 percent agreed, 29 percent were not sure, and 61 percent denied the proposition. Finally, a majority of the respondents, 57 percent, rejected the idea of government guaranteeing jobs for those who want to work, whereas 43 percent believed the government did have this obligation.

These three questions are strongly related to each other and have therefore been combined into an index of commitment to free enterprise. The distribution of cases on this index is as follows:

	Index Score	Percentage
Very low commitment	0	16
Medium low	1	22
Medium high	2	29
Very high commitment	3	33
		100
		(1,982)

Only 16 percent of the sample were unable to endorse any of the three measures of commitment to free enterprise. They were not prepared to say that free enterprise was the best economic system, that socialism was a worse system, or that the government should not guarantee jobs for everyone who wants to work. At the other extreme, 33 percent of the sample endorsed all three of these principles, and the next largest group, 29 percent, agreed with two of these positions.

We might expect that those who were hardest hit by inflation and the recession would be the ones who had lost confidence in the free enterprise system. Table 10.4, which deals with the inflation crunch variables and recession impact, bears out this expectation.

From the last column in each part of the table we see that commitment to free enterprise steadily declines as the impact of inflation and recession increases. Almost half of those whose financial situation had actually improved were totally com-

Table 10.4: Commitment to Free Enterprise by Measures of Inflation
Crunch and Recession Impact (percentages)

	Commitment to Free Enterprise				
	Low and Medium Low	Medium High	Very High		N
Objective Crunch					
Better now	22	31	47	100	(308)
Same	32	31	37	100	(493)
Little worse	39	29	32	100	(733)
Lot worse	54	25	21	100	(422)
Subjective Crunch					
Low	18	32	50	100	(457)
Medium low	28	32	41	101	(485)
Medium high	42	28	30	100	(434)
High	58	26	17	100	(606)
Crunch Typology					
Untouched	20	32	48	100	(565)
Stoics	28	31	41	100	(236)
Complainers	48	28	23	99	(361)
Suffering victims	52	26	22	100	(794)
Recession Impact					
None	27	30	43	100	(666)
Some	40	29	31	100	(617)
Considerable	56	25	19	100	(390)

mitted to free enterprise compared with only one-fifth of those
whose situation was a lot worse than previously. This relationship is even stronger for subjective inflation crunch with total
commitment declining from 50 percent to 17 percent as suffering from inflation increases. As for the crunch typology, we
find that the untouched and the stoics are committed to free
enterprise while the complainers and suffering victims tend to
be alienated from this system. Finally, those who were hard hit
by the recession were not nearly as likely to believe in free
enterprise as those who were untouched by the recession. The
ability of the recession to turn people off from free enterprise is
even more evident from the data on the unemployed. Fully
two-thirds of the people who had lost their jobs were alienated
from free enterprise compared with only one-third of the
employed.

Inasmuch as the underprivileged were much more likely to suffer from inflation and recession than the privileged classes— that is, the poor, the unskilled workers, the minority groups, and the poorly educated—it would come as no surprise that these groups have more radical perspectives, that is, oppose free enterprise and favor government guaranteeing jobs to those who want to work. The data show this to be the case. Only 33 percent of the poor sample scored high (2 or 3) on the index of commitment to free enterprise, compared with 58 percent of the working class sample, 76 percent of the white collar sample, and 67 percent of the retired. Income is also strongly related to the free enterprise index, with the rate of commitment rising from 42 to 79 percent as income rises. Occupation shows a similar pattern as does education. Finally, the minority groups were much less committed to free enterprise than the whites, as 71 percent of the whites, but only 37 percent of the blacks and 28 percent of the Spanish-speaking were in the two highest categories of the free enterprise index.

Do radical perspectives on the economy stem from one's social position in society irrespective of inflation crunch, or are the patterns just reviewed entirely a result of the impact of inflation? To answer this question we must reexamine the role of social position taking inflation crunch into account. Table 10.5 shows the results for subsample, income, occupation, and race-ethnicity when subjective inflation crunch is held constant.

The rows in each part of the table tell us what we already know, namely that subjective inflation crunch lessens commitment to free enterprise. The key findings appear in the columns of the table. They show that social position very much determines views on free enterprise independent of inflation crunch. Thus, whether they suffer from inflation or not, the poor are much less committed to free enterprise than the blue collar group, which in turn is less enamored of free enterprise than the white collar and retired samples. The same patterns appear for income. In both the low and the high crunch groups, income is strongly related to belief in free enterprise with the more well-to-do being much more accepting of free enterprise than the less well-to-do.

Table 10.5: Percentage Committed to Free Enterprise by
Selected Social Characteristics and Subjective
Inflation Crunch

| | Subjective Inflation Crunch | | | |
	Low Crunch		High Crunch	
Subsample				
Poor	52	(54)	29	(269)
Blue collar	73	(232)	48	(349)
White collar	82	(487)	64	(282)
Retired	75	(169)	57	(140)
Income				
Under $7,000	64	(93)	35	(302)
$7,000–$12,999	71	(139)	44	(251)
$13,000–$19,999	79	(207)	58	(228)
$20,000 and over	82	(325)	72	(137)
Occupation				
Higher white collar	82	(431)	61	(249)
Lower white collar	82	(170)	59	(126)
Higher blue collar	69	(137)	56	(207)
Lower blue collar	67	(204)	37	(458)
Ethnicity				
White	81	(812)	59	(652)
Black	52	(102)	32	(305)
Spanish-speaking	39	(18)	26	(70)

The occupational patterns are similar to those for income. Commitment to free enterprise steadily declines from the top to the bottom of the occupational hierarchy when subjective crunch is held constant, and the race-ethnicity data show that blacks and Spanish-speaking respondents are not nearly as committed to free enterprise as the whites regardless of inflation crunch. Clearly, inflation crunch does not explain the association between social position and belief in free enterprise. Another mark of privilege, education, shows the same patterns as the previous tables. As education increases, support for free enterprise increases both among those who were immune to inflation and those who suffered from it.

In sum, inflation plays a major role in how people feel about the dominant economic ideology of free enterprise, with those who suffered from it being more likely to reject this ideology.

But a person's location in the social structure, whether he is a member of the privileged or the underprivileged groups, is also an important determinant of belief in free enterprise. The underprivileged are much more critical of free enterprise than the privileged, and they are more likely to adhere to the socialist idea of the state guaranteeing employment for all those who want to work. These findings are in sharp contrast with those for lowering aspirations. There we saw that only inflation crunch was relevant and that one's social positions did not influence one's aspirations once inflation crunch was held constant. Commitment to free enterprise, by contrast, is very much class related.

The minority who were opposed to free enterprise elaborated on their views during the depth interviews. A forty-seven-year-old business executive earning over $40,000 a year, when asked about free enterprise, said:

> The free market presumes that the market is self-regulating and the mechanism has failed. We need to increase central economic planning.

The anomaly of the simultaneity of inflation and recession so baffling to economists was sufficient to shake this man's faith in free enterprise.

A forty-two-year-old advertising executive earning $45,000 was quite cynical about the role of the large corporations:

> I don't have much faith in capitalism. A competitive economy is the best thing to have but the big companies have gotten together to wipe out competition and competition is essential. . . . We should put capitalistic drive back into the economy, break up the big trusts and union power should be broken too. . . . In the past, wars kept the economy going. A war would put the economy back on its feet. It's terrible but true.

This man believes in free enterprise, but he feels that the system is not working because the large corporations have eliminated competition. He is sufficiently pessimistic about the economy to believe it can only thrive during war time.

Another respondent convinced that big business has sabotaged the free market by engaging in price fixing is a middle-aged merchandising manager employed by a large department store at a salary of $19,000:

> I don't think there is a free market. Competition has left us. The same model car costs the same give or take a few dollars whatever the manufacturer. I think they get together and unofficially agree on the price. They've found it easier to get together. I don't believe in government interference and regulation but I don't know how to stop it.

The ambivalence of this man is clear from his comment. He is opposed to price fixing but he is wary of governmental regulation and is at a loss as to how to stop price fixing.

A thirty-six-year-old mailman with a working wife and a joint family income of $20,000, is particularly bitter about big business:

> It's not really a free market. It's controlled by small groups of people. Big companies were servicing fascist regimes during the Second World War and today they are supporting dictators.

To this man, the country is pretty much in the control of a small group of business moguls.

A twenty-seven-year-old white woman with two children, currently a college student being supported by welfare, is also very bitter:

> It [free enterprise] doesn't work, obviously. It doesn't care about people. It's a bad situation when the President says that people don't really count and what counts is foreign aid to Arabs so that we can get oil at totally outrageous prices. Maybe we should have a revolution. It's so far gone that maybe we need a total disaster so that we can start rebuilding.

The theme that the people don't really count was reiterated by numerous respondents as we shall see later on.

A fifty-five-year-old brewery worker earning $14,000 a year lost faith in the free enterprise system because of the failure of the law of supply and demand:

> I never did have any faith in the free enterprise system. You can see right now that there's hardly any demand for cars; there are so many cars in the lots and in the garages. But in spite of low demand, they keep raising prices. How can you go by supply and demand?

This man's observations on the breakdown of supply and demand tells us a good deal about why many people have lost confidence in the free enterprise system. Prices, according to eonomic theory, should fall during a recession when demand declines. But the average citizen is only too well aware that prices keep climbing even when demand is off. Inasmuch as the basic thesis of free enterprise is proven false by day to day experience, small wonder that many people are losing faith in the system.

A fifty-year-old black woman whose husband works for the post office and who works herself as a saleswoman (family income of $24,000) gave a very thoughtful response when asked her opinion of the free enterprise system:

> I really believe that free enterprise has run its course. The time is right for government to take over big essential companies and hospitals. They could run more efficiently that way. We are our brothers' keepers. We could pay more taxes so that they could have nice homes for poor old folks. What difference would $100 in taxes a year mean to us when we would know that if you live to be a 100 you'd have a nice place to live? It shouldn't be run by private people. Capitalism played its part well, but it is now time for government to look after human needs. I think every child of ability should go to school. Poor people's children need help. With help they can do well.

As we have seen, this woman is still very much in the minority as the majority have no qualms about free enterprise and do not share her view that government should help the needy. Later on we shall hear from others in this minority who feel that government should be concerned with human needs.

Confidence in Government

The third major attitude area explored in this chapter deals with confidence in the federal government. The respondents were asked how much confidence they had in various institutions, including the three that comprise the federal government, Congress, the Supreme Court, and the presidency. In the post-Watergate era in which these interviews were conducted, confidence in the federal government was quite low, as only small minorities registered a lot of confidence in any of the branches of the federal government. Congress had the worst image, as only 11 percent had a lot of confidence in it, 58 percent had some, and 31 percent hardly any confidence in it. The presidency was only slightly better off, as 15 percent said they had a lot of confidence in it, 54 percent some, and 32 percent hardly any. The Supreme Court had the best image, as 23 percent had a lot of confidence in it, 54 percent some, and only 24 percent hardly any. If there is any comfort to the federal government in these results, it is that in no instance did a majority say they had no confidence in the institution. In every instance the majority had some confidence.

For the purposes of the subsequent analysis the responses to these three questions have been combined into an index of confidence in the federal government. Not surprisingly, the largest number fell into the low confidence category, 42 percent, with 35 percent in the medium confidence group and only 23 percent in the relatively high confidence category.

As we shall see in the next chapter, many people blamed the federal government for the economic ills of inflation and recession and therefore it is not surprising that those who were hardest hit by the inflation and recession had the least confidence in government. Table 10.6 shows how the various measures of inflation impact relate to confidence in government.

All of these measures of the impact of inflation and recession prove to be strongly related to confidence in government. Those whose financial situation had actually improved in the previous few years were not nearly as likely to have a low opinion of government as those whose financial situation had gotten much worse (first column in the upper part of the table). Subjective crunch is even more strongly related to confidence in government (first column in second part of the table). The crunch typology also shows this relationship with the untouched having more confidence in government than the complainers and the

Table 10.6:   Confidence in Government by Measures of Inflation Crunch
              and Recession Impact (percentages)

	Confidence in Government				
	Low	*Medium*	*High*		*N*
Objective Crunch					
Better now	34	38	27	99	(305)
Same	36	35	29	100	(477)
Little worse	43	37	20	100	(719)
Lot worse	51	31	18	100	(406)
Subjective Crunch					
Low	28	40	32	100	(452)
Medium low	41	34	26	101	(465)
Medium high	43	37	19	99	(422)
High	52	32	17	101	(583)
Crunch Typology					
Untouched	33	37	30	100	(549)
Stoics	36	38	26	100	(233)
Complainers	41	36	23	100	(353)
Suffering victims	51	33	16	100	(763)
Recession Impact					
None	36	35	29	100	(652)
Some	44	35	31	100	(607)
Considerable	50	31	19	100	(382)

suffering victims. The stoics again prove to be quite close to the untouched in their views. Finally, those who were hard hit by the recession were much more likely to have low confidence in the government than those who were not hurt by the recession. Inspection of the data shows that inflation and recession lead people to lose confidence in government completely. But even those who managed to escape the ravages of inflation and recession were not likely to have a high opinion of the government. Thus, in every instance only a minority had complete confidence in government regardless of where they stand on the inflation and recession variables. The critical distinction is whether people had no confidence or some confidence in government, and inflation and recession play a major role in this distinction.

Just as the various social characteristics were only weakly related to lowered aspirations, so these characteristics of privilege in society were only weakly related to confidence in government. For example, in the sample of poor families some 47 percent scored low on confidence in government; among the blue collar workers, the figure was 44 percent, for white collar workers 39 percent and for the retired 37 percent, for an overall percentage difference of only 10 points. Occupation also yielded a percentage difference of 10 points, as 37 percent of the higher white collar workers had low confidence in government compared with 47 percent of the lower blue collar workers. Income shows no relationship at all to confidence in government, as 44 percent of those in the lowest income group and 41 percent of those in the highest had low confidence in government. When ethnicity is considered, we find that one of the minority groups, the blacks, was slightly more likely to have low confidence in government than the whites, 49 compared with 40 percent, but the other minority group, the Spanish-speaking, was least likely to be turned off by government, as only 34 percent of them were in the low confidence category. Finally, education shows a weak relationship to confidence in government, as 45 percent of the most poorly educated reported low confidence compared with 37 percent of the best educated. What little differences these social characteristics make on the matter of confidence in government are largely explained by their connection with subjective inflation crunch. When subjective inflation crunch is held constant, these weak relationships tend to disappear. In short, however important these social characteristics may be for commitment to the ideology of free enterprise, they have virtually no bearing on confidence in government. Whether people have confidence in government is primarily influenced by whether they have been victims of inflation and recession and not whether they are rich or poor, black or white, well educated or poorly educated. The tendency is to blame the government and politicians for the messes in the economy, and those who have been victimized by these economic events are apt to lose confidence in government. Significantly, not many have a great deal of confidence in government, symptomatic of the post-Watergate cynicism that has swept the populace.

Those who said they had lost confidence in the American dream were asked to explain their view, and many elaborated by strongly criticizing politicians and government in general. Government was also mentioned when the respondents were asked their opinions on how the economy could be improved. Many of the respondents said they could no longer trust the government. Typical of these is a twenty-four-year-old mother of two living on welfare:

> I can't trust the government. They promise and then they don't keep their promises.

A fifty-year-old boiler operator earning over $20,000 said:

> I've lost confidence in the politicians. I don't trust the way they are running the country.

This lack of trust in government is related to the belief that government is no longer serving the needs of the people, but rather only the needs of the politicians. A sixty-seven-year-old retired businessman felt that the only way to improve the economy would be to alter the political system drastically:

> The system has come to the end of the line. We must change our system. Our government is out of hand. They are not our servants; we are theirs.

A twenty-two-year-old gas station attendant earning only $5,000 felt that the government was out of touch with the people:

> Everything is falling down in government. There is no interest in the people anymore. The politicians are only interested in themselves.

A sixty-two-year-old art director earning $25,000 also felt that the government was misleading the people:

> I just feel that we've been led down the primrose path without the government letting us know what they were doing. I think we need a change with honesty and truth in government.

Cynicism regarding the intentions of politicians is particularly evident in this comment by a fifty-one-year-old longshoreman earning $14,000:

> I find myself hating the politicians more. I despise them more than ever. They're all looking to hurt the little people. They're all out looking to make a buck for themselves, to get rich. They don't care who they hurt.

This idea of politicians betraying the public trust for their own selfish ends is made clear by a twenty-nine-year-old policeman whose wife works, giving the family an income of $28,000:

> Things were bad a couple of years ago, but they seem to be getting worse. Nobody really cares. You got these people in office, these politicians; they're getting high salaries and they don't care what's happening to the people. They don't seem to care about these thousands of people who have lost their jobs.

Implicit in these comments is the idea of dishonest public servants, a theme made more explicit by other respondents. A forty-nine-year-old mechanical engineer earning $19,000 said:

> I used to feel very patriotic. Now I feel cheated because I feel we are supporting a lot of crooks. I don't feel my vote counts anymore. We can only improve the economy by getting better politicians and honesty in government.

A sixty-three-year-old merchant earning $40,000 a year said he had lost confidence in the American dream

> because of cases like Watergate and the sex scandals of our present leaders.

A twenty-five-year-old designer in the automobile industry earning $17,000 also was perturbed by the sex scandals in Congress:

> The politicians should get a little less. A little less federal bureaucracy and a little less money for supporting things like Congressmen's mistresses.

Apart from viewing politicians as dishonest, a number of respondents saw them as incompetent. A twenty-nine-year-old repairman was of this view:

There's a whole lot of people in government who shouldn't be there. They are related to someone and they get appointed to office. We should cut back on government spending by getting rid of these people who don't know what they are doing.

A retired lawyer also felt that the incompetence of politicians was a major problem:

One way to improve things would be to get rid of politicians in government and put in experts. We need a strict control of government expenditures and we should make certain that nonpolitical minds explain to the country the necessity for every step taken.

A New York longshoreman placed all the blame for inflation and recession on politicians, whom he viewed as incompetent:

Everything stems from the politicians. They promise you everything and then when they get in office, they just don't do anything about it. And they put on the payroll all their friends who make all those big salaries which is uncalled for. They don't even get them on their merits. They don't even have to take a test. Mayor Lindsay when he was in office gave out 92,000 jobs which is not fair to the taxpayer.

Still another theme mentioned by some respondents was their disappointment in recent presidents, a view heavily colored by the Nixon fiasco. To these respondents the critical issue is having a strong, competent man at the helm of the ship of state. A well-to-do musician in New York who was interviewed in the early stages of the research expressed this view:

It's not the system but the people on top. We haven't had a good leader since Eisenhower. I'm surprised that we could withstand Johnson, Nixon and Ford. Eisenhower is a giant compared to them. . . . He knew when to put his foot down. A country that has the will to exist must find its man in its hour of peril. Now America needs someone, but he's not there.

A fifty-year-old black woman whose husband had lost his job and was now living on welfare, also felt the country needed a good president:

We have bad management. It's politics. I was around in Roosevelt's time. They were doing more things then. They had the WPA. They should bring back the days of Roosevelt's New Deal. *We need a good President but they don't live in these times. They get killed.*

Several respondents specifically blamed Nixon for the country's troubles. A middle-aged black woman living on welfare in New York, who was interviewed at the beginning of the study, blamed the economic ills of the country on Nixon:

It's all because of that lousy President Nixon, Tricky Dick. . . . Ford is just taking over where Nixon left off. They might as well have left Nixon in. They've got the wrong people running this country. The Vice President too. He doesn't care what happens. Rich people don't care what happens to the poor. As long as they stay President and Vice President, things are going to get worse.

The cynicism regarding politicians and government was quite widespread as evidenced by the large numbers who had lost confidence in government. Watergate and the congressional scandals were obviously major sources of this cynicism. But perhaps even more, the negative view of government stemmed from the economic ills of the country. Many people, especially the poor, concluded that politicians did not care about the people since they were ready to tolerate high levels of inflation and unemployment. And many felt that politicians were not making the same kinds of sacrifices that they were being forced to make because of the sharp rise in the cost of living. To them, the politicians were flourishing even while they were suffering. Carter, of course, made a big issue of the lack of trust in government and pitched his entire campaign to the theme that if elected he would restore faith in government. After more than a year in office, Carter is discovering that overcoming the public's cynicism regarding government is a bigger task than he anticipated. It may well be that the task cannot be accomplished until the economic ills have been cured.

Chapter 11

PERCEIVED CAUSES OF INFLATION AND RECESSION

The causes of inflation and recession are by no means known to the economists who spend their time studying these phenomena. To be sure, economists have identified two different types of inflation. In one model, prices rise when demand exceeds production, presumably because everyone is employed and the economy is operating at its full capacity and cannot produce more. Under these circumstances, demand exceeds supply and prices rise. In the other model of inflation, what is known as the push-pull model, prices rise in response to sharp rises in wages. If wages rise faster than productivity, then businesses can only remain solvent by raising their prices. In this model, the villains are the unions pushing for undeserved (because productivity has not increased) wages. But inflation can also be the result of the avarice of another villain, big business, determined to increase its profits. Higher prices mean higher profits, and since business is oriented toward profits, it has a built-in motive to raise prices. Of course the economists' model of inflation always took for granted a trade-off between unemployment and inflation. When unemployment is low, the economy can no longer expand and therefore prices must rise. But when production declines, prices fall and unemployment rises. What the economists with their models were totally unprepared for were the events of the mid-seventies when for the first time the country was beset with both high inflation and high unemployment. The causes of the simultaneity of these twin evils still escape the economists.

In view of the confusion among the experts about the causes of inflation and recession, there is perhaps some merit to examining what the general public thinks are the causes of these phenomena. Whatever the accuracy of their views, the public's thinking about inflation and recession has important implications for policy-makers. The public's willingness to tolerate one or another program for combating inflation or unemployment is very much related to its views of these phenomena. Moreover, what the public thinks about inflation and recession will tell us a good deal about its confidence in the American system and our government. In this chapter we shall examine three sets of data bearing on these issues. At one point in the survey the respondents were asked who they felt was most to blame for so much inflation. At another point they were asked if they had any ideas about how to improve the economy or prevent high inflation and unemployment. And in seventy-odd depth interviews, the respondents were questioned at length about their views of inflation and recession. Most of the material presented in this chapter will be based on the qualitative data generated by the survey question on ideas for improving the economy and the depth interviews. But before turning to the qualitative data, we shall first examine the quantitative data from the question of who is most to blame for inflation.

The Checklist of Villains

The respondents were presented with a checklist of potential villains for rampant inflation and asked to choose the group they thought was most to blame. The list consisted of (1) big business, (2) unions, (3) government, (4) politicians, (5) wel-

fare, (6) other, and (7) don't know. In the aggregate, 15 percent
of the respondents blamed big business for inflation and almost
as many, 14 percent, blamed the unions. Only 5 percent of the
respondents thought that inflation stemmed from the welfare
program. Six percent came up with some other villain apart
from the ones that were provided, and 14 percent said they did
not know who to blame. By far the most popular villain in the
eyes of the public is the government. Fully 30 percent of the
respondents placed the blame for inflation on the government,
and the second most popular set of villains was politicians,
mentioned by 17 percent of the sample. Since politicians work
in government, the percentage blaming government or politicians comes to 47 or almost half of the sample.

Are the people who suffered from inflation and recession
more likely to blame the government and politicians than those
who did not suffer from inflation? The answer is provided by
Table 11.1.

Hardly anybody blames welfare for inflation (about 5 percent) whatever the impact of inflation. Unions are more likely
to be the villains than big business among those who managed
to escape from inflation and recession, whereas the reverse is
true among those suffering from inflation and recession. They
are more likely to blame big business than unions. But the
striking pattern shown in Table 11.1 is the strong relationship
between being victimized by the economy and blaming government and politicians for inflation. As inflationary pressures
increase, so do the percentage blaming government and politicians for inflation. Clearly, those suffering from inflation and
recession hold the government accountable for their troubles.
Table 11.2 shows how the various social characteristics are
related to locus of blame for inflation.

The underprivileged social groups were much more likely to
be affected by inflation and recession than the more privileged
groups, and hence the patterns in Table 11.2 are quite similar to
those in Table 11.1. The more privileged social groups, whether
on income, occupation, or ethnicity, are more likely to blame
unions than big business, whereas the less privileged groups
blame big business more often than unions. But in every social

Table 11.1: Locus of Blame for Inflation by Measures of Inflation Crunch and Recession Impact (percentages)

	Locus of Blame					
	Big Business	Unions	Government and Politicians	Welfare	Other and Don't Know	N
Objective Crunch						
Better now	13	20	36	6	24	(307)
Same	15	14	49	5	17	(493)
Little worse	18	13	48	4	17	(732)
Lot worse	13	11	51	5	21	(422)
Subjective Crunch						
Low	13	20	39	5	24	(456)
Medium low	17	15	43	6	19	(484)
Medium high	16	14	46	5	19	(434)
High	15	9	57	4	15	(605)
Recession Impact						
None	17	16	43	5	19	(664)
Some	16	12	50	5	18	(616)
Considerable	14	6	56	5	19	(390)

214

Table 11.2: Locus of Blame for Inflation by Selected Social Characteristics (percentages)

| | Locus of Blame | | | | | |
	Big Business	Unions	Government and Politicians	Welfare	Other and Don't Know	N
Subsample						
Poor	14	7	56	5	19	(322)
Blue collar	18	6	53	6	17	(581)
White collar	15	19	42	4	19	(766)
Retired	13	24	38	3	23	(309)
Income						
Under $7,000	14	11	52	4	19	(395)
$7,000–$12,999	18	10	52	3	17	(390)
$13,000–$19,999	20	12	43	7	18	(435)
$20,000 and over	13	19	45	5	17	(461)
Occupation						
Higher white collar	14	21	40	4	22	(677)
Lower white collar	18	18	44	4	17	(296)
Higher blue collar	18	9	51	6	16	(344)
Lower blue collar	15	8	53	5	19	(662)
Race-Ethnicity						
White	15	17	42	5	21	(1,461)
Black	17	4	59	4	16	(407)
Spanish-speaking	9	7	65	8	11	(88)

215

group, whether privileged or underprivileged, the leading villain is government and politicians. Moreover, the underprivileged are harder on government and politicians than the privileged. This is especially true of the poor when compared with the white collar and retired and of the minorities, the blacks and Spanish-speaking, compared with the whites.

Table 11.3 relates the various measures of inflation-induced strain to locus of blame.

Those whose mental health and marriages suffered from inflation were more likely to blame big business and less likely to blame the unions than those whose mental health and marriages were not affected by inflation. They were especially likely to blame government and politicians, much more so than those whose mental health and marriages were not touched by inflation.

The various villains were also identified by the respondents in response to the open-ended questions about how to improve the economy and the causes of inflation that appeared in both the survey and the depth interviews. The rest of this chapter presents illustrative quotations from the respondents about these various villains.

The Respondents' Views of Inflation and Recession

The open-ended question asked of the survey respondents about how to improve the economy and fight inflation and unemployment and the depth interviews generated a wide range of perceived causes of these economic ills. The responses have been classified into twelve categories, five of which have to do with the major villain revealed by the quantitative data: government. The first category to be examined is antiunion sentiments; the second is a combination of antiunion and antibusiness views; the third is antibusiness, and the fourth a combination of antibusiness and antigovernment. The next four categories all have to do with government: government spending, government regulations, foreign aid, military spending, and the war in Vietnam. A ninth category of reasons for inflation and recession has to do with supply and demand theories of these

Table 11.3: Locus of Blame by Measures of Stress (percentages)

	Locus of Blame					
	Big Business	Unions	Government and Politicians	Welfare	Other and Don't Know	N
Mental Strain						
Low	16	17	41	5	22	101	(1,030)
Medium	16	14	47	4	19	100	(485)
High	13	8	59	6	14	100	(464)
Balance of Feelings						
Negative	13	7	57	7	17	101	(384)
Equal	20	7	46	7	20	100	(149)
1–2 positive	14	16	50	3	18	101	(604)
3–5 positive	17	16	41	4	22	100	(666)
None	15	23	38	5	18	99	(176)
Marital Strain						
Same	13	17	43	5	22	100	(697)
Better	21	13	46	5	16	101	(487)
Mixed	13	10	54	6	17	100	(324)
Worse	20	9	50	4	16	99	(236)

phenomena. A tenth category, mentioned by a few people, is automation, and an eleventh is the welfare system. Finally, a twelfth category consists of proposed solutions to inflation and recession. We begin this analysis by considering the views of the people who blame the unions for our economic ills.

UNIONS AND BIG BUSINESS AS VILLAINS

A fifty-three-year-old executive with the telephone company said:

> Free enterprise is no longer free. Unions cause high wages, force management to cut down on the number of jobs. The unions are the biggest violators of anti- trust. . . . Unions should be investigated and some of their activities outlawed. We cannot have them dictating every stage of business.

A forty-eight-year-old engineer in Detroit earning $35,000 shared this man's views of unions:

> In some way, we must decrease the power of the unions. We must stop the constant wage demands that constantly make wages go up unreasonably.

This man endorses the popular push-pull model of inflation, which holds that prices go up in response to sharp increases in wages. A twenty-nine-year-old policeman with a working wife and a family income of $28,000 also puts the blame for inflation on unions' demands for more wages:

> I guess everyone is out to make a buck. The more you have the more you want. Every time an employee's contract expires, they always demand a great deal more than they are entitled to get.

A forty-nine-year-old black woman on welfare also blamed the unions:

> Well, to start with, the unions have a lot to do with it. Every time the unions demand a higher salary, the things in the street go up. The transit union demanded a higher wage and the fare went up.

Farm workers demanded more and the price of food went up. Unions are not bad for their members, but they cause problems for other workers.

An engineer in his twenties earning $16,000 saw wage demands as fostering imports of consumer goods and drying up jobs in America:

The American worker is destroying himself. He's made such high union demands that buying has to go elsewhere. You can't buy an American baby carriage. He's unionized himself right out of a job.

A forty-two-year-old advertising executive earning $45,000 blamed our economic troubles on a drift toward socialism spurred by unions:

Costs increase because we are more and more socialistic. We're carrying the load of more and more people; pension funds, welfare; the unions have crushed individual incentive. This adds to inflation.

Some respondents took the position of a pox on both your houses as they held both unions and business responsible for inflation. A fifty-year-old sales executive in Detroit put it this way:

I think there should be fewer demands by labor unions and business should be willing to work on less profit. And there should be a complete revision of the pension plans.

A thirty-two-year-old marketing executive earning $25,000 had this plan for improving the economy:

Should have a national caucus of unions and ask them to hold back labor's increases and at the same time restrict big business from excess profits.

A forty-two-year-old plant layout estimator earning $19,000 said:

Government, business and the unions must sit down and discuss this problem and reach a conclusion. They always pull apart but they must work together.

A middle-aged woman employed as an editor and earning $20,000 also saw the conflict between labor and management as the problem:

> We have to prime the economy but the Republican party is opposed to this.... We're having an economic revolution—labor vs. management. Labor is demanding too much and management would like to knock labor out. Until they get themselves straightened out the economy will be screwy.

A musician earning $23,000 also blamed unions and business for inflation:

> Inflation is caused by unions and too high profit margins. Our government has been too lax.... We should put a freeze on wages and profit margins, and professional incomes. And we should stop giving people salaries when they don't work. I think the people on welfare should be made to work by paving roads or doing whatever is needed. That would sure help the economy.

This man also seems to be blaming the welfare system, a view we shall examine in some detail later on.

The idea that big business and the unions should get together instead of fighting was expressed by a black skycap for an airline earning $10,000:

> Big business and the unions should get together and stop fighting. And they should enforce some of the laws on the books. Get rid of those lawyers who are finding loopholes in the laws. They should get down to doing the job. May have to disappoint some people, but would be better off in the long run.

A fairly large number of respondents blamed big business for the economic troubles. Mixed in with these views is a strong populist sentiment attacking the rich.

A brewery worker earning $16,000 who saw big business as the villain, reported:

Big business has to take less profits and keep people working, instead of taking everything for themselves.

A fifty-five-year-old factory worker earning $14,000 said:

Corporations are trying to take too much profits out of the products. That's one reason for high prices. People are not able to buy things because the prices are so high and that's the fault of the corporations. The fault of government is letting the corporations keep raising their prices all the time, not putting a lid on prices. And naturally wages are not going up as fast as prices. Things are just out of hand. . . . The corporations want too much and they are not taxed enough. They want more and more and the little guy just can't compete. That's all there is to it.

A twenty-nine-year-old white woman attending college while on welfare was very cynical about the role of big business:

(The cause of inflation?) Big business and the puppets in government who do whatever they say. This inflation is phony. Sugar prices went up even when they were making enormous profits. And there was no shortage of sugar. Con Ed, the same thing. They always show a profit at the end of the year. An enormous profit. They spend money on commercials and brainwash the strongest people. They are doing it deliberately. They want power. They give us welfare and unemployment so that we'll fight among ourselves. There's more heroin getting into the ghetto and it's because they are letting it in. Our schools are getting worse because they allow it. They don't want people to get educated because we'd start to challenge them.

This woman sees the corporate elite carrying out a conspiracy to maximize its profits and keep the common man down.

A twenty-nine-year-old draftsman earning $9,000 said:

I have lost confidence in our system of business. Big business overpowers and controls all. The small man can't get ahead.

And a thirty-seven-year-old graphics designer earning $15,000 had a similar view:

I think big business should not expect so much profit. Then more of
the middle class people would benefit from the overall profit.

A thirty-one-year-old Atlanta woman earning $15,000 as an
assistant to a physician blamed big business and the government
for the economic troubles:

Have to cut down on the cheating in government and big business
shouldn't take big profits and get all the tax breaks. Tax breaks
should be geared to people who need them.

A thirty-nine-year-old assistant controller for a corporation
was also hostile toward big business:

We can't control our own destiny any more. You can't be a self-
made man anymore. Big business pushes you out. There's the lack of
control of big business.... Big business should invest in our resources. We shouldn't have to buy from other countries. We lost
many jobs in this country by doing that.

This respondent, like many others we talked to, was disturbed
by our dependence on foreign goods and what he perceived as a
loss of jobs as a result.

Another respondent, a postman with a working wife and a
family income of $20,000, voiced this same view, putting the
blame on the multinational corporations:

(What caused the recession?) I think it was the business interests.
They probably have as many people working for them as before but
they are in other countries.... You see all these imports of clothes
and automobiles and a lot of people have been laid off in these
industries. I think our priorities are out of line.... The government
has no money for New York City but gives billions to foreign
countries.... I blame it on big business and there's no government
intervention. A lot of things are monopolized, especially energy. The
government doesn't get involved and when they do, they support big
business.

This man sees imports as undermining our economy and causing
unemployment, and he is most cynical about the government
which he sees as big business's ally.

A surprising number of respondents saw the country's economic ills as the result of a conspiracy of a small group of very rich and powerful people. To these respondents such gross inequality was unfair and undemocratic. Here are some of the comments in this vein:

A twenty-seven-year-old roofer earning $10,000:

We've got to stop a few people from owning all the money. The money should be divided among all the people.

A New York mailman elaborated on this view:

Today we have many people living in luxury and many more people living in poverty. It shows the unequal distribution and the lack of true representation for the majority. After all, this is supposed to be a country that represents the needs of the majority.

A thirty-two-year-old black woman on welfare said:

It's not what it's supposed to be in this country. The rich get richer and the poor get poorer.

A middle-aged professional whose wife worked, providing a family income of $43,000, gave this view:

There's a lot of manipulation for the benefit of a few. It seems that we are heading toward a society of very rich and very poor with no middle class.

A twenty-nine-year-old black woman working as a teacher in a day care center and earning $8,000 also saw the middle class being squeezed:

I think more money should be spread around. I don't think it should be the type of system that is in upper and upper-upper class hands. What happens is that even the middle class suffers and winds up paying a tremendous amount of taxes. Lower class people have always suffered. . . . There are just a few families that control most of the money in the United States and I think that money should be spread out a little more. Then things wouldn't be so bad as they are now. . . . People say that people on welfare are lazy and that they're welching off the government. What people fail to realize is that in certain areas of the United States, certain counties, grants are given to farmers for not growing crops and these grants are very huge. They're not like $3,000 or $4,000 or $5,000 that people might get on welfare. They're like $100,000 for not growing crops. It's not called welfare, but in reality that is what it is.

This woman has a sophisticated view of the complex system of public benefits as she sees little difference between farm subsidies and welfare. And she too, like so many other respondents, is resentful of the concentration of wealth in the hands of the few.

A few respondents extended the conspiratorial theory of big business and the wealthy to include government.

A member of the working class put it this way:

We have poor leadership and poor management at the highest political levels, a political machinery that leans toward business rather than to the majority of the people. You got the multi-nationals in there and the import of labor. They've raised profits tremendously out of proportion and the government, especially the government of the last eight years, is probably in collusion with them. . . . There's no real power or party that's able to offset it, like a labor party, an organization of the people because the people are not well organized while this small industrial group is well organized. You read that the profits are at their highest and yet there's inflation and unemployment. Nobody cares about the workers. They don't really care about the prices as long as the profits are up. . . . A small group is getting richer and everybody else is getting poorer.

As we have noted, inflation and recession, by attacking the underprivileged while the more privileged groups are unscathed, tend to exacerbate class divisions and conflict. This man's views are a good illustration of this process.

A twenty-eight-year-old social researcher for a city agency earning $17,000 held a similar view:

Inflation and recession are both encouraged by those in power to serve as a labor disciplining device. I have a conspiratorial view. Government and capital are not interested in alleviating the effects of inflation and recession on working people. They benefit from having the people poor and struggling.

GOVERNMENT AS THE VILLAIN

Although many respondents placed the blame for inflation and the recession on big business and the very wealthy, even more blamed the government and its various policies, ranging from government spending and regulations, to foreign aid, the military-industrial complex, and the Vietnam War.

A real estate lawyer earning $30,000 saw the economic problems as a result of too much governmental spending:

> They are spending too much money, the government that is. They are spending more than they have. Also, I think it basically goes in cycles. Every 20 years or so, it is really good and then it gets really bad.

Apart from government spending, this man saw the economic ills as merely an expression of the normal business cycles.

A number of respondents saw the problem as too much governmental interference with and regulation of business. For example, a sixty-two-year-old manager of a warehouse earning $35,000 said when asked about improving the economy:

> Eliminate government edicts and bureaucratic tyranny. And reduce useless governmental expenditures.

A forty-six-year-old systems analyst earning $20,000 was even more emphatic:

> Get government out of big business. They interfere too much. Tell business that they have to give jobs to people that need them.

This man has a strange ambivalence about government interference with business. On the one hand he wants government to stop interfering with business, but on the other he wants someone to tell business they must give jobs to the people who need them. And who would give this message to business if not government?

A fifty-year-old night manager of a supermarket earning $19,000 was bitterly opposed to government regulation of business:

> We should get rid of all the bureaucracy that we have in the city, state and federal government. The government is strangling all sorts of business and they're causing prices to rise on everything. If I were on the outside looking in, I would think that the government is trying to strangle every type of business and trying to lift prices on everything, with all these controls they are imposing. They have people telling you it is for your own good but they don't tell you about the backfire from all these laws that they are imposing on people.

This man was particularly offended by the Ralph Naders of the world who in the name of the consumer interest lobby for laws that increase the cost of goods:

> Why the inflation? I'll tell you. It's the Ralph Naders who keep knocking American cars. You know the seat belts he said had to be installed on all cars? They cost money. The guy who buys a car has to pay $300 more for the seat belts and the light that goes on. That's just one example of regulation costing money.

A thirty-six-year-old business executive earning $31,000 was also opposed to government regulation of business, and he too gave the same example of the increased costs of automobile safety:

> There's too much government regulation. Take automobile safety. Who the hell wants an air bag? And we'll have to pay $300 more for it. Let people kill themselves if that's what they want. All these regulations make products more expensive.

A number of respondents were critical of the government's foreign aid programs and overseas involvement generally. Among these is a forty-four-year-old black widow, the mother of nine children, who worked as an educational assistant:

> (Why so much inflation?) Because America has given too much to other countries. Recession has come because they have given all the

money away. America's a very generous country. To everyone but
the poor right here. I think they should see to it that the poor have
decent housing and decent jobs so that they can take care of their
families. . . . I find myself hating society these days because society
isn't letting me take care of my family. They can bring others here,
foreigners, and give them decent jobs. I've been here all my life and
all I get is shit.

A thirty-three-year-old systems programmer earning $16,000
was also opposed to foreign expenditures by the government:

There are too many out of country expenditures and not enough in
country, leading to a high rate of poverty and welfare. I don't think
our military involvement has helped. . . . The economy started to dip
after Vietnam.

A twenty-eight-year-old New York taxi driver said:

There should be less aid out of the country and they should put
more money into the United States. There should be more jobs
available. I've become more politically minded. I'm trying to find a
party that works but I don't think there is any.

A twenty-nine-year-old black woman earning $8,000 as a
teacher in a day care center, was generally critical of government spending including foreign aid:

I think that one reason we have inflation is that the government of
the USA refuses to put more money into the cities and help the
urban population. I think that more people are becoming unemployed than in past years and I think there is a lot of fiscal
mismanagement on the upper USA levels. I think money is being
spent in other areas when it should be spent right here. I don't think
a lot of money should be spent on foreign aid. And I think that
sending people to the moon is a waste of money.

A forty-eight-year-old Detroit sales manager earning $35,000
was also critical of government spending:

I believe we are not getting the services from government for the
amount of money we are paying in taxes. I think we could bring

down inflation by not sending money out of the country. We send too much.

Apart from foreign aid, some respondents were resentful of immigrants and refugees, who they saw as taking jobs away from Americans. A forty-two-year-old black woman living on welfare expressed this point of view:

> They bring all those foreigners over here and then they can't help us people. They [the foreigners] get what they want and then they go home. Then they got the nerve to tell you they ain't got no money for you.

A thirty-four-year-old unemployed Puerto Rican had a similar view:

> Money is everything nowadays. Nobody cares about the poor. You gotta eat, but they don't care. Why give the Vietnamese jobs? We Americans are on the streets. Hold those immigrants back.

The idea that nobody cares for the poor was often voiced by the poor people we interviewed who saw our government as more benevolent to foreigners than to the people here at home.

A twenty-six-year-old black laboratory assistant earning $12,000 stated the matter even more generally:

> I think America should stop concentrating on foreign intervention and be more concerned with the problems at home.

Some respondents were highly critical of the large defense budgets and military spending, which they felt were hurting the country. Typical of these are the following comments. A retired army colonel said:

> I think all government has gone wild. I think it is ridiculous that we are spending more on defense today than in World War II, even though I'm a retired army man. They don't want to cut defense budgets.

A fifty-six-year-old longshoreman earning $15,000 said:

They spend too much money for defense and they shouldn't. They should think more of education and the elderly. The senior citizens don't get a damn thing.

A fifty-three-old adult education leader earning $32,000 said:

I would cut military spending. It does not always contribute to national security.

And a thirty-five-year-old financial planner earning $38,000 had a similar view:

Put an end to international defenses and nuclear spending.

Some other respondents were highly critical of the Vietnam War, and they saw America's economy as dependent on war. A twenty-eight-year-old black woman whose husband worked as a medical electronic technician, earning $11,000, expressed this sentiment:

Who is to blame for the high cost of living? I don't think you can blame a person. It's the capitalistic system. We're not at war. That's the problem. It's terrible to say, but we need a war to have a boom.

A thirty-six-year-old editor of a trade journal also saw war as important to the American economy:

Why the recession? Well, from the end of the Vietnam War there haven't been enough jobs to go around. There just aren't enough jobs without war.

A young school teacher whose wife worked and whose family income was $16,000 had a similar view:

We have unemployment because there's no more war. We were a war economy. We can't operate in peace.

A thirty-five-year-old public opinion pollster earning $43,000 blamed the war for inflation:

I think inflation is created by the war. Before the war, the economy was more stabilized.

These respondents held to the cynical, but not necessarily unreasonable, view that full employment in America was dependent on war.

SUPPLY AND DEMAND THEORIES OF INFLATION AND RECESSION

A number of respondents offered rather sophisticated theories of inflation and recession based on the principles of supply and demand. One respondent had this explanation for unemployment:

There's an old saying that the rich get rich and more rich and that seems to be where all the money is going. The prices of things are constantly going up and people can't afford to buy these things. And so the production of these things is cut down which means that the people making them have to be cut down, that is, they're let go.

To this man unemployment is a result of inflation's high prices. Because of high prices, purchasing power diminishes which in turn means cutting down production and hence jobs. A twenty-nine-year-old unemployed man who was planning to open his own business had a similar view:

We have a recession because there are no jobs. There's no money now and people don't spend. If people don't spend, the businesses aren't getting any money and that means they can't exist without money. So more businesses are failing and if businesses fail that means there are more people on unemployment.

According to this man when demand dries up, businesses suffer as well as employees.

If high prices can lead to reduced demand and thus unemployment, some respondents saw a reverse process. They pointed to sharp increases in demand which in turn pushed prices up in an inflationary spiral. Typical of these views is the comment of the middle-aged black wife of a postal employee who herself worked as a saleswoman, bringing the family income to $20,000:

> The chief reason for inflation is the high standard of living here in America. There's lots of money in circulation. There's no competition in business. They set the prices. You've got a lot of people making money now. The number of black people making more than $10,000 has quadrupled. If they can pay for it, they're going to have the "necessities," what they call necessities such as cars and good clothes. As long as people will pay the high prices they will stay up.

This woman saw high prices as the result not only of increased demand, but also of the absence of competition in business.

A forty-two-year-old business executive earning $35,000 shared this view:

> I think it is a matter of so many people wanting the same things. The demand pushes the price up. All the new consumers coming into the market place wanting a piece of the pie. I think supply and demand has to be the root of it.

A twenty-seven-year-old mother of two living on welfare also seemed to feel that inflation was the result of excessive consumer demand:

> I think it is the system in which we live. It's a consumer oriented system. It's like we keep producing more and more. There's just too much of a need to keep buying and buying. That's why the prices keep going up and up. It seems to me the government should just put a limit on everything.

AUTOMATION AS THE VILLAIN

A few respondents pointed a finger at automation as the chief cause of unemployment. A thirty-five-year-old black woman married to a motorman for the Transit Authority who earned $18,000 put it this way:

> The machines have taken over. They've knocked out a lot of jobs. Where it used to take 20 men, now 2 men can do it.

A thirty-three-year-old employee of the gas company earning
$14,000, when asked how to solve the problem of unemploy-
ment, said:

> Get rid of the computers and make people work for a living, not
> machines. People should work. Automation always means less work.

A forty-nine-year-old black woman living on welfare explained the recession this way:

> It's partially taxes. Because the businessman constantly has to pay
> more taxes, he's got to let someone go so he can offset the increase
> and still make a living. So he brings machines in and gets rid of
> people.

Just like the respondents who sought to explain rising prices
in terms of rising demand stemming from greater affluence, so
those who called attention to automation were identifying a
major process at work in society that does have an impact on
the health of the economy.

WELFARE AS THE VILLAIN

A number of respondents were upset with the system of
welfare in this country and they were prepared to blame it for
the economic ills of inflation and unemployment. These people
were resentful of the idea of people getting money without
having to work for it, and they saw the people on welfare as
lazy, or even worse, engaging in fraud. These views are even held
by some people who are on welfare. For example, a New York
Puerto Rican mother of three, being supported by welfare, said:

> There are too many lazy people. Too many who can work, but don't
> work because of the welfare system. People sit on their damn rumps.
> Without welfare, the city wouldn't be in all this trouble.

A twenty-seven-year-old dock man in the trucking industry
earning $15,000 also was opposed to the welfare system:

> I believe the government gives a lot of money away to people that

could be working. If they can't make top pay, they don't want to work. They give food stamps to people who do not need them.

This man was a blue collar worker, but hostility toward welfare recipients occurs on all levels of the social hierarchy. For example, a San Francisco physician, earning $41,000, said:

I have the feeling that some of the people who have welfare, have too much. Some don't deserve it and if they made some of them get out and work, they could use the money for something else.

A sixty-one-year-old businessman in Detroit had a similar view:

I think there are a lot of jobs that people could do if they really wanted to work. As it is, the working man is now paying for welfare.

A thirty-year-old supervisor in the automobile industry earning $20,000 also was hostile to people on welfare:

Unemployed people on welfare should be made to work at something so I don't see them on the rolls.

The wife of a sheet metal worker who earned $19,000 was particularly bitter about welfare mothers:

I think these active producers of offspring . . . something ought to be done about them. They're collecting welfare from four different families. You see a woman on TV with 6 or 7 kids and she's only 22. She doesn't care. The more kids, the more money she gets. That kind of system doesn't work.

The hostility toward welfare illustrated by these quotations was rather prevalent in the survey. But as noted earlier, a number of respondents that were subjects in the depth interviews at the beginning of the research were mothers on welfare. They were extremely bitter about the welfare system, which they viewed as degrading and humiliating. The enormous gulf between the welfare recipients and their critics outside the system is seen by contrasting the views just presented with those of the women on welfare. These women were particularly upset by the impersonal bureaucratic system they were forced to cope with. For example, a thirty-one-year-old black woman with five children, separated from her unemployed husband, had this to say:

> I want to get off welfare. They don't treat a woman right. They treat you like shit. You let a junkie in there and he gets his money right away. Every six months they send you down for these face to face interviews. They send me all the way to Queens. They don't care if you got the carfare or not. They'll cut you off immediately if you don't show. They cut me off in October and I had to go down the next day and explain why I couldn't make it. I'm sick of their shit. I had to keep the kids out of school for a week because I didn't have money to buy them clothes. That's when they cut my check. My husband was supposed to send me $25 a week, but he wasn't sending the money and they cut the check anyway. These people don't care. I've been in and out of courts and I'm tired. . . . They make the old and the sick people sit around waiting for hours. When I'm there, I'm afraid to go to the bathroom to piss because I'm afraid I'll lose my turn. I hate going there. If I could get a good job, I wouldn't tolerate this.

To the outsiders opposed to welfare, the people on welfare are lazy and do not want to work. But to the people who are on welfare, a decent job would be their salvation, and they are distressed because such jobs are not available to them.

A forty-two-year-old black woman with five children and one grandchild to care for had a similar story:

> That face to face interview shit is getting on my nerves. I don't care if they are black. I have to bring all those papers and then they ask me all those crazy questions. Every six months you got to go. It's like a jail, but you've got to eat. Not all of them are nasty. One black woman was very nice. The three-year-old boy, they said, had to have a social security card. What the hell he needs a social security card for? He ain't goin' to work no job at three. Just more time they waste and money; yet they don't have more to give you.

A forty-four-year-old black woman with seven children to care for, worked as a teacher's aide but was receiving supplementary welfare. She was especially bitter about her situation:

> They always said, get a good education and you'll get a good job. I bust my ass and what do I get? Things have been very difficult. I'm always angry about what I don't have. I'm angry when I read in the papers and see them giving away so much and I'm here in America and I ain't got nothing. America, the home of the free and the home of the brave. Here I am, and I ain't got shit. What do they say—we're shiftless and lazy. We don't want to work they say, we just want welfare. But nobody wants to be on welfare when they can get a decent job. But the kinds of jobs they give us ain't good enough to support our families. We're better off sitting at home and getting that little bit of check. . . . They just don't want black people to do better.

Whereas the welfare critics view the recipients as unwilling to work, the recipients, such as this woman, see the larger society as engaged in a conspiracy to prevent the welfare recipients from obtaining decent jobs. Such is the gulf between the two groups.

The critics of welfare make a big issue of what they consider to be rampant cheating by the recipients. By far the most common form of welfare cheating is the receipt of unreported income. One welfare mother of five children explained why off-the-books income was necessary to survival:

> I had a job when I was on welfare. Even though, technically, being on welfare, I wasn't supposed to be working. But I just couldn't live on welfare alone. Most women on welfare must have some job off the books. Or they have some friends who help them, because the money people get on welfare is really not enough.

As we saw in Chapter 5, off-the-books income is not only essential for welfare recipients, but for many families not on welfare as well, as they struggle to make ends meet in the face of sharply rising prices.

PROPOSED SOLUTIONS TO INFLATION AND RECESSION

Many of the views of the causes of inflation and recession already presented contain at least implicitly suggestions of how to solve these problems, for example, cutting back on foreign aid, military spending, and welfare. But a large number of respondents were quite explicit in proposing solutions to these problems. For example, a number of respondents felt that the way to solve unemployment was for the government to take responsibility for creating jobs.

A twenty-eight-year old black woman whose husband earned $11,000 as a technician made a strong case for the government providing jobs for everyone who wants to work:

> I think there is so much wrong with this country. I can't accept that they can't make work for people who want jobs. Jobs could be created over night if federal funding was voted. When I go over to the East 80s, I notice those people aren't suffering. They've got plenty of expensive clothes, cars and fancy apartments. Nobody told them there's a recession and inflation out there.

On the basis of the data of this study, this woman's perceptions are fairly accurate. As we have seen, the people who are really suffering from inflation and recession are the poor and the working class; the upper class and the middle class have not been nearly as affected.

A twenty-year-old part-time student who was self-employed and earning $12,000 also felt that jobs should be provided for everyone who wanted to work:

> Provide no cash dole for anybody but do provide jobs for everyone, except for those who simply can't work. Also there should be a limit to income. Young people should be turned away from values of greed and competition toward humanitarian values.

This kind of idealism was by no means rare among the respondents. For example, a fifty-three-year-old designer of ladies' coats and suits earning $25,000 had a similar notion:

> Instead of welfare, people should work at whatever job they can and they should be subsidized so they get a decent wage. The people

who can't work should get welfare and the military establishment should be trimmed to the minimum.

A forty-nine-year-old black woman living on welfare felt that the CCC program of the New Deal should be revised:

I think they should bring back the Citizen Conservation Corps for the boys 17 to 24. It didn't pay a lot but it gave them a place to stay and it taught them a trade. They sent them upstate back in the thirties. They had to build their own barracks. They really taught them how to take care of themselves. They need to get some of the boys around here together and send them to a place like that. The program was really good. It didn't just help the young people. Adults who were unemployed got jobs at the camps teaching the boys. It was good all the way around. There are a lot of ways they could make jobs if they wanted to.

A twenty-nine-year-old scoial worker earning $7,000 had a similar view:

The government should find ways to find jobs for people, like the conservation corps; real work programs.

A fifty-eight-year-old unemployed black woman living off of unemployment insurance also saw job creation as the solution to the country's ills:

We have to get together. We need jobs. Put the people back to work. Give them something to think about besides evilness. If people were working they wouldn't have time to think about crime. We need jobs.

And a fifty-year-old school teacher earning $20,000 had an idea for creating jobs:

I'd like to see more training at trade schools for children who do not want to go to college, so that they are not poured into the work force with no skills. There should be some provisions for incompetent people in any occupation or profession. They are not protected by laws enacted to protect the competent people.

This man is concerned about the job needs of the less talented and less competent, who he feels make up a large percentage of the unemployed. Finding work for such people would do much to solve the recession problem in his opinion.

If job creation was the most popular solution to the economic ills offered by the respondents, perhaps the next most popular idea was controlling wages and prices as a way of solving the problem of inflation. A fifty-one-year-old butcher earning $14,000, who believed that this would solve the problem of inflation, put it this way:

> Freeze everything, wages, gas, food and doctor bills.

A retired army colonel who was quoted earlier also believed in wage and price controls as well as public service jobs to handle the recession:

> I think the government will have to come up with price controls. We need wage and price controls to put the lid on things. As for the recession, we need public service jobs. Put unemployed people to work to improve the national parks, to make bike paths and things like that.

A retired businessman also saw price and wage controls as the solution:

> They should put everything under control. If wages and prices are controlled, prices will come down.

And a forty-six-year-old customer representative for the telephone company earning $22,000 had the same solution:

> I'd like a freeze on everything. No raises in wages and in the costs of items.

The idea of wage and price controls is considered to be highly controversial by the politicians, and they go to great lengths to point out that they will never advocate such drastic measures. But were a careful public opinion poll conducted, the politicians might well be surprised by the large scale public support for such "drastic" measures.

Still another much discussed policy measure that found some resonance among the respondents was the idea of tax reform. As a twenty-eight-year-old manager of inventory control earning $16,000 put it this way:

> There are too many tax loopholes. Too many businesses are making windfall profits and the unions are getting outrageous too.

A thirty-three-year-old fireman earning $19,000 said:

> Things would be much better if everyone was taxed the same—no loopholes—no oil depletion allowances. Also CCC camps and WPA should be reinstated.

A merchandising manager for a large department store earning $19,000 also called attention to tax loopholes:

> The problem is the poor tax structure. There should be less tax loopholes and more tax on corporate profits.

Creating jobs, controlling prices and wages and reforming taxes were ideas that a number of respondents mentioned as ways of solving the economic problems. But a number of respondents had more unusual solutions to our economic ills, some of which are worth presenting. A thirty-year-old free-lance photo editor who also taught economics on the side, had this scenario for our economic problems:

> I'm an economist. That's what I teach. I would offer a steady monetary increase, a balanced budget. Cut the military budget and divert it to job training programs. Be prepared to subsidize worker relocation. Tax automobile horsepower and gasoline and divert the taxes to mass transit. Reduce dependence on the automobile industry.

A forty-two-year-old business executive earning $35,000 saw our economic problems stemming from the problems of the construction industry:

Construction is the second largest industry in the country. Because
of inflation, money isn't available to the builders and hundreds of
thousands of workers are laid off. This is true of other industries as
well. The high cost of money. Until we can control interest rates,
lots of workers are going to be laid off.

To this respondent the villain is high interest rates. Other
respondents had even more esoteric plans for revitalizing the
economy. A twenty-eight-year-old newscaster for a radio station
earning $21,000 had a novel solution:

If everyone could have a piece of land for the raising of food—there
is enough land for everyone—vast amounts of land are owned by the
government.

His quaint idea is to turn over public lands for private gardens
to insure that everyone will eat well.
A thirty-two-year-old truck driver had a similar idea:

Start teaching people to be more self-sufficient. Get them to grow
their own gardens. They now teach the opposite—more spending.

A thirty-year-old high school teacher earning $11,000 in
Atlanta was troubled by the high costs of medical care and
when asked how the economy could be improved, said:

Socialization of medicine would help and supplementary income for
everyone.

A taxi driver who earned $6,700 in 1975 had an interesting
comment on how to improve the economy:

Change the tax structure, make jobs available to everyone and make
useful products instead of all the excessive, useless products that are
made now.

This man was offended by the profligacy of our affluent,
consumer-oriented society in which people are trained to want
useless products.

The middle-aged housewife of a former baker now living on a disability pension of $8,000 a year also thought there was something wrong with our consumer society:

> I think there's too much advertising that forces the prices up. The kids see all these things on television and they want them. But if they didn't put it on television, the kids wouldn't see it and they wouldn't want it.

To this woman the advertising industry conspires with the television industry to make people, especially children, want useless products.

Finally, a vegetarian, a twenty-one-year-old black woman attending college, and supported by her sister, felt that she knew the true villain in our economic turmoil:

> They should take meat off the market. Stop feeding their brains with garbage. Stop spending all that money raising those animals to eat and use the grain and nuts to feed the poor starving children. People are so hung up on this system that they can't distinguish their need from their desire. We think that what we desire is what we need. This is the case in the United States. The whole standard of living in this country needs to be changed. Income should be redistributed.

This woman is impressed by the irony that valuable grain is used to feed animals for the simple reason that we are a meat-loving society. In her view, the problems of starvation in the world could easily be solved if only people would join her in vegetarianism.

With this quixotic solution to the economic ills of America, we bring to a close this chapter on the respondents' views of the causes of inflation and recession and their opinions on how these problems could be solved. We need only note that many of their theories have been taken seriously by government officials, and the views of the common man are not that far out of line with the views of the experts.

Chapter 12

SUMMARY AND CONCLUSIONS

The study of inflation and recession reported in the previous chapters is intended as a definitive record of how American families have coped with these calamities that have beset the economy in the seventies. Not since the great depression has the country experienced such a severe recession as that of 1975, a recession that arrived almost simultaneously with the highest rates of inflation in this century. Recession and rampant inflation have been the central domestic issues in our society since 1973. Like the weather, everyone talks about rising prices and unemployment, and yet very little has been done to solve these problems. Given their persistence, it is important for policy-makers to know how damaging these dire economic events have been to the social fabric of society. More precisely, what families have been affected by inflation and recession, and what have these economic events done to the families that have been affected by them? This report has tried to answer these questions.

Rather than do a national survey, we concentrated on four major metropolitan areas—New York, Detroit, Atlanta and San

Francisco—areas that represent the Northeast, the Midwest, the South, and the Far West. In each of these areas roughly 500 interviews were conducted for a total of 1,982. To insure that the two groups widely suspected as being especially vulnerable to inflation, the poor and retired, would be well represented, we deliberately oversampled these groups within each city. Roughly 15 percent of the sample consisted of poor families with incomes under $7,000, 15 percent of retired families, and the remaining 70 percent was divided between blue collar and white collar families. (Through the accidents of sampling, we ended up with more white collar than blue collar families.)

Part I of the report dealt with the impact of inflation and recession. The first analytic chapter (Chapter 2) dealt with the question of how many families found their income falling behind rising prices, that is, experienced inflation, and how many experienced the recession in that they had either lost their job, worked less overtime, or had to work harder because coworkers had been laid off. In this four city sample, interviewed in the spring of 1976, we found that 41 percent had been able to keep up with rising prices and 59 percent had fallen behind. A more refined picture of the financial situation of these families showed that 16 percent had actually experienced an improvement in their financial situation, 25 percent had managed to stay even, 37 percent were a little worse off than they had been a few years earlier, and 22 percent were a lot worse off financially than previously. Some 9.6 percent of the chief wage earners in these families who were still in the labor force were unemployed, a rate well above that for the country as a whole at that time, indicating that major cities were particularly hard hit by the recession. When other aspects of the recession's impact on employment were taken into account, we found that 40 percent of the wage earners were untouched by the recession, 37 percent had felt some impact, and 23 percent experienced considerable impact from the recession, the latter group including, of course, the unemployed.

As these findings indicate, not all families were affected by these economic crises. Some 41 percent escaped completely from the ravages of inflation, as their incomes kept up with

rising prices, and 40 percent of the wage earners were completely untouched by the recession. The question naturally
arises as to how the families that escaped these calamities differ
from the families that were affected by them. A number of
social characteristics of the families were related to inflation
and recession impact, notably the type of subsample (poor, blue
collar, white collar, or retired), income, occupation, race-ethnicity, and education. These social statuses are symbolic of
prestige and privilege in society, and several of them bear
directly on the hierarchical arrangement of social classes. A
major finding of the research was that the more underprivileged
in terms of these status hierarchies—the poor, the semiskilled
and unskilled, the poorly educated, and the blacks and Spanish-
speaking—were much more likely to be hit by inflation and
recession than the more privileged groups of the well-to-do,
well-educated, higher white collar workers and whites. It was
suggested that these economic catastrophes serve to exacerbate
the natural cleavages in society between the more and less
privileged and for that reason are potentially dangerous to the
basic stability of society. The very fact that the victims of
inflation were much like the victims of recession indicated that
these economic events are related to each other, and indeed the
analysis showed this to be so. Those who suffered most from
recession were the very ones suffering most from inflation. This
finding calls attention to the extraordinary human cost of the
simultaneity of these economic events, which all economic
theory predicts cannot possibly happen at the same time. While
the have-nots suffered much more than the haves from both
inflation and recession, they were especially vulnerable to the
recession. Almost all of the unemployed were confined to the
poor and the blue collar samples, and blacks and those of low
income were much more likely than whites and those of high
income to have been touched by the recession. The more
general impact of inflation, reaching minorities of the middle
classes as well as the poor, no doubt explains why inflation
seems to be more feared by the public and politicians than high
unemployment. The victims of recession, unlike inflation, are
almost always the powerless groups in society.

In the third chapter we introduced a second dimension of inflation, the degree to which families were hurting because their incomes were not keeping up with rising prices. The gap between income and rising prices we identified as "objective inflation crunch." This objective gap is to be distinguished from the more subjective dimension, the degree of suffering produced by inflationary pressures. Families in the same objective situation with regard to inflation, may nonetheless experience it quite differently depending on a host of factors ranging from their financial resources and aspirations to their consumer needs. An index of this subjective dimension of inflation crunch was constructed from a series of questions that measured the ways in which families were hurting from rising prices. Obviously, the objective and subjective dimensions were strongly related, but there were nonetheless a number of families that were high on one dimension and low on the other. One striking finding was that the retired, who were almost as likely as the poor to have fallen behind rising prices, were not suffering too much from inflation. The poor families were most likely to be suffering from inflation, followed by the blue collar families. The white collar families were most likely to escape the pain of inflation for their rate of suffering was far below that of the poor and the blue collar families. But the retired, living on fixed incomes, were nonetheless very close to white collar families in this respect. Perhaps because they are at that stage of life when consumer needs and wants are minimal, the retired are better able to adjust to rising prices than those still in the labor force, particularly those still struggling like the poor and many blue collar families.

When the results for objective inflation crunch were compared with those for subjective inflation crunch, a striking finding emerged. The more privileged groups were even less likely to suffer from inflation than to experience it. In every instance, whether we looked at those in the highest income group, the highest occupational group, the highest educational group, or the whites, we found that more of these privileged people found their incomes falling behind rising prices (objective inflation crunch) than were suffering from this experience.

In contrast, the less privileged, the poor, the blue collar workers, the poorly educated, and blacks and Spanish-speaking, were as likely to be suffering from inflation as experiencing it. This finding can only mean that the more privileged have resources that enable them to better withstand the scourge of inflation.

The two dimensions of inflation crunch, although related to each other, generated a typology of inflation crunch. The families that were low on both the objective and subjective dimensions were labeled the "untouched," and they constituted 29 percent of the sample. Those who were high on objective but low on subjective crunch were called the "stoics" and made up 18 percent of the sample. The obverse of the stoics were the families that managed to keep up with rising prices but nonetheless claimed that they were suffering because of rising prices, a group that we named "the complainers." They constituted 12 percent of the sample. Finally there were the families who were high on both objective and subjective' inflation crunch, a group we called the "suffering victims." They were the largest group, comprising 41 percent of the sample.

Not surprisingly, the more privileged classes were most likely to be untouched by the inflation, the poor and the minority groups were most likely to be suffering victims, and the retired were most likely to be the stoics, the people who grinned and bore the inflation. The complainers were rather evenly distributed in the various groups but were somewhat more likely to be concentrated in the blue collar group.

Chapter 4, based on qualitative data generated by depth interviews, showed how people in the various subsamples were affected by inflation and recession. We saw that for the poor, inflation meant a struggle for survival, as virtually all the poor families told us of their efforts to cut corners and get by from day to day. The time span of these poor families was extremely constricted. They could not think very far ahead, as all their energies were consumed in trying to get through each day. The blue collar families were not as bad off as the poor. Most of them were also forced to tighten their belts, curtail their consumption, and postpone plans, but some of them were not suffering from inflation. When we examined the middle class families that were interviewed, we found many who were not hurting at all from inflation. The typical middle class response to high prices was to cut back somewhat on the food budget by avoiding high-priced meats, but apart from cutting back on the frequency of steaks and roasts, the middle class families seemed to manage very well. The big cost to the middle class of inflation was the undermining of their long range plans to improve .their lot in life. Many of the middle class families we spoke to were unable to save and had to postpone their plans to buy a house or some other expensive commodity. As we noted, inflation wreaks havoc with the present lives of the poor and many working class families whereas it interferes with the future of the middle class families.

Part II dealt with some consequences of inflation and recession, both positive and negative responses. Chapter 5 dealt with strategies for coping with the pressures of inflation. The disparity between income and expenditures suggested a three part model for closing the gap: increasing input (income), reducing output (consumption), and increasing efficiency whereby the same income is used more effectively. This in turn led to a consideration of five strategies for coping with inflation: raising income, curtailing expenditures, greater self-reliance, bargain hunting, and sharing with others, the last three relating to efficiency. Each of these strategies was related to the others, suggesting that people will try everything they can to close the gap. Employing these strategies was very strongly related to inflation crunch, and the people who were most hurt by inflation were also the ones most ready to use these strategies with one exception. Successfully raising income is not merely a matter of effort. Many people were unable to work harder even though they wanted to; they could not get more overtime or find another job, and their spouses were unable to find a job. The poor and those of low income generally were not as successful as the more well-to-do in raising their income, especially among those who were hard hit by inflation. Inflation impact also explained why families curtailed consumption and resorted to sharing with others. These strategies were not related to the social chracteristics denoting privilege once subjective inflation crunch was held constant. But two of the strategies continued to be used more often by the have-nots even when inflation crunch was taken into account: greater self-reliance and bargain hunting. These might be considered the poor man's strategies for coping with inflation. In addition to these five coping patterns we considered a sixth way in which families might have tried to come to terms with rising prices, reliance on consumer credit. This turned out not to be a significant strategy, as many more families reported using credit less often than said they were using credit more often than formerly. It is important to note that we inquired only about consumer credit, the idea of buying goods on time, and did not consider other forms of credit, such as mortgage debt.

In Chapter 6 we considered the impact of inflation and recession on the family. A measure was developed that indicated whether financial pressures had strengthened or weakened the marriage. Some 40 percent of the sample said that the inflation had no impact on their marriage; 28 percent said that financial problems had drawn them closer to their spouse; 19 percent mentioned negative as well as positive consequences; and 14 percent said that inflationary pressures had only made their marriage worse. This measure of marital strain was strongly related to inflation crunch and recession impact. Those who were hard hit by inflation and recession were especially likely to report strains in their marriage. The social characteristics found to be related to inflation crunch were also related to marital strain, but these relationships turned out to be due to the connection of both to inflation crunch. When subjective crunch was held constant, the underprivileged were no more likely than the privileged to experience marital strain. Apart from the marital relationship, inflation was shown to have some impact on the parent-child relationship as well. The respondents were asked whether they had to deny things to their children because of financial pressures, and some 43 percent of the parents answered affirmatively. Both marital strain and child denial were related to the various coping strategies, suggesting that one reason why families make efforts to cope with inflationary pressures is the damage inflation does to their family life.

The impact of inflation and recession on mental health was examined in Chapter 7. Two measures of mental health were developed, one relating mental health directly to economic pressures and the other a more general measure of psychological well-being based on the balance of positive and negative feelings. The first index, what we called mental strain, showed that 52 percent of the sample managed to avoid any mental strain as a result of inflation, 24 percent experienced some strain, and 24 percent considerable strain as a result of inflationary pressures. The balance of feelings index showed that a majority of the sample had a favorable balance of feelings, with 27 percent reporting either more negative feelings or the same number of negative as positive feelings. These two measures of mental health were strongly related to both objective and subjective inflation crunch. The more people suffered from inflation crunch, the more likely was their mental health to suffer. The social characteristics related to inflation crunch were also related to mental health. The underprivileged in terms of income, occupation, ethnicity, and education reported much more mental strain than the privileged. When inflation crunch was introduced as a test variable, we found that these social characteristics continued to be related to mental strain among those who were suffering from inflation crunch. Among those who were not hurt by inflation, the social characteristics were not related to mental strain. In this group the have-nots were just as healthy mentally or emotionally as the haves. But when inflation caused suffering, the underprivileged were much more likely than the privileged to have this suffering translate into mental strain. This is yet another sign of the greater resources of the more well-to-do. Even when they are hit so hard by inflation that it hurts, they are still able to retain their equanimity. But when the have-nots are hurt by inflation, their mental health begins to crumble.

Part III of this book dealt with resources that might mitigate the impact of inflation and recession. Chapter 8 considered the role of welfare benefits in easing the pain of inflation and recession. Some 27 percent of the sample were receiving public benefits in the form of social security, unemployment insurance, welfare, or food stamps. When the retired were excluded, this number dropped to 16 percent of the sample. The recipients of public assistance were much more likely than the nonrecipients to have been hard hit by the inflation and recession, and they were much more likely to belong to the underprivileged groups in society, the poor, the semiskilled, and unskilled, and the blacks and Spanish-speaking. The critical question was whether receiving public assistance mitigated the pain of inflation and recession. To answer this question, we compared those who were suffering from inflation and recession and receiving assistance with those who were suffering to the same extent from these calamities but not receiving public assistance. In every instance we found that the recipients of public assistance were hurting more, not less, than the nonrecipients once objective inflation crunch and recession impact were held constant. Thus, on every level of inflation crunch and recession impact, those who received public benefits were more likely than those who did not to be suffering from inflation, to report marital strain, to have mental strain stemming from inflation, and to have a negative balance of feelings, a sign of unhappiness. Clearly, receiving public assistance did not make people whole again. Rather, it would seem that public assistance had the consequence of keeping people from going over the brink rather than restoring them to mental and social health. The data show that the stereotype of the recipients of assistance as living off the fat of the land is clearly wrong. They suffer much more than their brethren who were hit as hard by inflation and recession but were not receiving benefits.

Chapter 9 looked at the role of a most important asset in mitigating the impact of inflation and recession—home ownership. Most Americans own their own home, and this asset provides considerable protection from the ravages of inflation and recession since the value of the house appreciates considerably in inflationary times. The economist Alan Greenspan has noted that mortgage borrowing has risen to more than 60 billion dollars a year, which is roughly equal to the amount that homes appreciate in a year. This suggests that many people have been refinancing their homes and using the money they obtain to tide them over inflationary pressures. Unfortunately, we did not inquire about refinancing of homes and thus do not know the extent to which this strategy was employed in the sample surveyed. But we were able to compare homeowners with nonowners on how they were able to adjust to inflation and recession, and we found that in every instance the homeowners suffered less from inflation than the nonowners. Thus they were not as vulnerable to objective inflation crunch, they did not suffer as much as the nonowners from inflation, their marriages were less impaired, and they were better able than the nonowners to maintain their mental health. Clearly, home ownership is an important antidote to the pressures of inflation and recession.

Part IV of this book examined the impact of inflation and recession on the minds of the respondents, that is, such components of mind as values, attitudes, and beliefs. Given the impact of inflation and recession on the lives of many people, it seemed reasonable to expect that these economic crises would force people to rethink their orientations to life and change their ideas of what is important and unimportant. Chapter 10 explored these possible impacts of inflation and recession on selected attitudes and values. A measure was developed of lowering aspirations, and the data showed that those who were hard hit by inflation and recession were much more likely than the others to lower their aspirations. They were much more willing to lower their standard of living, to forego owning expensive things, and to lose confidence in the American dream. A second attitudinal area dealt with in Chapter 10 concerned faith in the free enterprise system. Three items that tapped this faith were belief that free enterprise is the best economic system, rejection of socialism as an alternative, and rejection of the idea that government should meddle in the job market by guaranteeing jobs to those who want to work. A majority in the sample accepted the dominant economic ideology in this country in that they had complete faith in free enterprise as the best economic system and were opposed to government interfering with the job market, that is, guaranteeing jobs. But those who were hard hit by inflation and recession were more opposed to this ideology than those who had escaped from inflation and recession. The underprivileged classes were much less committed to these ideologies than the privileged even when subjective inflation crunch was taken into account. Commitment to free enterprise is very much class related in our society independent of the pressures of inflation.

The final set of attitudes examined in Chapter 10 dealt with confidence in the various institutions of the federal government, Congress, the presidency, and Supreme Court. In the aftermath of Watergate, confidence in these institutions was quite low in general, and those who were hard hit by inflation and recession had even less confidence in the federal government than the others. Unlike commitment to free enterprise, confidence in government was not linked to the social statuses of privilege once subjective inflation crunch was controlled. The only reason the have-nots were more likely to lose confidence in government was that they were hard hit by inflation. When they did not suffer from inflation, they had about as much confidence in government (which was not very much) as the more privileged groups.

Chapter 11 dealt with the respondents' views of the causes of inflation and recession. We saw that most respondents blamed government and politicians for inflation rather than business and unions. The underprivileged were more likely to blame business while the more privileged were more likely to blame the unions. This chapter presented extensive qualitative data on the causes of inflation and recession, ranging from the greediness of unions and big business to the failures of various governmental programs, such as foreign aid, regulation of business, and welfare. Among the solutions to these economic problems offered by the respondents were government-guaranteed jobs, wage and price controls, and closing tax loopholes.

What all the findings that have been reviewed indicate is that inflation and recession did hurt many families, especially the underprivileged, but there was no wholesale breakdown of social or psychological life because of these economic setbacks. Many people escaped the ravages of inflation and recession altogether; most people did not have their marriages damaged by inflation and recession; most people did not experience mental strain because of these economic upheavals; and most people retained their faith in the free enterprise system even in the face of clear evidence that the system was not working well, i.e., inflation and recession. All of this is in keeping with the seeming equanimity of the populace in the face of these economic crises, the absence of marches, riots, and any signs of radicalization.

It may well be that public benefits, which keep the recipients from going over the brink even though they do not restore them to social health, and home ownership are the secret weapons that allow America to weather the storm of these economic disasters. But as noted, these economic calamities exacerbate the class divisions in society, and policy-makers would do well to solve the problems of inflation and recession before the class divisions break out into open conflict.

How Matters Stand Today

The research reported in this study, as noted, was carried out in the spring of 1976, when the inflation rate had declined from the 1974 peak of 11 percent to the more modest rate of 6.2 percent. As this is written in 1979, the inflation rate has soared back to double digits, and inflation continues to be the most pressing problem facing the nation. For more than six years now, the country has been suffering from rampant inflation, and there is every reason to believe that this problem will be with us for many years to come. President Carter's voluntary controls, in effect now for more than six months, have done little to stem the inflation tide as the figures released by the Bureau of Labor Statistics each month show an ever-increasing rate of inflation. Mandatory wage and price controls, although advocated by some, have been discredited by the Nixon administration's experience with price controls, which were effective in the short run but introduced serious distortions in the economy and resulted in rampant inflation when lifted. As this is written, the ship of state is very much adrift on the inflation issue. A solution is not in sight, and the long range effects of inflation can well prove disastrous to society as we know it.

In 1974, the highly prestigious journal *Skeptic* (Special Issue No. 3, October) published by the Forum of Contemporary History, devoted a special issue to inflation. The lead editorial of this issue warned that inflation can sap our freedom and bring down our democratic society in much the way that Weimar Germany was wiped out by inflation giving rise to Nazi Germany, and Uruguay in the past decade has been transformed from a thriving democracy to a bankrupt dictatorship under the pressure of inflation. To quote from this editorial,

> As stiff as inflation's toll has been up to now, it is nothing compared to the cost which confronts us at the end of the road. Unless we check inflation, it will cost us our freedom. And if that sounds too apocalyptic, consider the ways in which inflation has already chipped away at freedoms we have taken for granted. Our options in the marketplace are more limited than they used to be. . . . Our freedom of movement is circumscribed by the rising costs of operating a car. . . . Our freedom to locate where we choose is limited by soaring rents and real estate prices. . . . Our freedom to make plans of every imaginable sort, from having a baby to taking a vacation has been diminished by inflation. . . . Inflation has narrowed our choices and options. In the end it threatens to eliminate them entirely (p. 5).

Since this was written in 1974, our freedoms have diminished substantially more as the cost of living has climbed almost an additional 50 percent. The price of gasoline has doubled since then and the price of homes has soared as has the price of everything else. In 1976, when our survey was conducted, 35 percent of the people had lost confidence in the American dream and under the relentless pressure of inflation since then, the number who has lost confidence in the dream of success has risen substantially and is probably a majority of the population today. In 1976, it was primarily the poor and the working class who were suffering from inflation, and as our data showed, most of the middle class were relatively untouched by inflation. But polls since then show that inflation has now intruded upon the middle class as well. A March 1979 poll by Louis Harris shows that fully 69 percent of the population is having "a harder time making ends meet," an increase of 14 percent over the 55 percent who gave this answer in September of 1978. During the same period, the number of families who believe that inflation will outpace their incomes also increased sharply, from 30 to 49 percent.

As we saw in Chapters 10 and 11, many people are angry, angry with politicians whom they feel have betrayed them, angry with the myth that hard work will result in success as they find that their own hard work has not improved their lives in any way. In 1977, the movie Network achieved much acclaim as a satire of the television industry. One of its chief characters was a rather crazy, charismatic news commentator who won a large following through his outrageous declarations. At one point he urges the viewers to open their windows, stick out their heads and shout, "I'm mad as hell," and across the country millions of people carry out his instructions. This funny scene may not be too far from the mood of the country today. It is just conceivable that some charismatic figure might come along and unleash the reservoir of anger in the country today with untold consequences for the fabric of our society. Our democratic institutions seem so secure through the years that it is most unlikely that our country would slip into some kind of totalitarian state. But then we have never before known the shrinkage of our freedoms resulting from runaway inflation and, for that reason, even that dark outcome cannot be dismissed out of hand.

Certain forebodings are already at work in society. Proposition 13 was the manifestation of mindless anger with totalitarian overtones. The overwhelming majority who voted for Proposition 13 were ready to cut public services primarily to the underprivileged to protect their pocketbooks and, in so doing, they delivered a major bonanza to the landlords and corporations of California. The movement for a constitutional convention to pass a "balanced budget" amendment is another sign. This movement is based on the far from proven notion that inflation is caused by the federal government's deficit spending. Some twenty-eight states have already voted for such a convention, only six short of the necessary number. Meanwhile, civil libertarians and constitutional scholars are deeply worried about what might transpire at such an unprecedented event. They fear that other amendments might be pushed forward and adopted such as an antiabortion amendment or a school prayer amendment that would further reduce our freedom.

INFLATION AND THE ENERGY CRISIS

A major villain blamed for inflation has been the sharp rise in the price of oil brought about by OPEC (The Organization of Petroleum Exporting Countries). In the past six years, the price of oil has increased sharply. But the energy crisis is not merely a matter of scarcity of natural resources. It is also very much a political problem. There are vast reserves of natural energy in this country that wait to be developed. America has the largest coal supplies in the world that could be converted to oil; there is an enormous amount of oil locked into shale, and there are vast amounts of natural gas buried in the ground of America to say nothing of nuclear and solar energy. All it takes to develop these resources is money. But energy in America is the domain of private industry and the profit motive that guides private industry does not warrant vast expenditures of money on energy development. The only agency that has the capacity to carry out this development is the federal government, but were it to invest its billions in converting coal to oil and developing processes for extracting oil from shale or developing the natural gas fields, the cry would go out that this was socialism and not the American way. But some activities are reserved for the federal government such as the defense of the country and the exploration of space. No one objected when the Kennedy administration pledged billions of dollars to deliver a man to the moon nor have there been strong objections to the federal government spending hundreds of billions of dollars on defense. The reason is simple. Space and defense are not the turf of private industry. But were the federal government to move into energy development in a big way, it would be stepping on the toes of the seven big sisters, the gargantuan oil companies. And in America, corporate power pretty much runs things its own way. If the American public were given the opportunity to vote on whether it would permit the energy problem to be solved by the direct investment of federal monies, for example, whether it would approve of diverting billions of dollars from the space and defense budgets to energy development, there is little doubt how it would decide. And yet the American people is never given the opportunity to make such decisions.

INFLATION AND THE MILITARY BUDGET

If deficit spending by the federal government is a cause of inflation, then certainly the vast billions that are spent annually on defense must be a major cause of inflationary pressure. This military budget grows by leaps and bounds in spite of Arms Limitation Treaties with our major adversary, the Soviet Union. Even in 1979, when the Carter administration was determined to trim the federal budget to combat inflation, it still approved of a 3 percent increase in the military budget beyond the inflation rate. Serious critics of the military budget, such as the MIT physicist Philip Morrison, have pointed out that the country could be adequately defended with a defense budget only a third as large as the current budget of 127 billion dollars.[1] As Morrison points out, we do not need tens of thousands of nuclear warheads to present a devastating threat to the Soviet Union. And in an era in which the aircraft carrier is rapidly losing its utility just as the World War I hero, the battle ship, lost its value in World War II, there is no need to maintain thirteen aircraft carriers each with a large complement of supporting ships. Two or three would be adequate for this nuclear age. A recent Op Ed in the New York *Times* by the eminent scholar Alan Wolfe (April 18, 1979), entitled, "America's 'Frenzied Madness'" points out that the United States is in the process of destroying itself by spending sorely needed public funds on defense because of the mistaken notion that the Soviet Union is a military threat to it. As Wolfe points out, the Soviet Union is in the worst shape it has been in years. "Facing a

1. *The Price of Defense,* The Boston Study Group. New York: Times Books, 1979.

paralyzing economic crisis, dependent on the United States to provide bread to its own population suddenly surrounded by antagonistic superpowers on all sides, the Russians are acting like any weak power: They are spending more on arms in order to gain the illusion that they are strong." As Wolfe goes on to say, "the fantasists of American intelligence, mistaking this spending for belligerence, call for the United States to meet the threat."

There is even more concrete evidence that the Soviet Union is far from the belligerent enemy that threatens America's security. At no point during the years of devastation heaped upon its close ally Vietnam, did it come to the defense of that country against America's military might. And more recently the Soviet Union stood by while a presumably less powerful country, China, invaded Vietnam. It may well be that the Soviet Union has a major aversion to war stemming from the devastation of World War II which wiped out millions of Soviet citizens. If so then the Soviet Union poses little threat to any country, much less a mammoth superpower like the United States.

Were the "frenzied madness" that has swept America and its leaders to miraculously disappear and our defense budget reduced by two-thirds, the United States would be in a position to solve all its pressing problems. Inflation would disappear as would unemployment as the billions of dollars diverted from defense were invested in the civilian economy. It would be possible to solve once and for all the problem of poverty and· have a national health insurance system that would save Americans the billions they now spend on health care. The deteriorating cities could be rebuilt and eventually taxes could be reduced. This nirvana only awaits a return to reason, an end to the "frenzied madness."

APPENDIX

AUDITS & SURVEYS, INC.
One Park Avenue
New York, N.Y. 10016

5-1

INFLATION-RECESSION STUDY
SCREENING SHEET

Interviewer's Name _____ Respondent's Name _____

Interviewer's # _____ Telephone # ( ) _____
                                              Area Code

Location # _____ Address _____

Validated By: _____ City/State _____

Date of Validation: _____

Time Interview Started: _____
Time Interview Ended: _____
Total Time: _____

Date of Interview :: _____
                  Month   Day

COMPLETE A SCREENING FORM FOR <u>ALL</u> RESPONDENTS AND
RETURN WITH YOUR MATERIALS:

BE SURE TO ATTACH EACH COMPLETED SCREENING FORM TO
THE COMPLETED QUESTIONNAIRE.

Hello, may I speak to the man or lady of the house?

Hello, I'm _____ of AUDITS & SURVEYS, a national research company. We are doing a survey of how families are coping with the economy, that is, rising prices and the recession. We would like to ask you a few questions.

1.   First, how many people live in this household?

_____   21-22

IF ONE, TERMINATE

2.   Would you tell me the names of the people in this household, starting with yours, then the name of your spouse, followed by the other family members, in order by age, and would you tell me their relation to you, such as son or daughter?

3.   Now, would you tell me their actual ages?

First Name	Relation		Age	
	wife			33
a. _____	husband	23 ___		34
	husband			35
b. _____	wife	24 ___		36
				37
c. _____	___	25 ___		38
				39
d. _____	___	26 ___		40
				41
e. _____	___	27 ___		42
				43
f. _____	___	28 ___		44
				45
g. _____	___	29 ___		46
				47
h. _____	___	30 ___		48
				49
i. _____	___	31 ___		50
				51
j. _____	___	32 ___		52

4.   Who is the chief wage earner in the family?

Respondent, male head.   1   53
Respondent's spouse, male head. . .   2
Respondent, female head   3
Respondent's spouse, female head .   4
Other (specify)   5
No wage earner (unemployed)   6
No wage earner (retired)   7

5.   What is your (his) (Chief Wage Earner) regular occupation?   54
                                                                       55
       _____   56

6.   In what kind of business (industry) do you (does your spouse) generally work?

                                                                       57
                                                                       58
       _____   59

CLASSIFY OCCUPATION OF CWE

Blue Collar.   1   60
White Collar   2
Unclassified   3
Retired   4

IF "UNCLASSIFIED," TERMINATE. OTHERWISE GO ON TO THE INTERVIEW.

7a.   Over the past couple of years, has your income kept up with the rising cost of living or has it fallen behind?

Kept up.   1   ASK 7b   6
Fallen behind   2   ASK 8

IF "KEPT UP" TO 7a, ASK:

7b.   Are you better off financially now than you were a few years ago, or are you just staying even?

Better off.   1   7
Staying even   2

IF "FALLEN BEHIND" TO 7a, ASK:

8.   Are you a little worse off or a lot worse off now than you were a few years ago?

                              Little worse off.   1   8
                              A lot worse off   2

ASK QUESTIONS 9 THROUGH 14 IN TERMS OF THE CHIEF WAGE EARNER (CWE)

9a.   Are you (is the CWE) currently employed?

                              Yes.   1   ASK 9b   9
                              No   2   ASK 14a

      IF "EMPLOYED" IN 9a, ASK:

9b.   How many jobs do you (does the CWE) have?

                              Number of jobs _____   10

      IF MORE THAN 1, ASK 9c; OTHERWISE SKIP TO 10.

      IF MORE THAN ONE JOB IN 9b, ASK:

9c.   What is the other job?

                                                                                     11
                                                                                     12
                              _____   13

9d.   How many hours do you (does he) work at it?

                              Number of hours _____   14–15

9e.   Did you (he) have to take a second job in order to increase your income?

                              Yes.   1   16
                              No   2

10.   Are you (CWE) self-employed?

                              Yes.   1   17
                              No   2

11a. Is the kind of job you (CWE) now have your (his) regular occupation?

                              Yes.   1   ASK 12a   18
                              No   2   ASK 11b

IF "NO" TO 11a, ASK:

11b. What is your (his) current job?

                                                   19

                                                   20

           _____   21

11c. Why aren't you (isn't he) working at your (his) regular occupation?

               Laid off. 1   22
               Other (specify) 2

               _____

12a. In the past few years, did you (CWE) lose a job because of a down-turn in the economy?

               Yes. 1   ASK 12b 23
               No 2   ASK 13

    IF "YES" TO 12a, ASK:

12b. How many times did this happen?

               Number of times _____   24

12c. Was that your main job or secondary job?

               Main job 1   25
               Secondary job. 2

12d. How many weeks were you (was he) out of work?

               Number of weeks _____   26–27

13. How worried are you (is he) that you (he) will lose your (his) job — very worried, somewhat worried or not at all worried?

               Very worried 1   28
               Somewhat worried. 2
               Not at all worried 3
               NA. 4

IF "NO" TO 9a (CWE UNEMPLOYED), ASK 14a-d. OTHERWISE SKIP TO 15a.

14a. How did you (he) lose your job?

_____   29

14b. How many weeks have you (has he) been unemployed?

Number of weeks _____   30–31

14c. Are you (is he) collecting unemployment insurance?

Yes.   1   32
No   2

14d. Are you receiving public assistance?

Yes.   1   33
No   2

15a. Did anyone else living in this household lose a job because of the recession?

Yes.   1   ASK 15b   34
No   2   ASK 16a

IF "YES" TO 15a, ASK:

15b. Who?

Husband   1   35
Wife   2
Son.   3
Daughter   4
Other (specify)   5

_____

16a. Did anyone living in this household have to stop work in the past few years for other reasons?

Yes.   1   ASK 16b   36
No   2   ASK 17a

IF "YES" TO 16a, ASK:

16b. What was the reason?

_____   37

17a. Has anyone in this hosehold been forced to work a shorter week because of the downturn in the economy?

Yes.............	1	ASK 17b 38
No	2	ASK 18a
NA.............	3	

IF "YES" TO 17a, ASK:

17b. Who?

CWE.............	1	39
Spouse	2	
Both.............	3	
Child.............	4	
Other (specify)	5	

_____

18a. Was anyone in the household forced to work less overtime?

Yes.............	1	ASK 18b 40
No	2	ASK 19a

IF "YES" TO 18a, ASK:

18b. Who?

CWE.............	1	41
Spouse	2	
Both.............	3	
Child.............	4	
Other (specify)	5	

_____

19a. Has anyone in this household been forced to work harder because of layoffs or staff shortages?

Yes.............	1	ASK 19b 42
No	2	ASK 20

IF "YES" TO 19a, ASK:

19b. Who?

CWE.............	1	43
Spouse	2	
Both.............	3	
Child.............	4	
Other (specify)	5	

_____

20. During the recession, were a lot of people laid off where you (CWE) work, some, or hardly any?

A lot	1	44
Some	2	
Hardly any	3	
NA	4	

21a. Does your wife (do you) have a job?

Yes	1	ASK 21b	45
No	2	ASK 22a	

IF "YES" TO 21a, ASK:

21b. What kind of work does she (do you) do?

46
47
_____ 48

21c. How worried is your wife (are you) that she (you) will lose her (your) job? READ LIST.

Very worried	1	49
Somewhat worried	2	
Not at all worried	3	

ASK QUESTIONS 22 AND 23 IN TERMS OF THE CWE.

22a. Do you (does CWE) belong to union?

Yes	1	ASK 22b	50
No	2	ASK 23	

IF "YES" TO 22a, ASK:

22b. Which one?

51
_____ 52

23. Are your wages (CWE's wages) tied to a cost of living increase so that your (his) pay goes up if the cost of living goes up?

Yes	1	53
No	2	

24a. In the past few years, has someone in your family been forced to go to work to help make ends meet?

Yes.	1	ASK 24b	54
No	2	ASK 25	

IF "YES" TO 24a, ASK:

24b. Who?

Spouse	1	55
Child.	2	
Other (specify)	3	

_____

25. Have you (CWE) tried to work more overtime in order to make ends meet?

Yes.	1	56
No	2	
NA	3	

26. Compared with your friends, would you say you have been hit harder by the inflation and recession than they have, less hard or about the same?

Harder.	1	57
Less hard	2	
Same.	3	

And now some questions about how you have changed your spending patterns.

27a. Have you changed your food shopping or eating habits to save money?

Yes.	1	ASK 27b	58
No	2	ASK 28a	

IF "YES" TO 27a, ASK:

27b. In what way?

_____ 59

_____ 60

28a. Have you changed your transportation patterns in any way so as to save money?

                    Yes. 1   ASK 28b   61
                    No 2   ASK 29a

IF "YES" TO 28a, ASK:

28b. In what way?

        _____   62
        _____   63

29a. Have you changed your clothes buying patterns in any way to save money?

                    Yes. 1   ASK 29b   64
                    No 2   ASK30a

IF "YES" TO 29a, ASK:

29b. In what way?

        _____   65
        _____   66

30a. Have you changed your vacation patterns so as to save money?

                    Yes. 1   ASK 30b   67
                    No 2   ASK 31

IF "YES" TO 30a, ASK:

30b. In what way?

        _____   68
        _____   69

31. Do you eat out in restaurants now less often than you used to?

                    Yes. 1   70
                    No 2

32. Do you go to the movies and other entertainment less often now than you used to?:

                    Yes. 1   71
                    No 2

33. Have you had to put off medical care for yourself or your family to save money?

> Yes. 1   72
> No 2

34. Have you had to put off dental care to save money?

> Yes. 1   73
> No 2

35. Have you had to get rid of any pets because you couldn't afford to feed them?

> Yes. 1   74
> No 2
> No pets 3

36. Have you moved to a different place (to live) in order to save money?

> Yes. 1   75
> No 2

37a. Have you made any other changes in your way of life in order to save money?

> Yes. 1   ASK 37b   76
> No 2   ASK 38

IF "YES" TO 37a, ASK:

37b. What?

> _____   77
> _____   78

38. Because of the high cost of living, have you joined any groups, like a food buying club, to save money?

> Yes. 1   79
> No 2

39a. Because of the high cost of living, have your friends been helping you . . . (READ LIST) (RECORD UNDER 39a BELOW)

39b. Have you been helping your friends . . . (READ LIST) (RECORD UNDER 39b BELOW)

	39a			39b		
	Yes	No		Yes	No	
with repairs?	1	2	6	1	2	12
by lending money?	1	2	7	1	2	13
by babysitting?	1	2	8	1	2	14
by sharing food?	1	2	9	1	2	15
by exchanging clothes?	1	2	10	1	2	16
by sharing transportation?	1	2	11	1	2	17

40. Do you now make household repairs or auto repairs yourself when before you used to hire people to do this?

Yes. 1   18
No 2

41. Have you taken in boarders, relatives or friends to save costs of housing or rent?

Yes. 1   19
No 2

42. Have you doubled up with another family to save housing costs?

Yes. 1   20
No 2

43. Have you taken out any loans in the past year or so?

Yes. 1   21
No 2

44. In order to make ends meet, have you sold any stock, jewelry, insurance, property or any other valuables?

Yes. 1   22
No 2

45. Do you spend more money now than you used to on lotteries, sweepstakes, the numbers or horses in hopes of hitting it rich, less, or about the same?

More.   1   23
Less   2
Same.   3
Never gamble   4

46. Were you in more financial trouble a year ago than you are today,
     less or about the same?

More.   1   24
Less   2
Same.   3

47a. During the past year or so, have you made any major purchases, such
      as furniture, appliances or cars?

Yes.   1   ASK 47b   25
No   2   ASK 48a
      IF "YES" TO 47a, ASK:

47b. What did you buy?

_____   26

48a. Are you now planning to make any major purchases?

Yes.   1   ASK 48b   27
No   2   ASK 49a
      IF "YES" TO 48a, ASK:

49b. What?

_____   28

49a. Have you postponed any major purchases that you would normally
      have made?

Yes.   1   ASK 49b   29
No   2   ASK 50
      IF "YES" TO 49a, ASK:

49b. What?

_____   30

50. Do you and your friends talk about the high cost of living a lot, somewhat, or hardly at all?

A lot	1	31
Somewhat	2	
Hardly at all	3	

51. Are you buying more things on credit than you used to, less, or about the same?

More	1		32
Less	2	ASK 51	
Same	3		
Never use credit	4	ASK 54	

52. Are you having difficulties maintaining the payments on your credit purchases?

Yes	1	33
No	2	
NA	3	

53. Are you now behind on your payments?

Yes	1	34
No	2	
NA	3	

54. How much are you worried about your debt burdens – a lot, somewhat, or not at all?

A lot	1	35
Somewhat	2	
Not at all	3	

55. In the past few years, have you had anything you bought on time repossessed?

Yes	1	36
No	2	

56. Have you had your wages garnished in the past few years?

Yes	1	37
No	2	

57a. Have you seriously considered filing for bankruptcy?

       Yes. . . . . 1 ASK 57b 38
       No . . . . 2 ASK 58

  IF "YES" TO 57a, ASK:

57b. Did you in fact file for bankruptcy?

       Yes. . . . . 1 ASK 58 39
       No . . . . 2 ASK 57c

  IF "NO" TO 57b, ASK:

57c. Why didn't you?

      _____ 40
      _____ 41

58. I'm now going to read to you a list of statements about inflation that might apply to you. For each one, tell me whether you agree or disagree. (READ LIST)

	Agree	Disagree	DK/NA	
a. Inflation is depressing me; it's as if it will never end.	1	2	3	42
b. The economy is getting better; soon things will be as good as ever.	1	2	3	43
c. I'm earning more than I ever did and can't save a penny.	1	2	3	44
d. Things are so bad that I've had to go into my savings.	1	2	3	45
e. We can't afford to send our children to college because of the high cost of education.	1	2	3	46
f. We are on the brink of poverty.	1	2	3	47
g. It is easier to make ends meet now than it was a year ago.	1	2	3	48
h. We've never been hurt so hard before; everything is turning into a hardship.	1	2	3	49

58.   (CONTINUED)

		Agree	Disagree	DK/NA	
i.	The money we earn is becoming worthless.	1	2	3	50
j.	Because of inflation, we are scrimping and doing without.	1	2	3	51
k.	We mostly buy the things that are on sale.	1	2	3	52
l.	Things have always been bad for us; inflation makes no difference.	1	2	3	53
m.	To economize on food, I sometimes skip a meal.	1	2	3	54
n.	We've stopped buying any luxury items.	1	2	3	55
o.	We've even stopped buying many things we need.	1	2	3	56
p.	As a result of inflation, we buy lower quality items.	1	2	3	57
q.	We have had to cut back on our insurance policies.	1	2	3	58
r.	We now repair a lot of things we used to throw away.	1	2	3	59
s.	Things have gotten so bad that many people have to do illegal things in order to survive.	1	2	3	60

59a.   What is your current marital status?

Married	1	ASK 60 61
Divorced	2	ASK 59b
Separated.	3	
Widowed	4	ASK 68a
Single	5	

IF "DIVORCED" OR "SEPARATED" TO 59a, ASK:

59b. Did recent financial problems contribute to the breakup of your marriage?

                Yes. 1   62

                No 2

SKIP TO 68a.

60. Have the financial pressures drawn you and your wife (husband) closer together?

                Yes. 1   63

                No 2

61. Have the financial pressures contributed to tensions in your marriage?

                Yes. 1   64

                No 2

62. Do you and your wife (husband) quarrel more these days about money than you used to?

                Yes. 1   65

                No 2

63a. Do you think your wife (husband) could do a better job than he (she) is now doing to save money?

                Yes. 1   ASK 63b 66

                No 2   ASK 64

IF "YES" TO 63a, ASK:

63b. Are you annoyed because your wife (husband) is not doing a better job?

                Yes. 1   67

                No 2

64. Do you and your wife (husband) spend more time at home than you used to?

                Yes. 1   68

                No 2

65. Have the economic pressures led you and your wife (husband) to understand each other better?

> Yes.   1   69
>
> No   2

66. Have the economic pressures confronting you family made your marriage better, worse, or has it remained the same?

> Better   1   70
>
> Worse   2
>
> Same.   3

67. Everything considered, how would you describe your marriage? Would you say your marriage is very happy, pretty happy, or not too happy?

> Very happy   1   71
>
> Pretty happy   2
>
> Not too happy   3

68a. Is there one person in your family who has been particularly hurt by the combination of inflation and recession?

> Yes.   1   ASK 68b   72
>
> No   2   ASK 69

IF "YES" TO 68a, ASK:

68b. Who?

> Husband   1   73
>
> Wife   2
>
> Child.   3
>
> Other (specify)   4

_____

68c. Why?

_____   74

69. Do you or your spouse have any dependent children who do not live in this household?

> Yes.   1   75
>
> No   2

IF NO CHILDREN IN HOUSE OR NO OTHER DEPENDENT CHIL-
DREN, SKIP TO 76a.

70. Do your children understand the financial pressures you're under?

Yes. 1   76
No 2
Children too young 3

71. Do they cooperate in trying to save money by being careful about
electricity, household supplies, and groceries?

Yes. 1   77
No 2

72a. Have you found it necessary to deny your children things they have
wanted because of a lack of money?

Yes. 1   ASK 72b   78
No 2

IF "YES" TO 72a, ASK:

72b. Has this led to quarrels and tensions with your children or have they
understood the problem?

Led to tensions 1   79
Understood problem . . . 2

5–4

72c. Does it bother you to deny your children things they want?

Yes. 1   6
No 2

73. Have any of your children had to postpone going to college because
of the money pinch?

Yes. 1   7
No 2
NA. 3

74. Have any of your children had to postpone plans for marriage
because of the economic situation?

Yes. 1   8
No 2
NA. 3

75. Has the economic situation led any of your children to stay at home, when ordinarily they would have moved out on their own?

          Yes. 1   9
          No 2
          NA 3

76a. Has the economic situation had any effect on your plans for (more) children?

          Yes. 1   ASK 76b   10
          No 2   ASK 77

    IF "YES" TO 76a, ASK:

76b. In what way?

          _____   11
          _____   12

Now, I'd like to ask you some questions about how you're feeling these days.

77. Because of the financial pressures, do you find yourself frequently depressed?

          Yes. 1   13
          No 2

78. Do you find yourself worrying a lot about how you're going to make ends meet?

          Yes. 1   14
          No 2

79. Do you find yourself easily irritated and annoyed these days?

          Yes. 1   15
          No 2

80. Because of financial pressures, do you find yourself so mad that you're almost ready to hit somebody?

          Yes. 1   16
          No 2

81. Do the financial pressures ever make you want to scream or shout in anger?

    Yes. 1   17
    No 2

82. Do you find yourself more forgiving these days of people who resort to stealing in order to get by?

    Yes. 1   18
    No 2

83. Because of the economic pressures, have you considered doing things that might be illegal in order to make ends meet?

    Yes. 1   19
    No 2

84. Have you surprised yourself with how you have been able to save money and cope with things?

    Yes. 1   20
    No 2

85. Has the economic squeeze led you to discover certain talents that you didn't know you had, like fixing things yourself?

    Yes. 1   21
    No 2

86a. Have the economic pressures led to a drinking problem for any member of your family?

    Yes. 1   ASK 86b   22
    No 2   ASK 87a

    IF "YES" TO 86a, ASK:

86b. Who?

    Respondent 1   23
    Spouse 2
    Child. 3
    Other (specify) 4

Now, I'm going to read you some statements and I'd like you to tell me whether they are true or false as they apply to you. (READ STATE-MENTS)

		True	False	
87a.	When I make plans, I'm certain that I can make them work.	1	2	24
87b.	Many times I feel I have little control over the things that happen to me.	1	2	25
87c.	What one gets out of life is more a matter of luck than anything else.	1	2	26
87d.	I feel I can get pretty much what I want out of life if only I work at it.	1	2	27
87e.	People like me have nothing to say about how things are run in this country.	1	2	28

88. Compared with how you used to feel, during the past few weeks have you frequently felt: (READ LIST)

		Yes	No	
a.	Nervous and tense?	1	2	29
b.	Headachy?	1	2	30
c.	Particularly excited or interested in something?	1	2	31
d.	Lonely and remote?	1	2	32
e.	Bored?	1	2	33
f.	That things were going your way?	1	2	34
g.	Dizzy?	1	2	35
h.	Pleased about having accomplished something	1	2	36
i.	Upset because someone criticized you?	1	2	37
j.	Proud because someone complimented you on something?	1	2	38
k.	Very unhappy?	1	2	39
l.	On top of the world?	1	2	40

Now, I'd like to ask you how inflation and recession have affected your beliefs in things.

89. First off, who do you think is <u>most</u> at fault for so much inflation? (READ LIST)

Big business   1   41
Unions   2
Government   3
Politicians   4
Welfare   5
Other (specify)   6

90. Do you think our free enterprise economy is the best economic system or do you think some other system is better?

Yes.   1   42
No   2
Don't know   3

91. Do you think a socialist kind of system would be better or worse than what we have now?

Yes.   1   43
No   2
Don't know   3

92a. Has the combination of inflation and recession led you to change your views about the political party you support?

Yes.   1   ASK 92b   44
No   2   ASK 93

IF "YES" TO 92a, ASK:

92b. In what way?

_____   45
_____   46

93. Do you consider yourself now a Republican, Democrat, Independent, or what?

Republican.   1   47
Democrat.   2
Independent.   3
Other   4

94a. Do you think you will vote in the Presidential election next fall?

Yes.	1	ASK 94b	48
No	2	ASK 95	
Don't know	3	ASK 94b	

IF "YES" OR "DON'T KNOW" TO 94a, ASK:

Republican.	1	49
Democrat.	2	
Other	3	
Not sure	4	

95. How would you describe your political orientation: would you say you are a conservative, moderate, liberal, or radical?

Conservative.	1	50
Moderate	2	
Liberal	3	
Radical	4	

96. Do you think that government is obligated to find a job for everyone who wants to work?

Yes.	1	51
No	2	

97. I'm going to name a number of institutions in our society. For each one, tell me whether you now have a lot of confidence in it, some confidence, or hardly any confidence at all. (READ LIST)

	Lot of Confidence	Some Confidence	Hardly Any Confidence	
a. Labor unions	1	2	3	52
b. Big business	1	2	3	53
c. Congress	1	2	3	54
d. The Supreme Court.	1	2	3	55
e. The Presidency	1	2	3	56
f. The medical profession. . .	1	2	3	57
g. The legal profession.	1	2	3	58
h. Religious institutions	1	2	3	59
i. T.V. news shows	1	2	3	60
j. The schools	1	2	3	61

98.   Do you find yourself, <u>more</u> interested in owning expensive things than you used to be, <u>less</u> interested, or has there been no change?

More.   1   62
Less   2
No change   3

99.   Would you be willing to give up some of your comforts if this would insure a solution to unemployment and inflation?

Yes.   1   63
No   2
No comforts.   3

100. Compared to a few years ago, would you say your standard of living is higher, lower, or about the same?

Higher.   1   64
Lower.   2
About the same.   3

101. Have you decided to lower your standard of living so as to make ends meet?

Yes.   1   65
No   2

102a. Do you find that the events of the past couple of years have led you to lose confidence in the American dream?

Yes.   1   ASK 102b 66
No   2   ASK 103a

IF "YES" TO 102a, ASK:

102b. In what way?

_____   67
_____   68

103a. Do you have any ideas about how to improve the economy or prevent high inflation and unemployment?

Yes.   1   ASK 103b 69
No   2   ASK 104a

IF "YES" TO 103a, ASK:

103b. What?

           _____ 70

           _____ 71

Finally, a few questions about your background.

104a. In what state were you born?

                                            72

           _____ 73

194b. What about your wife (husband)?

                                            74

           _____ 75

105a. Were you brought up mostly on a farm, in a town, a small city, or a large city?

Farm.	1	76
Town	2	
Small city	3	
Large city	4	

105b. What about your wife (husband)?

Farm.	1	76
Town	2	
Small city	3	
Large city	4	
NA	5	

5–5

106a. What kind of work did your father (guardian) do for a living when you were growing up?

                                            6

                                            7

           _____ 8

106b. What about your wife's (husband's) father?

                                            9

                                           10

           _____ 11

107a. When you were growing up, was your family's financial situation above average, average, or below average?

Above average.	1	12
Average	2	
Below average.	3	

107b. What about your wife's (husband's) family?

Above average.	1	13
Average	2	
Below average.	3	
NA	4	

108a. What was the highest grade of school that you completed? (DO NOT READ LIST)

8th grade or less	1	14
Some high school	2	
High school grad	3	
Technical school	4	
Some college	5	
College grad	6	
Postgrad	7	

108b. What about your wife (husband)? (DO NOT READ LIST)

8th grade or less	1	15
Some high school	2	
High school grad	3	
Technical school	4	
Some college	5	
College grad	6	
Postgrad	7	
NA	8	

109a. In what religion were you raised?

Protestant	1	16
Catholic.	2	
Jewish.	3	
Other	4	
None.	5	

109b. What about your wife (husband)?

Protestant	1	17
Catholic.	2	
Jewish.	3	
Other	4	
None.	5	
NA	6	

110a. What is your religion today?

Protestant	1	18
Catholic.	2	
Jewish.	3	
Other	4	
None.	5	

110b. What about your wife (husband)?

Protestant	1	19
Catholic.	2	
Jewish.	3	
Other	4	
None.	5	
NA	6	

111. How religious would you say you are: very religious, somewhat religious, or not at all religious?

Very religious	1	20
Somewhat religious	2	
Not at all religious	3	

112. Do you own your own home?

Yes.	1	21
No	2	

113. Did your family have any income last year from rent on property you own?

Yes.	1	22
No	2	

114. Did your family have any income last year from stocks and bonds?

Yes.	1	23
No	2	

115.   Are you or your wife (husband) receiving social security?

                              Yes.   1   24
                              No   2

116.   Do you get any money from a pension?

                              Yes.   1   25
                              No   2

117.   Do you get any money from public assistance?

                              Yes.   1   26
                              No   2

118.   Are you now getting food stamps?

                              Yes.   1   27
                              No   2

119.   Are you (is your wife) receiving alimony or child support?

                              Yes.   1   28
                              No   2

120a. Do you have any other sources of income?

                              Yes.   1   ASK 120b 29
                              No   2   ASK 121a

       IF "YES" TO 120a, ASK:

120b. What?

                              _____   30

121a. Are you (is your husband) paying alimony or child support?

                              Yes.   1   ASK 121b 31
                              No   2   ASK 122a

       IF "YES" TO 121a, ASK:

121b. What percent of your (his) income do you pay in alimony or child support?

                              _____%   32–33

122a. Taking everything into account, what was your total family income
before taxes last year (1975)?

$_____   34–37

IF "DK" OR "REFUSED," ASK 122b. OTHERWISE SKIP TO 124a.

122b. Would you tell me which of these income categories was your total
family income of last year? (SHOW INCOME CARD)

Less than $3,000.   1   38–39
$4,000 to $4,999   2
$5,000 to $6,999   3
$7,000 to $8,999   4
$9,000 to $10,999.   5
$11,000 to $12,999.   6
$13,000 to $14,999.   7
$15,000 to $16,999.   8
$17,000 to $19,999.   9
$20,000 to $24,999.   10
$25,000 to $29,999.   11
$30,000 to $34,999.   12
$35,000 or more   13
Refused.   14

123a. What do you think will be your total income from all sources this
year?

$_____   40–43

IF "DK" OR "REFUSED," ASK 123b. OTHERWISE SKIP TO 124a.

123b. Would you tell me which of these income categories you think will
be your total income from all sources this year? (SHOW INCOME
CARD)

Less than $3,000.   1   44–45
$4,000 to $4,999   2
$5,000 to $6,999   3
$7,000 to $8,999   4
$9,000 to $10,999.   5
$11,000 to $12,999.   6
$13,000 to $14,999.   7
$15,000 to $16,999.   8
$17,000 to $19,999.   9
$20,000 to $24,999.   10

123b. (CONTINUED)

                $25,000 to $29,999. 11
                $30,000 to $34,999. 12
                $35,000 or more 13
                Refused. 14

124a. Now, think back three years to 1973. What was your total family income back in 1973?

                $_____   46–49

IF "DK," ASK 125b. IF "REFUSED," ASK 124b. OTHERWISE SKIP
TO 126.
TO 126.

124b. Would you tell me which of these categories was your total family income in 1973? (SHOW INCOME CARD)

                Less than $3,000. 1   50–51
                $4,000 to $4,999 2
                $5,000 to $6,999 3
                $7,000 to $8,999 4
                $9,000 to $10,999. 5
                $11,000 to $12,999. 6
                $13,000 to $14,999. 7
                $15,000 to $16,999. 8
                $17,000 to $19,999. 9
                $20,000 to $24,999. 10
                $25,000 to $29,999. 11
                $30,000 to $34,999. 12
                $35,000 or more 13
                Refused. 14

125a. IF "DK" TO 124b, ASK:

Will you earn more money this year than you did in 1973, the same amount, or less?

                More. 1   ASK 125b 52
                Same. 2   ASK 126
                Less 3   ASK 125b

IF "MORE" OR "LESS" TO 124a, ASK:

125b. How much more (less): 10 percent, 25 percent, 50 percent, or what?

                _____%   53–54

TO BE COMPLETED BY THE INTERVIEWER FOLLOWING THE INTERVIEW.

126.   Total length of time of the interview.

Hours _____   55
&   56
Minutes _____   57

127.   Race of respondent.

White   1   58
Black   2
Spanish-speaking   3
Oriental.   4
Other (specify)   5

_____

128.   Sex of respondent.

Male   1   59
Female   2

129a. Was anyone else present during part of the interview?

Yes.   1   ANS. 129b 60
No   2   ANS. 130

IF "YES" TO 129a, ANSWER:

129b. Who?

Spouse   1   61
Children   2
Other (specify)   3

_____

130.   In general, what was the respondent's attitude toward the interview?

Friendly and eager.   1   62
Cooperative, but not
particularly eager.   2
Indifferent and bored.   3
Hostile   4

131. Type of dwelling.

Single family, detached. . . .	1	63
Single family, attached	2	
Two, three units	3	
Four to six units	4	
Small apartment house	5	
Large apartment house	6	

132. Condition of furnishings.

Good	1	64
Average	2	
Poor	3	

133. Condition of neighborhood.

Expensive houses.	1	65
Modest houses	2	
Run-down houses	3	

134. Is this a racially segregated neighborhood?

Yes.	1	66
No	2	

INDEX

INDEX

American dream, 188, 190, 207, 252, 255
Anxiety, 139
Aspirations. See Lowered aspirations
Assets. See Homeownership, Savings
Atlanta, 26, 31, 40, 173
Automation, 218, 231

Balance of feelings index, 167-168, 170, 175, 250-251
"Balanced budget" amendment, 256-257
Bargain hunting, 91, 97, 98-99, 102, 106-110, 112, 117, 130, 248-249
Blue collar workers, 26, 28, 32-33, 35, 41, 46, 51, 64-74, 87, 104, 107-109, 112, 126, 128, 132, 134, 150, 152, 165-166, 198, 245-248
  homeownership, 174, 179-180
  reliance on credit, 115
Bradburn, Norman, 141, 143-144
Business, 200-201, 211-213, 216, 218-222, 224-225, 253, 258
  regulation of, 216, 225-226, 253

Carter, Jimmy, 10, 209
  administration of, 254, 258
Causes of inflation and recession, 211-212
Children, effect on, 131-137, 249
Cities, impact on, 23, 26, 30-31, 36, 244
City University of New York, 60
Confidence in government, 18, 188, 202-209, 253
Congress, confidence in, 203, 209, 253
Conspiratorial theory of economic control, 221, 223-225
Consumer demand, 231, 240-241

Consumer interest lobby, 116, 226
Consumption, curtailing of, 10-11, 17, 41, 86-87, 91, 94-97, 102, 104, 106, 108-110, 114, 123, 130, 132-134, 247-248
Coping strategies, 11, 18, 114, 129-131, 135, 137, 151, 212, 248. See also Bargain hunting; Curtailing of consumption; Efforts to raise income; Self-reliance, Sharing of resources
Cost of living, 9, 21-24, 37, 255
Credit, 91, 114-117, 173, 184, 249, 251-252
Crime, 62-64, 94, 133

Depression, 140, 146. See also Mental strain
Detroit, 26, 31, 40, 173
Double digit inflation, 9, 21

Economic growth, 11
Education, 28, 30, 33, 36, 42, 46-48, 51, 107, 117, 127-128, 132, 134-135, 165, 167, 174, 183, 198-199, 205, 245-247, 259
  and mental strain, 150, 152, 154-156
Energy crisis, 257-258
Ethnic groups, 32-36, 41-44, 46, 48-51, 106-107, 111-112, 117, 136, 165-166, 174, 182-183, 198-199, 205, 213, 216, 245-247, 250-251
  attempts to raise income, 104, 111
  marital strain, 127, 137, 182-183
  mental strain, 150, 153-154, 156
  public assistance, 165-167
  reliance on credit, 115

Familial stability, 11, 22-23, 119-125, 135-136. See also Children, effect on; Marital stress
Family planning, 135-137
Family size, 24, 29-30, 43-44, 51, 107, 132, 136
  and marital strain, 128, 136
Fixed incomes, effect on, 10. See also Retired persons
Food costs, 61, 95-96
Food stamps, 11, 17, 57, 162, 250
Ford Gerald R., 9
Free enterprise, 18, 188, 195-202, 205, 252-254
Frustration, 139
Full employment, 229-230

Germany, 255
G.I. Bill, 69
Government:
  regulation, 216, 225-226
  role of, 6, 8, 162, 195, 200, 212-213, 216, 222, 224-230, 253
  spending, 216, 225-230, 236, 256-259
  See also Confidence in government
Great Depression, 10-11, 17, 30, 161-162, 184, 243
Greenspan, Alan, 173, 251

Happiness, 141, 143, 145, 148, 168, 170-171, 175, 178-180, 251
Harris Poll (March 1979), 255-256
Health care costs, 58, 60, 77, 95-96, 240, 259
Homeownership, 17-18, 67, 71, 75, 87, 174, 179-183, 251-252, 254. See also Property values

Illegal activities, 62-64, 92-93, 235
Income, 10-11, 23-25, 27-30, 35-36, 41-44, 46, 48-51, 53-64, 87, 101, 104, 106, 108-110, 134, 136, 150, 153, 156, 165-166, 174, 179, 181-183, 205, 209, 213, 236, 245
  and marital strain, 127-128, 136
  and public assistance, 165, 251
  and reliance on credit, 115
  declining, 34, 42-43, 163, 244

efforts to raise, 17, 91, 92-94, 102, 104-105, 108-114, 116-117, 235, 248
  illegal, 93
  reduced by:
    layoffs, 16, 31-32, 34-35, 112-113
    less overtime, 31-33, 69, 244
    shorter work week, 31-33, 112
Inflation, impact of. See Objective inflation crunch; Subjective inflation crunch
Inflationary spiral, 230
Interest rates, 240

Job loss, 162, 187, 244
  to immigrants, 228
Jobs guaranteed by government, 36, 195-196, 198, 200, 225, 236-239, 252-253
Jobs, multiple, 50-51, 65, 72, 81, 92, 94, 104, 109

Keynesian economics, 9

"Last hired, first fired," 35
Lowered aspirations, 18, 187-195, 200, 204, 252

Marital strain, 119-131, 135-137, 147, 149, 151, 157, 167-168, 170-171, 173, 175, 177-183, 194-195, 216, 249, 251-253
Medicaid, 57. See also Health care costs; National health insurance
Mental health, 11, 17-18, 139-141, 148. See also Mental strain
  measures of, 141-146, 154-156
Mental strain, 17, 140-141, 145-147, 150, 152-156, 167-168, 175, 178, 194-195, 216, 250-252, 254
Military spending, 216, 225, 228-229, 236, 258-259
Minority groups. See Ethnic groups
Morrison, Philip, 258

National health insurance, 58, 72, 259
National Opinion Research Center, 23-24
New Deal programs, 10, 237
New York City, 26, 31, 40, 173

Nixon, Richard M., 208-209

Objective inflation crunch, 25-26, 28,
    30, 37, 40-41, 44-45, 102-104,
    115, 129, 131, 134, 148, 155,
    163, 169-170, 176, 246-247, 250-
    252
Occupational status, 26-30, 32-36, 41-
    42, 46, 112, 165-166, 174, 183,
    198-199, 205, 213, 245-246, 250
    and marital strain, 126, 136-137
    and mental strain, 150, 152, 154-156

OPEC, 257

Pension income, 69
Political parties, 161
Politicians, 206-209, 212-213, 216, 238-
    239, 253, 256
Presidency, confidence in, 203, 208, 253
Presidential election of 1976, 10
Proletarianization of middle class, 85, 87,
    117
Property values, 17-18, 173, 184, 251
Proposition 13 (California), 256
Public assistance, 161-169. See also Food
    stamps; Social security; Unem-
    ployment insurance, Welfare
Public policy, 18, 36, 58. See also Jobs
    guaranteed by government; Na-
    tional health insurance
Public service jobs, 238
Push-pull model of inflation, 211, 218

Race. See Ethnic groups
Radicalization of population, 184, 254
Recession of 1975, 17, 161-162, 243
Resources, allocation of, 59-60
Retired persons, 10-11, 23, 26, 28, 30,
    41, 46, 85-87, 97, 104, 106, 108-
    109, 112, 150, 152, 163-169, 192,
    198, 205, 245-247, 250
    and marital strain, 126-127
    and public assistance, 163-165, 169
    homeownership, 179-181
    standard of living, 192
Rising prices, 10, 16, 30, 37, 41-42, 44-
    46

San Francisco, 26, 31, 40, 173

Savings, 39, 78, 82-85, 87, 248
Second jobs, 29-30, 50-51, 65, 72, 81,
    92, 94, 104, 109
Self-reliance, 91, 97-98, 102, 106-108
Sharing of resources, 91, 99-102, 106-
    109, 111, 117, 248-249
Skeptic, 255
Social privilege, indicators of. See Educa-
    tion; Income; Occupational status
Social Science Research Council, 10
Social security, 17, 57, 162-163, 165,
    169, 250
Social stability, 161, 245
Social unrest, 161-162
Socialism, 196, 218, 252
Soviet Union, military threat posed by,
    258-259
Stagflation, 10
Standard Metropolitan Statistical Area,
    11-12, 15
Standard of living, 18, 51-52, 75-76, 81,
    87, 91-92, 95, 116, 119, 188-
    190, 192, 195, 231, 252
Stress, 170-171, 176, 178-179, 181. See
    also Marital strain; Mental strain
Subjective inflation crunch, 40, 42-45,
    95, 102-104, 107-108, 112-113,
    115-116, 125-126, 128-129, 131,
    134-135, 148, 152, 154-156, 163-
    164, 168-169, 174-176, 192-194,
    197-199, 203, 205, 246-250
    defined, 37, 39
Supply and demand, 201-202, 211, 216,
    230-231
Supreme Court, confidence in, 203, 253

Tax reform, 239, 253, 259
Theft, increase in, 94

"Underground economy," 92-94
Unemployed persons, 33, 42-43, 51, 58,
    109, 114, 147, 174, 176-178, 197,
    244
    reliance on credit, 115
Unemployment:
    benefits, 11, 17, 56, 92-93, 162, 250
    rising, 9-11, 21, 23, 30-31, 36, 48,
    161, 211-212, 245
Unions, 212-213, 216, 218-222, 253

Values, 18, 252. See also Lowered aspirations
Vietnam War, 216, 225, 229-230, 259

Wage and price controls, 238-239, 253-254
Welfare, 11, 17, 162, 167, 169-170, 212-213, 250-251, 253-254
  recipients, 54-55, 58-60, 62-64, 93, 101, 147, 169
  state, 162

system, 17, 218, 220, 224, 232-236, 255-257
White collar workers, 26, 28, 32-33, 35, 74-85, 87, 104, 106-109, 112, 117, 126, 128, 132, 134, 150, 152-153, 165-166, 174, 177-180, 192, 198, 205, 216, 245-246, 248
WIN campaign, 9
Wolfe, Alan, 258-259
WPA, 10

ABOUT THE AUTHOR